A Moral Military

A Moral Military

Revised and Expanded Edition, with a New Chapter on Torture

Sidney Axinn

TEMPLE UNIVERSITY PRESS
Philadelphia

For June

Temple University Press
1601 North Broad Street
Philadelphia PA 19122
www.temple.edu/tempress

Copyright © 2009 by Temple University
All rights reserved
Revised and Expanded Edition published 2009
First Edition published 1989
Printed in the United States of America

♾ The paper used in this publication meets the requirements of the American National Standard for Information Sciences—Permanence of Paper for Printed Library Materials, ANSI Z39.48-1992

Library of Congress Cataloging-in-Publication Data

Axinn, Sidney.
A moral military / Sidney Axinn. — Rev. and expanded ed.
    p. cm.
Includes bibliographical references and index.
ISBN 978-1-59213-957-6 (cloth : alk. paper) — ISBN 978-1-59213-958-3
(pbk. : alk. paper) 1. Military ethics. 2. War—Moral and ethical
aspects. 3. Kant, Immanuel, 1724–1804–Ethics. 4. Kant, Immanuel,
1724–1804—Influence. I. Title.
U22.A95 2008
172'.42—dc22

2008021675

2 4 6 8 9 7 5 3 1

Contents

Preface to the Revised and Expanded Edition

S ince the first edition, the subject of torture has received a lot of attention. Many books, editorials, and congressional discussions have been devoted to the matter. Therefore I have added a chapter, Chapter 10, to consider recent arguments about when, if ever, it is permissible or prudent or moral to use torture. There are also various smaller additions to increase accuracy and relevance to the present.

I must thank many audiences for discussion of the material in this edition. A sophomore class at West Point; many classes at Temple University, Philadelphia; and Temple University, Tokyo have used the first edition as a text. I also thank the class members at the University of South Florida in the spring of 2007 for their assistance. In addition, I have also been regularly helped by my daughter, Constance Axinn Johnson, who has led me to relevant material, and done occasional proofreading. My editor, Micah Kleit, is an expert at knowing when to give an author some extra rope, and when to pull on that rope: both actions were necessary for me and much appreciated. I'm grateful to someone I have never met, Bobbie Dempsey, who was the copy editor and made great improvements in the readability and the sense of the manuscript. I'm also particularly grateful to my friend/partner, Christeen Brady, who has gone to great lengths to make it easy for me to work, and for her impressive thoughtfulness.

Because it is often misunderstood, I should say something again about the title of this book. Immanuel Kant distinguished between political morality and moral politics: political morality would be determined by political requirements, not by morality. He also distinguished ethical theology and theological ethics: Theological ethics would be theology, not ethics. The title A Moral Military is governed by moral matters: quite different would be A Military Morality, governed by military rather than moral thinking. While I point out this distinction in Chapter 9, many readers have apparently not reached that part of the book.

Sarasota, January 2008

Preface to the First Edition

I have many reasons for wanting to write a book on the scope and limits of moral military activity. My father served in the first World War, and my childhood memories include his telling stories and my looking at the pictures of Camp Upton and France that he kept in an old shoebox. My brother and I served in World War II, he in the Pacific and I in North Africa, Corsica, and Italy. These experiences alone should have forced me to organize my thinking about warfare and about World War II in particular. But, like millions of others after their discharge from the military, I wanted to forget the war and hoped just to get on with a normal life. However, the moral issues central to the war against Nazism could not be easily ignored.

A copy of Spinoza's *Ethics*, stamped with my Army serial number, traveled in my barracks bag to North Africa, Europe, and back. I had decided on a career before the war and was lucky enough to be able to carry out my plans. I became a member of a strong philosophy department, teaching and writing about the classical, familiar subjects in that academic field. During the Vietnam War, however, I found myself giving a course called "Philosophy of War." I had been using military examples more and more in my other philosophy courses. The Vietnam War forced college students to think about military service, and an effort on my part to apply philosophical thinking to military issues seemed most appropriate.

As far as I could tell, military training typically reached the subject of ethics only in a course called Leadership. There apparently were no courses called Followership. Ethics, the study of the theory of morality, seemed to be a matter for leaders only. Followers simply carried out the orders, including those that involved serious moral matters. But each individual is a moral agent, and each must give him- or herself the moral command. A command from outside the individual may be effective, but it is not a moral command unless it is self-imposed.

Readers of moral theory will immediately recognize that my views of morality and of human nature come from German philosopher Immanuel Kant. This entire book can be called "Kantian." It is an effort to continue the application of Kant that Francis Lieber started in the set of rules that he wrote for the U.S. military forces. Lieber was a political scientist, educated in Germany, who was engaged for the task by Abraham Lincoln. One of the objectives of this study is to explore the moral assumptions behind the well-known military position holding that all, but only lawful, orders must be followed; those that are not lawful are not morally required. This position implies that everyone, including enlisted personnel, the "followers," must be aware of his or her responsibility as a moral agent. I believe that this approach will increase, not decrease, the fighting strength of such troops—where fighting strength is understood to measure the ability to win a war, not merely a battle. A war is won only if a desirable peace is sustained.

Military morality is formulated in the Hague and Geneva Conventions on the conduct of warfare; therefore, it is necessary to give significant time and effort in military training to their study. These war conventions are an impressive moral code. Basic assumptions about natural law and human rights are the foundation. The goals of the Conventions are to avoid unnecessary suffering, to safeguard fundamental human rights, and to help restore peace. Pursuit of these goals presupposes an educated population, both military and civilian.

Because of the obvious importance of knowledge of the Conventions, the nations that signed them included the statement that they would try to teach the contents to their military and civilian populations. I hope that this book and various other materials that are available will help increase the knowledge of both military and civilian groups about the Conventions. Ideally, before leaving high school, everyone should have a unit of study on the Hague and Geneva Conventions. At the age of eighteen, a young person can become a member of the armed forces in many countries, often to be trusted with lethal power. It takes some time to understand the war conventions, and that understanding is important whether a person is going to be involved directly in military action or not. To protect against war crimes, everyone has to know what they are.

The war conventions stand up well under examination. The military have a code in which to take pride, a code that is sometimes assumed must be carried out by men of honor, by professional soldiers who can be trusted to behave honorably. That assumption raises a very old and significant question in the history of philosophy. The problem of teaching honesty, of whether it can be taught, is a classical question that Plato considered and that we still face. The hope is that education will produce officers, enlisted personnel, and civilians who at least understand what is the right thing to do. The essential mechanism for forcing people to obey the code is apt to be the fear of being caught in violation of it. That fear, rather than the romantic hope of producing soldiers who are absolutely honest, is our protection that the code will be followed. The fear of being caught requires that there be widespread knowledge of just what the code requires, of what a war crime is. The need for that knowledge is the reason that the framers of the war conventions agreed that all nations signing them would try to teach their contents to both military and civilian communities. Unfortunately, the subject is almost never presented formally to civilian students.

Does studying the war code make wars more likely? I doubt it. Not studying it, however, can make wars more terrible than necessary. I assume that we shall eventually move to a single world government and eliminate wars among nations, but there will still be a need for a military, an international police force to uphold international law. The members of such an international force will still need the concepts of military honor and a code of the same general sort that we have now in order to be trusted to police the world. So, while I hope that narrow and fanatical patriotism will end, I expect that there will always be a need for a moral military force. That military force, like any other, will have to be loyal to moral principles if it is to succeed. I also hope that those parts of this book that refer only to military actions among nations will quickly become out of date. Until they do, however, we must think about those parts as carefully as we can.

It is a commonplace to note that war, like sex, is judged differently by different people. Opposite principles are taken to be moral. I have tried to avoid the extremes of chastity and overindulgence, of never and always. In terms of my predecessors, I have tried to use both Epictetus and Edmund Wilson. Epictetus expresses the ancient attitude toward military duty: "You must stand by your friend and share your country's danger." But along with this, Edmund Wilson makes the point (in his Introduction to *Patriotic Gore, Studies in the Literature of the American Civil War*) that "this is the time to think . . . because as soon as a war gets started, few people do any more thinking about anything except demolishing the enemy."

I have tried to write for an audience that appreciates both points of view. The duty to fight must not deny Wilson's call for "the time to think." Both points have their dangers, but one without the other is even worse. It may be as immoral to act without the time to think as it would be to think without the courage to act.

I owe thanks for assistance to many people, particularly to Lt. Colonel John Nugent, formerly Commanding Officer of the Temple University ROTC, for years of thoughtful comments on these subjects. I immediately add that Colonel Nugent must not be held responsible for the results here, but certainly for stimulation. Early encouragement came from Captain John Odell, who also served at one time with the same ROTC. Russell Weigley's military histories, lectures, and generous comments on earlier papers have been of great value. Constance Axinn Johnson gave her typically clear and sensible comments on early papers and located copies of the publications on the effects of the atomic bombing of Hiroshima and Nagasaki. William Wisdom and George Deaux cheerfully helped with an early version of the test in Appendix 3.

The students in Philosophy 228 at Temple University Philadelphia and Temple University Japan have used material included here in several chapters and have certainly improved it. For the very comfortable living and working environment in Tokyo, I must thank President Chikara Higashi, Dean George Deaux, and the administration of Temple University Japan, as well as President Peter Liacouras and the administration of Temple University Philadelphia. I must also mention the expert advice that came to me from an anonymous reviewer for the Temple University Press. A perfunctory salute is hardly enough thanks for the great help of his or her thoughtful and detailed suggestions.

I gratefully acknowledge a study leave granted by the Trustees of Temple University in the spring of 1976 for the purpose of working on the first draft of this book.

As those fortunate authors who have had Jane Cullen as an editor know, she has almost no resemblance to the caricature of a first sergeant— almost none—but they both get the job done. Jane Cullen does it with charm, flattery, and real expertise. I join many others in expressing thanks for that. It is a pleasure to mention the copyediting skill, humor, and grammatical superiority of Mary Capouya.

Those who know us need not be told of the effect that June Axinn has on almost anything I do. Just expressing appreciation would be an enormous understatement.

Tokyo, Japan, May 1988

1

Introduction

The Kind of Question Involved in Moral Military Action

Should a soldier ever disobey a direct military order? Are there restrictions on how we fight a war? What is "military honor," and does it really affect the contemporary soldier? These questions lead to a number of ethical problems, including the odd but basic one: Is human dignity possible under battlefield conditions? This book considers views on several sides of these matters, analyzes the "laws of warfare," and concludes that the answer is "yes" to each of the above questions. Military honor matters, morality restricts military choices, and human dignity can be won or lost.

If military honor and "laws" of war do exist, what acts do they forbid, if any? Here are a few of the problems: Can a prisoner of war be threatened with torture or death in order to get information that can save the lives of one's comrades? Can the enemy's water supply be poisoned? Can the enemy be told that its country has surrendered, when this is not true? Can an enemy soldier be assassinated, shot by a soldier who is out of uniform and dressed as a local native? If the enemy is found to have tortured captives, may the other side do the same to its captives? Can ammunition be stored in a church? These are some of the questions that arise during war. They are ethical questions because each of these actions certainly can be carried out, but it is far from clear that they should be permitted. These are examples of the issues that are part of the subject of moral military activity—the part dealing with choices about *how to conduct warfare.*

The individual soldier is not left to exercise personal whims when moral questions arise. He or she must consider both written and unwritten codes of military conduct. Military honor and the laws of warfare partly express the present stage of civilized man's morality. These codes do not answer every possible question that a battlefield can raise, but they go an impressive distance toward the answers.

Soldiers make and act on decisions *during war.* Such decisions are at the center of this study. We will not consider the classical question of the justification of war or of particular wars, although this is certainly a prior and basic matter. The decision to go to war is political; Decisions on the conduct of war are military. This distinction between the political and the military is crude, because no question is purely one or the other. Political choices depend on the military power to enforce them, and military choices presuppose the political will to sustain them. However, our subject matter is the moral reasoning called for in a wide variety of situations in which persons in military uniform may find themselves. They may involve life or death in actions ranging from the display of loyalty and honor to the most inhumane kinds of cruelty and unnecessary suffering. Some of these decisions resemble those that are common among employees and executives in large institutions, civilian as well as military, although most are unique to the military. Such moral questions as stealing from an institution, false reporting, careerism, and whistle-blowing will not be considered here. Our concern is with the essential military mission—protecting the nation by force—and that leads us to moral questions that arise before, during, and after combat.

The object of this study is to establish the basic modern framework for moral military action. A secondary object is to assist military personnel in the analysis of their own professional ethic. It takes courage as well as knowledge to remain within the bounds of morality—and courage, we all suspect, cannot be poured out of a book.

Must Every Order Be Obeyed?

To say that soldiers make decisions means that they do not automatically carry out orders. One essential moral problem for each of those below the rank of commander-in-chief is this: "Should I obey or disobey the order that I was given?" Although the individual U.S. soldier, when inducted into the armed forces, swears to uphold the Constitution of the United States and to obey the orders of the commander-in-chief and subordinates, this does not mean that every order must be obeyed. The Department of the Army's Field Manual (FM) 27-10, *The Law of Land Warfare,* has a significant section titled "Defenses Not Available." At a court-martial of a soldier accused of committing a war crime, the fact that the act in question was carried out under "an order of a superior authority, whether military or civil, does not deprive the act in question of its character of a war crime, nor does it constitute a defense in the trial of an accused individual."[1] Clearly, a soldier does not give up all personal responsibility for what he or she does. One may *not* carry out an order to do something that is a war crime and then claim in defense that the order had to be obeyed. The Army Field Manual dictates that "members of the armed forces are bound to obey only lawful orders."[2] Of course, if the individual did not know, and could not reasonably have been expected to know, that the act ordered was unlawful, he or she may use that ignorance as a defense.[3]

Because members of the armed forces are held responsible if they commit war crimes, they must be provided with the clearest possible understanding of what these crimes might be. To make the laws of warfare govern the actual practice as closely as possible, the laws must be well known. Therefore, the governments that signed the Geneva Conventions agreed "to disseminate the text of the present Convention as widely as possible in their respective countries, and, in particular, to include the study thereof in their programmes of military and if possible civil instruction, so that the principles thereof may become known to the entire population."[4] Each government publishes a manual on the Conventions to be used in training its own armed forces. What is of most concern is how much of the time available for military education is spent on the subject of military ethics and which tests are used to evaluate understanding.

In addition, we need to consider the agreement to try to make the entire population aware of the subject. The laws of warfare could certainly be taught to students at the secondary-school level, perhaps in connection with courses on government or international agreements. Understanding the nature of the international conventions—and the language in which they are phrased—requires no more than a secondary-school level of education, if that. Thinking about the combination of the obligation to serve one's country, along with the obligation to disobey orders when required by higher morality, is a proper subject for people in their middle teens. The minimum age for military duty is seventeen; however, a young soldier may need several years of training on such a crucial and complicated subject before having to make any decision.[5]

The question of the limits of military obedience is involved in every chapter of this study and comes to a decisive focus in Chapter 8, "War Crimes, Remedies, and Retaliation (Dirty Warfare)." There we consider the nature of war crimes and the specific basis for the decision to obey or disobey an order.

Forbidden Weapons? Nuclear Weapons? Terrorism?

Nuclear bombs and nuclear weapons systems raise new questions in the history of warfare. Are they so terrible that they should be forbidden, as certain kinds of gas warfare have been forbidden?[6] If not forbidden, do they make "conventional warfare" obsolete? Can there be, at most, one more brief war that would bring about either the end of humankind or the rise of an international government? Does listing a weapon as forbidden mean that it should never be used, even in reprisal against its use by an enemy? Are there circumstances in which the decision to use such weapons can be morally defended? Is there an essential moral difference between small and large or tactical and strategic nuclear weapons? Chapter 4 deals with the issues involved in international agreements on forbidden weapons and tactics and develops the principles that apply. Chapter 9 considers the application of these principles to each of these questions.

Terrorism raises questions that go beyond the old concept of a war crime. In a fair study, we have to consider the arguments both for and against those military actions that we call terrorism.

The Good Soldier

The primary concept of the good soldier is that of an individual who agrees to sacrifice his or her own life, if necessary, for the welfare of others. The idea of military discipline is just this: The soldier will do as ordered, regardless of personal peril. Discipline means sacrifice—almost automatic sacrifice. The question arises immediately: Why would a rational individual accept the position of a soldier and become essentially a slave to a master's goals? We have to consider this matter in some detail, but first we must add to the notion of obedience the equally dramatic notion of honesty.

Soldiers operate openly, publicly, wearing uniforms that announce their goals. The combination of sacrifice and of honesty—unselfishness and truthfulness—are the components of military honor. Because humans are so obviously selfish and dishonest, the romance associated with military honor is a heady source of excitement and appeal. To be able to look with superiority at civilians, to have the notion that they depend on you but not the converse, is to have achieved a certain value for your life. This aspect is not stressed in the literature, perhaps because it is embarrassing to discuss superiority and, thus, contempt. However, all values are contextual, requiring comparison with something else that does or might exist. So, it is perfectly natural for soldiers to compare their potential danger to that of civilians.[7]

Perhaps another reason for the lack of attention to the role of the soldier's contempt for the non-soldier is that much of the writing about military ethics and the military profession seems to have been done by present or former officers rather than by enlisted personnel. Officers must be more discreet, or "gentlemanly." They are the group that must persuade civilians to finance the enterprise.[8] In military training, the problems of *leadership* are considered in great detail; the correlative problems and thinking of *followership* are not given the same attention.

Relations between Officers and Enlisted Personnel

Colonel Malham M. Wakin reminds his readers of some of the origins of military thinking in a very interesting article, "The Ethics of Leadership."[9] He mentions "the story of those peasants of southern Germany who fought for their emperor in 1078 against knights of the feudal armies who, upon defeating the peasants, castrated them for daring to bear arms, a privilege reserved for the aristocratic knights. . . . Military honor . . . involved the practices of chivalry, including duels, but extended only to aristocratic peers."

Appendix 2 includes a discussion of the relations between officers and enlisted men, as well as a discussion of whether two distinct classes are needed. The topic ends with the remark that ignoring the dignity of enlisted personnel may be a pattern that will have to be abandoned—that has already been abandoned in certain areas—in a world in which extremely technical positions are held by enlisted men. As Major Daniel M. Smith put it recently, "Enlisted soldiers are not subordinates or of a lower rank than officers; they are simply in a lesser pay grade."[10] We have come a long way since the story about the eleventh-century German knights. Enlisted men outnumber officers; they often take on the highest risks to life and the most difficult and technical jobs. In addition, just as all humans are, they are required to make moral decisions. Certainly the problems of military followership can stand some analysis.

The Moral Foundations of Soldiering

What makes something moral or immoral? Is it *action* that is to be judged, or is moral judgment properly restricted to the *intention* of an individual, because the consequences of one's intentions may be beyond control? Chapter 2 develops four different ways of thinking about morality and ways of applying each to military situations.

There is an important distinction between *military morality* and *a moral military.* In the first term, *military morality,* the subject of morality is modified or made to fit the requirements of the military. But modified morality is no longer morality. In the second term, *a moral military,* the military is required to meet the demands of morality. That is a different matter; that is the application of morality to judging military questions—hence, the title of this book. Like others, I find myself using both *military morality* and *military ethics,* but these phrases are shorthand for our serious subject, the nature of a moral military.[11] (See the Preface of this edition for additional details about this matter.)

Before taking a detailed look at alternative theories of morality, we should take a general view. This study accepts a definition of the term *moral action* developed by American philosopher William James. His sense is that *moral action* is "action in the line of the greatest resistance."[12] The greatest resistance to moral action apparently comes from within the individual: There are within us both a moral and a selfish incentive. The moral battle takes place on the level of personal incentives—for example, a person chooses between what he or she thinks is right and what he or she thinks is safe. When an individual's own personal selfish goals are clear and strong, it takes the greatest resistance from outside the individual to overcome selfishness. In this viewpoint, to act morally is to act for the benefit of someone or something other than the individual's selfish advantage. In plain language, to act morally is to sacrifice some part of oneself. What part does one sacrifice, and for what? The next chapter deals with these questions.

In military terms, the question of morality—the matter of sacrifice—is this: "What, if anything, is worth dying for?" The soldier's answer is clear: "My country." However, the extent of the soldier's sacrifice, or willingness to sacrifice, is hardly clear. One will offer his or her life, if necessary. Will the soldier also sacrifice personal honor? Honor requires honesty: Will a good soldier lie, cheat, kill women and children, and torture and mutilate for the sake of country? The answer that this study presses is "No. A soldier offers to sacrifice his or her life, but not honor." One purpose of this study is to develop, argue for, and publicize that limit. Certain civilian misconceptions about the military may be eased by understanding this matter; certain patterns in the military may be corrected by attentively acting within those limits of acceptable action.

We must analyze the West Point motto, "Duty, Honor, Country," so that we have a sense of the scope and the limits of each of these three concepts. Without a notion of the limits and the competing principles for each, we are left with fanaticism. A fanatic has a conception of his or her goal, his or her heaven, and takes this conception to be perfect in every way. A healthy human, a non-fanatic, must also have goals and priorities; however, healthy people understand that their goals are not perfect, and they can find some sympathy and appreciation for different goals. Healthy people understand that an enemy, who has different goals, is also human.

Returning to the West Point motto, the term *duty* is here understood as *obedience,* the term *honor* is taken to be *honesty,* and the concept of *country* leads to the notion of *sacrifice.* Of course, these one-word synonyms merely indicate the area of analysis. Each term needs full consideration and examples. And, as mentioned above, each of these terms stands for a concept that has to be understood in light of its rational and moral limits. None of these terms is absolute.

Chapter 3 discusses our dual duties to both country and morality. Morality is often understood as following the military code, and the duty to follow that code ranks with, and perhaps above, the duty to country. The three parts of the West Point motto are not always independent; there are moral costs involved.

One military version of the moral question is this: Is it better to lose a war morally or to win immorally? Chapter 2 contains an analysis of four different moral positions—religious, individualist, social, and universal—and the way each responds to this question.

The Order of Topics

The next chapter is devoted to the subject of morality, presenting a way of classifying all possible moral positions and considering the military implications of each. It also offers a novel way of relating moral theories based on an Aristotelian square of opposition. However, those readers who need no introduction to moral and ethical theory may skip Chapter 2.

Chapter 3 follows with a study of military honor and the laws of warfare. The term, "Geneva Conventions" *is* familiar to many people, but the Conventions are rarely read or understood outside of certain military training programs. The Hague Conventions are much less well known. While a few excerpts are widely used in basic training, that usage hardly provides an adequate philosophical analysis of their foundation and broad significance. Civilians without military experience ordinarily fail even a simple test (like the one found in Appendix 3) on their contents. In the last few years, military personnel have been given a much-improved set of materials and have spent more time training soldiers in the Conventions. But even more attention should be given to the morality involved.

The term *professional military ethics* is now well recognized. Military and other journals publish on the subject regularly. The U.S. Army established an Ethics Task Force at Fort Benjamin Harrison in Indianapolis (since reorganized and moved to an Ethics Division at Fort Leavenworth in Kansas) and has done an impressive job of producing teaching materials. I hope that this effort will continue to be supported. In 1982, the appearance of a brief but thoughtful book published by the Hastings Center, *The Teaching of Ethics in the Military,* was another helpful and promising development.[13]

The problem with these "enlightened" efforts is that thinking about ethics is both very important and very dangerous. It is important because the dignity of human beings requires that they think, that they know the reasons for their actions; it is dangerous because a serious effort to think may have an unpredictable outcome. Such efforts may lead to embarrassing conclusions. Ethics is a part of philosophy, and philosophy involves the art of raising the most basic questions. I think, however, that if we have the courage to take the risk, we will find acceptable answers—not perfect answers but, all things considered, acceptable ones.

My own experience with learning the Conventions in World War II was this: In basic training, if we were on a rain-day schedule, a noncom read something about the Geneva Conventions to a group of about one hundred recruits. There was no discussion and no testing to check understanding. If it did not rain, even the minimal lecture was omitted. So, an introduction to the Conventions, their purpose and methods, seems appropriate. The concept of military honor depends on understanding both the written and unwritten "customary laws of warfare," as we will see.

Chapters 4, 5, and 6 consider specific details of the military code, the laws of warfare. These three chapters follow the sequence found in FM 27-10, the Department of the Army Field Manual, *The Law of Land Warfare*.[14] Starting with the procedure for declaring war, Chapter 4 considers many, but not all, battlefield situations and specifies acceptable and unacceptable actions. Chapter 5 deals with prisoners of war and Chapter 6 with spies—those not protected by all of the prisoner-of-war rules.

Chapter 7 goes on to nonhostile relations with an enemy. This topic involves the increasingly important subject of occupation forces, as well as the treatment of civilians, women, children, and the aged. Some wars end with and some end without an army of occupation; some political situations are now managed by outside forces occupying borders. While occupying forces have great advantages over those engaged in active hostilities, certain new problems need to be solved. However, because we are particularly interested here in the morality of combat, these topics are, for the most part, ignored. Chapter 7 deals with the process of ending hostilities, which means specifying the machinery of an armistice and some of the concepts involved in a surrender.

Chapter 8 analyzes the concept of a war crime, the central notion in the military code. This concept involves questions of whether war crimes can be avoided during a war, possible remedies to such crimes, and the law of retaliation, leading to some of the issues concerning terrorism. The relationship between terrorism and war crimes is but one obvious matter. Another is the delicate question of a possible moral defense for acts of terror. If we adopt a broad construction of terrorism, quite a bit of modern military history can be so classified. If we take a narrow view, we seem merely to be covering up our own history.

Chapter 9 presents the dirty-hands theory of command, the idea that it is impossible to govern a large institution properly without doing things that one knows to be immoral. This theory goes on to hold that those who are overly concerned with their own moral purity are too prissy to command effectively, presenting a serious moral challenge.

Chapter 10 considers the history and definition of torture. The chapter includes arguments both for and against the use of torture, and those arguments are judged by the war conventions and by moral matters.

Chapter 11 takes on questions about nuclear devices and low-intensity conflicts. Along with terrorism, these are topics of the day. Are tactical and strategic nuclear weapons different? Are nuclear weapons acceptable in some construction of the laws of war? The second section of this chapter turns to the many moral problems involved in "special" kinds of warfare, covert warfare, and variations that are referred to as *low-intensity conflicts* and a *war against terrorism*. Some believe that these are new sorts of activities and so we need new moral categories and new rules of engagement in order to deal with them.

Finally, the concluding chapter reviews a number of questions that have appeared along the way. Are the laws of war a moral and an adequate basis for contemporary action? What is the reality and seriousness of military honor? The needs for certain kinds of publicity and certain kinds of education are stressed. Publicity is one of the mechanisms for encouraging obedience to the laws of war, and this publicity involves the military education of both sides in any potential war. The chapter argues that both civilians and military personnel must be educated in the laws of war.

In the history of philosophy, a great difference has been noted between the views of Thomas Hobbes and Immanuel Kant on warfare. Hobbes held that when peace is impossible, one may "use all helps and advantages of war." For Kant, one must behave within certain bounds so as to make peace possible again. This controversy revolves around whether there are such things as war crimes. The concluding chapters offer an analysis of Hobbes and of Kant that brings their positions closer to each other. The analysis takes the Kantian position that a war crime is not a "help and advantage in war," because the object of war is to have the enemy surrender and remain that way—surrendered. To behave in so vicious and cruel a manner as to cause the enemy never to forget and never to forgive is not to have won the war. To win a war, one must end the war on favorable terms, and the war must stay that way—ended. To have the war really end, the enemy must agree to surrender and remain surrendered. That resolution requires behavior with military honor, with some respect for the human rights of the enemy; otherwise, the war does not end. We have some of these situations in the modern world, such as in Northern Ireland and the Middle East.

This book started out as a philosophical commentary on FM 27-10, the Army's presentation of the Hague and Geneva Conventions. I hope that it serves that purpose, as well as interesting the philosophical and the general public. Morality cannot be left to professional experts because, as Kant explained[15], there are none.[16]

The Scope and Limits of This Study

There are many excellent histories of particular wars and many fine studies of almost every aspect of war, including military professionalism in its many ramifications. And, as mentioned above, the last decade has seen a great increase in attention to the teaching of ethics in the military. In the last few decades, the concept of the "just war" has been reconsidered from contemporary religious and historical viewpoints. The issues in nuclear deterrence have provoked a great number of programs at meetings of professional philosophers and others and have led to some stimulating publications. The scope of this book is much more limited, and somewhat different, from those many important and useful developments.

This study is essentially confined to examining the Geneva and Hague Conventions in an effort to discover their philosophical structure. They purport to be the codification of the laws of warfare and to provide a standard for the morality of honorable combat. I will conclude that they are, indeed, an impressive basis for a moral military and that their principles cannot be ignored without great moral cost.

The Geneva and Hague Conventions were not the first efforts to limit military violence, and they are not fixed and established in detail for all time. A history of restrictions on military action would have to give a prominent place to a significant American development, the Lieber Rules and President Lincoln's role in promulgating them. However, this book is not a history of that subject; it is an analysis of the modern focus of thinking. Historians have noted that "Francis Lieber, while teaching Americans the Kantian moral philosophy, worked the premises of Kant's book, *Perpetual Peace,* into the code for the conduct of armies which President Lincoln commissioned. This last was only one of the ways that Kant's proposals were shepherded into the international law of the nineteenth and twentieth centuries."[17] Because our interest is in the philosophy rather than in the history behind modern thinking about the subject, we will give special attention to the theories of Kant and ignore or slight the details of codes and conventions earlier than the twentieth century. Our discussion of the twentieth-century codes is far from complete; the various protocols added to the Geneva Conventions in the seventies and the recent conferences and statements on terrorism are also slighted. The protocols and the terrorism agreements certainly call for serious attention, but that must wait for future efforts.

The main object of this study, again, is to formulate the basic contemporary framework for moral military action. The second object is to offer some philosophic assistance to military personnel in their analysis of their own code, their own professional ethic.

Florence Nightingale once said that, at a minimum, hospitals should not spread disease. American logician Morris R. Cohen repeated her remark and added his own hope that his book, *A Preface to Logic,* would not spread fallacious thinking. If nothing else, I hope that this book does not spread casualness about war crimes.

2
Morality

Why Sacrifice Myself?

What Are Moral Questions?
What Is the Meaning of Duty?

Moral questions concern choices between the alternative paths of satisfying *either* one's personal, individual goals *or* the goals of some entity outside of and different from one's self. Such questions arise on almost every page of this book. During a war, should one risk one's life as a soldier or flee the country? Should one follow the Geneva Conventions on the treatment of prisoners, or may prisoners be shot to preserve one's own personal safety? Should a soldier keep his or her word, even if personal convenience, safety, or advancement suggest otherwise? Should a soldier use torture to obtain possible valuable military information? Should a soldier follow an order to certain death?

Strict egoism holds that there is no entity outside of the individual for which that person ought to agree to be sacrificed. Nothing, no one, is more important. More complex kinds of egoist theories hold that even the most self-centered goals must include some outside entity, that humans are essentially social beings who can approach personal happiness only by some sacrifice for an outside entity. The non-egoist positions insist that there is some entity more important than the individual, and therefore individuals ought to make sacrifices on its behalf. For every viewpoint other than strict egoism, there is the problem of specifying this outside entity and explaining why it is worthy of personal sacrifice. And for egoism, there is the matter of clarifying the notion of the self and explaining what is and what is not to its real advantage. We will call this matter of deciding what is of highest importance *the problem of the moral object.*

In addition to this first problem, locating and defending the status of the moral object, there are two other assumptions in any complete moral theory: the moral question—Can the goal of a moral act be phrased as a clear question?—and the moral method—How are we to answer the moral question? To characterize a theory, we must specify these three features: its *moral object,* its form of *moral question,* and its *typical method.*

The Four Different Theories of Morality

The Moral Object

The purpose of moral theory is to locate principles by which to govern the relations among people. The pragmatic question—that is, the question of purpose—cannot be avoided. For whose advantage are these moral principles to be chosen? Who, or what, is to be the moral object? A famous and easy way of classifying the alternatives is Aristotle's pattern for arranging kinds of opposition.[1] When we consider the subject of humanity and the moral object, we face four possible positions:

1. *All* members of humanity *are* to be the moral object.
2. *Some* members of humanity *are* to be the moral object.
3. *Some* members of humanity *are not* to be the moral object.
4. *None* of the members of humanity *is* to be the moral object.

Each of these alternatives has been expressed in a well-known moral theory, and we have to consider their advantages and disadvantages. First, we will look at a brief characterization of each, followed by more detailed comments.

Universal Fairness

The universal fairness position assumes that all members of humanity are equal moral objects; there is no preference for certain people over others. *The questions* taken to be essential here are: Can everyone intend to follow the same rule? Does the same principle apply equally to all? *The method* to be used in responding to this formulation of the moral question is logic or reason. Reason can test for consistency in application. Historically, well-known versions of this position, Kantianism, were developed by Immanuel Kant in the eighteenth century, by John Rawls in our time, and by others. Human rights theories often assume the notion of universal fairness—that all members of humanity are equal moral objects.

Suppose food or medical facilities are in short supply. Must what exists be shared equally with prisoners of war (POWs), with civilians, and between officers and enlisted personnel? On the basis of this position, no one can be used merely as a means to the goals of others; each person is to be treated by a principle that applies to all. No one can be made a slave to another, no one starved for the sake of another. While there are great complications involved in applying this view to all situations, the spirit and consequences of it contrast sharply with the other alternatives to be considered.

Social Utility

In this position, *some* members of humanity are to be the moral object (e.g., a certain social group). In the version that we will consider, the majority within a particular nation is the favored group, the moral object. *The moral question* becomes this: Does this group, the majority, benefit more by the act (or rule) in question than it would by an alternative act (or rule)? *The method* used to answer this question might be a democratic vote, or it might be a decision only by representatives of the majority or by one or more specially empowered individuals. From this viewpoint, what is useful to the majority is taken to be right and good. What is useful to many produces more good than what is useful to a few. Aspects of this position, utilitarianism, have been developed and defended by Jeremy Bentham and John Stuart Mill in earlier centuries and by Richard Brandt and others in the recent past.

In this view, questions concerning such issues as sharing scarce food and medical supplies or torturing captives for information are to be answered by an estimation of the benefit to the majority. If the only way to save a large number is to starve a few, then social utility holds that it is the right thing to do.

Individualism

The position of individualism holds that some members of humanity are not to count as moral objects. More exactly, this variation takes the only moral object to be the individual alone. Here, "some of humanity are not to count," leaves just one who does count, me. For someone to count, his or her feelings must be consulted and, on this viewpoint, that means only the individual who is making the moral judgment, choosing one act or another. Other people do not count unless the moral actor feels their claim.

Individualism is called selfishness by its opponents. In the history of moral theory, one obvious name associated with individualism is Thomas Hobbes.

The essential *moral question* is this: Will a proposed action be more advantageous to the individual than any alternative action? How is such a question to be answered? More than one method can be applied to the problem; however, here we will look only at the consequences of choosing *the method of introspection*. Introspection is the technique of looking within, of searching within one's own mind and feelings for the answer to certain questions. The goal of increasing the individual's advantages might also be pursued by other methods—for example, an external or objective estimation of various courses of action.

Should scarce resources be shared with POWs? According to individualism, the proper answer depends on what would most likely increase the power of the person who is making the decision. According to extreme individualism, no external law, code, or textbook should overrule the individual's own estimate of his or her own security.

Religious Foundations

One variation of the position that no human is to be the moral object holds that the moral object is God, or a group of gods. Of course, there are alternative conceptions of God, as well as religious positions without gods. The essential moral question here is this: What does God, or do the gods, desire? The method for answering this question may require sacred writings or revelations from the gods. Prophets or religious leaders are sometimes taken to serve as required parts of the method used to answer the question. Religious positions have been developed in a great variety of ways—for example, in the Old and New Testaments, the Koran, other sacred writings, and the works of such commentators as St. Augustine, St. Thomas Aquinas, Luther, and Maimonides. This chapter, unfortunately, must ignore the non-Western religions and, thus, a major part of the world's population.

Should scarce supplies be shared with POWs? The answer may depend on which sacred writing, or which passage of that writing, is taken to be the word of God and pertinent to the question. Notoriously, interpreters may differ.

It must have occurred to some readers that, beyond the four views noted above, there is still another possible attitude toward the question of a moral object. Perhaps the matter cannot be decided because there is no such thing as a moral object. Perhaps there are no duties, nothing for which we *should* sacrifice—not even for ourselves. The terms *should, ought,* and *duty* are empty. This view is known as moral skepticism, and we have to pay attention to it before reaching a firm and dependable moral position. For the moment, it can be considered a variation of the fourth position: None of humanity is a moral object, and neither is anything else.

Now that we have briefly described each of the four different choices of moral beneficiary, the problem of evaluating them remains. Our special interest is in the role that these choices may play in various military contexts. Each of the four has certain advantages and disadvantages. We next turn to a more detailed consideration and indicate their scope and limits—that is, how they may each be used to some extent and in certain situations.

It would be *moral optimism* to assume that every possible situation has a perfect moral solution, and it would be *moral pessimism* to assume that no situation has a perfect moral solution. We conclude, modestly, that many, but not all, do. Further, the moral *monists* take it that a single theory is basic and perfect for all situations, The *pluralists* hold that several theories are equally basic. The monists have the problem of convincing us that their choice of theory is quite perfect; the pluralists, for their side, must show us when to use which theory. First, we will give each of the four theories a chance to present itself and to show us its strong and weak points.

Universal Fairness

We start with a position that sounds comfortable: *All of humanity are equal moral objects.* This has both familiar and unfamiliar aspects. For Christians, it may sound like a consequence of "Love your enemies, bless them that curse you, do good to them that hate you, and pray for them which despitefully use you, and persecute you" (Matthew 5:44). The familiar part is the notion that all humans are in the same situation, that they have the same nature and the same ultimate history: They are to die, and they know it. With regard to the brotherhood of man, the unfamiliar aspect is the insinuation that it is not natural *and right* to fight against one's enemies. It is quite understandable to feel that, while all men are brothers, one may be justified in fighting against one's brother on some occasion. If all humans are equal moral objects, how shall we think about war?

The assumption that each of us is an equally significant moral object has several direct implications. For one, we ought to be treated equally: Equality or fairness means that we must all play by the same rules. Whatever the activity (or game), we must all follow the same set of rules because no one of us deserves more than another. Applied to individuals, this assumption means that each of us must act only by principles that we could understand applying to everyone. Does this part of the position rule out war? No, but it does rule out *unfair actions.*

What are unfair actions? If we act on a principle that could not apply to both sides, our action is unfair. The principle, the overall rule, must be such that all parties could act on it. This is the ordinary concept of fairness: The same rules should apply to all parties concerned. If the enemy must not use the Red Cross symbol to conceal ammunition storage, we may not either. The Hague Convention states this clearly.[2] If we must not tell them that their government has agreed to an armistice when it has not, they also must not lie to us about such matters. As the Department of the Army put it, "It would be an improper practice to secure an advantage of the enemy by deliberate lying . . . or when there is a moral obligation to speak the truth. For example, it is improper . . . to broadcast to the enemy that an armistice had been agreed upon when such is not the case."[3] Why improper? Because the objective is to win by fair means, if we are all of equal moral value. If we use a principle or rule that they cannot use, we are unfair. If we know the truth and they do not, we—but not they—are able to use the liar's rule, the rule that the speaker may convince the audience of something that he or she knows to be false. So, fairness requires that if one side cannot properly lie, neither can the other.

Many examples of fair and unfair rules are obvious. What happens, though, when one side takes an action, but the other side cannot retaliate in kind? For example, under the notion of a fair application of the same rules, can one individual kill the other? If successful, the other party, now dead, cannot personally retaliate. If this action takes place under rules and agreements that both sides follow, it can be called a fair fight. But there is another aspect of the view of a moral object that we have not yet considered.

To hold that all humans are equal moral objects has both a negative and a positive implication. We have briefly considered the negative—the idea that we must not follow rules that do not equally apply to all parties. The affirmative aspect of moral equality is expressed in the idea that each human life must be understood to be as sacred or absolute a goal as any other human life. No one may be exploited or made a slave to anyone else's goals. As one philosopher has put it, a person must be treated, "always at the same time as an end, and never simply as a means."[4] Not only are we to follow rules that apply equally, but we are to treat others as if their own goals were never to be subverted to ours. Their purposes are not to be thwarted merely for our own sakes. Even this reasoning is, of course, a somewhat negative formulation. To be clearer: If others are moral objects equal to us, we must try "to further the ends of others."[5] This is the positive implication. We must try as far as we can *to further the ends of others*. To love our enemies is to try to have them succeed *in their goals*. Can we adopt this position and still carry on warfare?

One answer to this question is that there is an end or purpose even more important and absolute than the purposes of the individual. This end or purpose is the preservation of the human species.[6] If we find a situation in which the human species is really strongly threatened with extinction, we can justify using individuals as the means of furthering the more general goal. However, as soon as we say this, we find that we have moved from the position that each individual is to be an absolutely ultimate moral object to the view that the social utility of preserving the species may justify exploiting individuals for the sake of the species. Are these views consistent? Can there be *degrees* of absolute respect for individuals?

To take individuals as moral objects requires that there continue to be such individuals. If the continuance of such moral entities requires the risk of exploiting them, this risk must be suffered. An appropriate analogy might be the necessity of amputating a limb (an individual) to preserve the life of the body (species).[7] The obvious wrong of subverting the integrity of an individual, killing or wounding him or her, can be justified only by the most careful and strenuous effort to exhaust all other alternatives first. There remains, however, the principle of the lesser evil. The answer, then, becomes: War *may* be justified under certain circumstances. These special circumstances include not only the threat of the end of the human species but also danger to the individual. Kant, the philosopher best known for developing this position of universal fairness, has also insisted that it operate so that "A man is authorized to use coercion against anyone who by his very nature threatens him."[8] Fairness allows coercion against coercion. The limits of "coercion," if any, are not spelled out by many—apparently shy—authors.

As we have seen, respect for the goals, the rights, of all humans may still allow warfare, but there must also be rules for the conduct of that warfare. The Geneva and the Hague Conventions are efforts to construct just such rules. The details of the war conventions are considered in the next few chapters of this book; the basic principles behind them include the view that all humans have equivalent dignity, have equivalent rights even when taken prisoner, and *are to be treated as people with whom a peace treaty will be negotiated.* Therefore, as Kant put it, "It is forbidden to employ any such treacherous measures as would destroy the mutual faith that is required if any enduring peace is to be established in the future."[9] The Department of the Army uses almost identical language to make the same basic point.[10]

A parallel question to ours about war is often raised from the viewpoint of the universal fairness position: Can capital punishment be justified if every person is an equal moral object? One answer to this difficult matter is based on the idea that fairness allows (requires?) that an equal amount of loss (or pain or punishment) be inflicted on one who has caused a loss. This idea is the principle of *lex talionis,* the Roman law of retaliation, which holds that punishment can properly be equal to the offense. Accepting this principle provides a rationale for capital punishment and, under parallel circumstances, for war.

Of course, to hold that punishment can be equal to the offense does not mean that it *must* be equal. The principle that all of humanity's members are equal moral objects is also a common assumption for pacifists. One pacifist view is that because all humans are equal ultimate moral objects; war and capital punishment are simply not permitted. To kill a human is to violate the idea of equal moral status. To love our enemies obviously forbids war against them. A parent who mildly punishes a child may still love the child; a soldier who intentionally kills another soldier can hardly be said to love his victim.

Both the pacifist and the militarist positions have advantages and disadvantages. The advantage of the pacifist is that he or she avoids the error of killing someone who does not deserve to die, someone who either was not really guilty or who may live to impressively atone for the crime. The disadvantage that the pacifist risks is that he or she becomes partly responsible for the crime already committed, by apparently condoning it, and thus becomes a passive accomplice of future crimes. The militarist has the advantage of not risking the error of condoning the crime and of taking steps to avoid future crime. He or she does, however, risk what the pacifist avoids: the errors of killing possibly innocent humans and of postponing the date of peace.

We need not adopt either the militarist or the pacifist postures as absolutes for every situation. We can imagine wars in which one side was justified in fighting and wars in which neither side had a just cause. Therefore, we need not fight at the slightest insult nor abandon our friends and families if they are under vicious attack. We can choose a response, and a style for that response, on the basis of the facts of the situation and the pattern of risk of error that we find our duty demands. At the conclusion of this chapter, we return to this matter of choosing a moral strategy.

The advantage of this first position, universal fairness, lies in the reasonableness of the notion that all humans have equal moral rights. The very definition of morality seems to require it. The disadvantage lies in the demand that neither ourselves nor our dearest companions receive more special consideration than is given to absolute strangers. We may agree that the same laws apply to all, but do we agree to love everyone equally? To sacrifice equally for everyone? As stated earlier, the negative part of universal fairness is difficult enough—the same rules must apply to all. The positive aspect, that we are to love all equally, seems not to be psychologically serious. If we love everyone, we love no one; there is no longer the essential exclusivity. A remark comes to mind about a person who deeply loved humanity but loved no one in particular. For the advantages that it has in reason and in logic, this view seems to cost heavily in ordinary human loyalties. The loyalty to one's native land or adopted country is also threatened by this position. If all humans are equal moral objects, why have separate sovereign nations? Why not world citizenship?[11]

Of course, we would like to have the advantage of rationality without the disadvantage of the lack of love and loyalty. However, there are three other choices of moral object to consider. Although the next alternative will promulgate group loyalty, it may have some problems with the rationality or fairness of its position.

Social Utility

We now turn to one of the most familiar of the moral alternatives: the view that a certain social group ought to be the beneficiary of our actions. That group is *the majority* of our fellow citizens. The moral question is then obvious: Which act would be most useful to the majority? The use, *the utility* in producing happiness for that group, is to decide all serious questions.

Immediately one asks, "Why just a majority of one nation? Why not a majority of all humanity?" or "Why prefer just one nation? Why not prefer the goals of a majority of the world's nations?" Perhaps the utilitarians—those who hold this *social utility* position—will eventually agree that a majority of all humanity is their ultimate reference group. The sacred principle of social utility is, after all, "the greatest good for the greatest number." Utilitarians, however, may fall back on two assumptions for restricting their principle to their own nation: (1) It is not "practical" to consider populations in more than one nation because of their diverse cultural and other institutions. (2) One particular nation is somehow favored by history (or chosen by God) to lead humanity into the best of all possible worlds. These assumptions both look provincial. As we have seen, the notion of "world citizenship" is an embarrassment to both the social utility and the universal fairness positions, and it must also be dealt with by religious positions. Only egoism can consistently avoid it. For present purposes, however, we will take social utility to mean a utilitarianism limited to the borders of one's own country.

The advantages of social utility are its apparently clear decision rule and its seeming naturalness. There need be no ambivalence over conflicting values. Let everyone vote who is eligible to do so, and we have a rule for making decisions. If it is not practical to have a vote, let representatives of the majority make decisions and be subject to some eventual recall or impeachment by the majority.

What could be immoral in such decision making? For one thing, the majority might be wrong about its own interests. Determining their rightness or wrongness, however, requires a strong theory presenting an alternative source of wisdom. Still, it is frequently held that as the world's knowledge becomes more and more technical, the general population will have to rely on "expert" decision making. Even a democracy needs a scientific or political "elite." On the other hand, as J. S. Mill wrote, there are dangers in relying on a class of powerful experts: "All privileged and powerful classes, as such, have used their power in the interest of their own selfishness."[12] If the majority keep ultimate control of their destiny in their own hands, they have a technique for accepting or rejecting expert opinion, and so a decision principle can exist.

To take the majority as the moral object is ordinarily to deny the others their goals. Is it *natural* to sacrifice a minority to the welfare of the majority? It is, according to the moral intuition of this viewpoint. What can be said on this matter? First, we do expect that in a conflict a strong individual or group will in fact defeat a weaker individual or group. Is this expectation a basis for the *morality* of the outcome? Should we prefer to have the powerful defeat the weak? Does might make right? Yes, according to the democratic position. It is better to serve a large number than a small number. And, if that is better, then the sacrifice of the small number is justified. Let us consider some possible objections to this notion of what is natural.

One issue is revealed in the example of the ten people on the island. Suppose ten people go off to a place called Minyan Island and plan to live according to the principle of social utility. All differences are to be decided by a secret ballot, and the majority wins. Everything goes smoothly the first six days, but Sunday looks to be boring. So, nine of the group think that they would like to hang one little fellow, the weakest one on the island. Hangings were said to have drawn great crowds when they were done publicly. Should they do it? Would it be right? The principle of social utility makes the matter clear. A secret vote is taken, no one knows how anyone else has voted, and the result is nine-to-one in favor of the hanging. The democratically chosen one is hanged, to the great fascination of the community. All goes well until the following Sunday. Again, it is thought that perhaps, to alleviate boredom, the next smallest person might be tied to a stake and burned. This event also attracted great crowds of appreciative spectators in the old days of witch burning. Again, a secret vote, eight-to-one, makes the plan perfectly honorable, and it is done. On the following Sabbaths, individuals are shot, guillotined, drowned, and tortured. When the population drops to two, they give up democratic social utility and sail back to the mainland.

What can be said about the moral history of the ten people on the island? We might say that they need a bill of rights to prevent the taking of life merely for amusement. Suppose that they had killed these weaker individuals not merely for amusement but for the safety of the rest of the population. Would that have made the killing moral? Had these individuals been sacrificed to the gods of agriculture so that the population of the island would not starve, would we approve of the morality? Is it morally justifiable to sacrifice a few individuals so that others, perhaps many others, may live?

Suppose that Minyan Island had been attacked by the barbarians from the next island. Would it be moral to vote for a suicide squad to sail over and destroy the fleet of the enemy island? If their military and naval intelligence establishes that the only way to avoid defeat is to muster a suicide squad, is it moral to sacrifice some for the others? Should this matter be put to a vote and the decision to use a suicide squad be so determined? Suppose only two members of the group who are between the ages of eighteen and twenty-five are able to sail and swim. These skills are essential to the naval mission. If these two members do not volunteer, should they be drafted to sacrifice their lives for the welfare of the community? The utilitarian is inclined to say, "Yes." But, from the standpoint of the two candidates for the draft, why should they die rather than desert? Because, they are told, it is natural to want to save the majority, even at the sacrifice of the minority. If they don't find this "natural," if they advocate surrender to the enemy rather than accept their own deaths, are they choosing an immoral position?

To a utilitarian, the answer to the last question is, "Yes." It is immoral to refuse to accept whatever produces the greatest pleasure for the greatest number of fellow citizens. The utilitarian gains force from the negative version of the moral question: Does any group other than the majority deserve to be the moral object, the beneficiary of critical decisions? As we consider the utilitarian's question, it must occur to us that the boundaries of the majority can be expected to change and that anyone may find him- or herself sometimes within and sometimes outside the majority group. Beyond the question of personal luck, there is the matter of fairness and rightness.

Let's sum up the advantages and disadvantages of this position: There is a clear decision rule, an understandable method for reaching a decision. A secret ballot gives impressive scope to individual participation. While an individual may not always get the result preferred, there is the consolation that no other individual has a greater ability to decide the result. At least in an ideal voting situation, each voter would have an equal amount of power—money—with which to electioneer for his or her own desires. With such assumptions, *the method for reaching a decision* looks to be eminently fair. But, we must judge separately the morality of the result and the morality of the method used to reach that result. A perfectly fair and democratic method might produce something that is tyranny to the minority. The greatest good for the greatest number might be the greatest harm to a smaller number. To the advocate of the social utility position, this is as it should be.

Those who are concerned by the ability of the majority to impose their will on various minorities usually look either to a bill-of-rights technique or to one of the other moral positions. The bill-of-rights technique consists of an effort to specify limits for the majority. If the majority, assumed to be in control of the legislative power, is forbidden to make laws concerning religion, to restrict free speech and assembly, or to compel self-incrimination, then there are at least some nominal restrictions on its powers. The U.S. Constitution is, of course, an example of this pattern. It was written to preserve the advantages of social utility while protecting individuals and minority groups from being the victims of complete majority domination.

In addition to the power of the Bill of Rights (the first ten amendments to the U.S. Constitution), this Constitution has the significant feature that the powers of government are divided into three branches. The legislative, executive, and judicial branches are always in some tension. Each desires more power than it currently has, and so it presses on the domains of the other two. Each branch may consider that "national security" requires that it temporarily take on new duties that the Constitution denies it, and the other branches are expected to fight against such efforts. This continual tension among the three parts of the government was apparently one goal of the authors of the Constitution. By establishing legal machinery that gives the majority great but not complete power, the intention was to avoid the results of the parable of the ten people on the island, while keeping the advantages of social utility. As we have seen, like each of the other moral alternatives, this one also has desirable and undesirable features. The individual can be sacrificed. The next alternative reverses this completely.

Individualism

According to this viewpoint, the only moral object is the individual him- or herself. Consequently, *the moral question* becomes this: What is to the greatest advantage of the individual? The preservation of the individual's life is an obvious advantage, and this goal explains and justifies anything. What are the advantages and weaknesses of this self-interested or egoistic position? Is it a defensible basis for moral decisions?

First, consider its strength. Why accept a goal unless it is to your advantage? To persuade yourself of the force of a command, you must, apparently, come to see that obedience will be more to your advantage than disobedience. Why else pay attention? The individualist starts with this commonsense advantage. In addition, there is the argument that the dignity of the individual depends on taking him- or herself to be of major significance in the world. A slave is pressed into service for someone else, a free person lives for him- or herself. The dignity of freedom seems to require that individuals do not sacrifice themselves. To sacrifice is to give up something desirable, presumably for the sake of something more desirable. If the sacrifice requires that someone give up his or her life, the entity for whose sake this is done must have impressive credentials. A rational person bent on following self-interest may often abandon one desirable goal for the sake of other goals, but these other goals must also be personal. If they are not personal goals, then one is a slave who sacrifices for the benefit of another.

While the selfish individual starts with the apparent advantages of common sense and personal dignity, he or she faces certain dramatic problems. What first looked to be common sense—the clear preference for self-interest—turns out to be complicated by the basic need for friends, for loved ones, for others. Therefore, from the narrowest point of view that an individual can take, he or she may still not really prefer the life of a hermit. If the motto "I come first" is obvious to those around me, there may not be anyone who cares to come second. Thus, the purely selfish individual has the awkward problem of having to conceal that selfishness. In a way, the most selfish hope is that one not be merely selfish. The so-called common sense of selfishness turns out to be neither completely common nor sensible because we need other people for our own happiness. (Here I am merely stating this rather than arguing for it in detail.)

Turn to the second assumption behind individualism, the view that dignity requires that one be free of obligation to anyone else. Certainly dignity requires that one have a strong sense of his or her own significance. However, as philosopher Thomas Hobbes put it in his masterpiece based on individualism, "during that time in which men live without a common power to keep them all in awe, they are in that condition which is called war."[13] If you depend on your own power to protect yourself, you are sovereign and at war with all other self-defenders. You are at peace with others if neither you nor they are self-defenders. To be at peace requires that you and the peaceful neighbors are more in fear of a common ruling power than you are of each other. But why is it desirable to depend on a common ruler rather than to preserve the dignity of depending merely on your own strength? Hobbes insists that, "there is no man who can hope by his own strength, or wit, to defend himself from destruction without the help of confederates."[14] The dignity of being sovereign is a romantic myth. To depend on one's self for protection is to be in "continual fear, and danger of violent death; and the life of man, solitary, poor, nasty, brutish, and short."[15] The last word is significant: to go it alone is to have a *short* life.

The trouble with complete individualism, as Hobbes, its most powerful analyst, has put it, is that life would be short, in addition to being solitary, poor, nasty, and brutish. In a so-called state of nature in which each of us must defend him- or herself, must be at war with everyone else, life is short. Such a war cannot be won. Therefore, Hobbes holds that the first and fundamental law of nature for reasonable individuals is *to seek peace and follow it*. A rational person wants to live and so must prefer peace; however, Hobbes quickly adds, when peace cannot be obtained, a person "may seek, and use, all helps, and advantages of war." If peace cannot be had, he points to the right of nature, which is, "by all means we can, defend ourselves."[16]

This analysis of the features of individualism leaves us with several consequences. First, the dignity of relying on one's self must be balanced against the problem of the shortness of such a lifestyle. As an admittedly selfish individual, the most effective thing to do is to be a pacifist, to seek peace. If the first and basic effort to live in peace should fail, are there any limits to how one may fight? We have already seen Hobbes's first response to this question, "use all helps and advantages of war." That sounds like the view that all is fair in love and war: no restrictions, no agreements, no war crimes—no meaning to such things. However, it turns out that even hardheaded Hobbes advises us to honor agreements with the enemy as laws of war, "If I covenant to pay a ransom, or service, for my life, to an enemy; I am bound by it: for it is a contract."[17] And, he repeats the point, "Therefore prisoners of war, if trusted with the payment of their ransoms, are obliged to pay it."[18] Apparently, then, there are limits to how a selfish individual should fight if he or she is rational. A *rational* individual must honor certain agreements with the enemy.

What are the pluses and minuses of individualism at this stage? As a test question, we might consider this position from the viewpoint of the nation. Will someone who holds this view of the moral object sacrifice him- or herself for a political goal? If the sacrifice is to be a sacrifice of one's life, then the benefit of the victory goes not to the individual but to others. Why should an individual sacrifice his or her life for others? That person should do so only if he or she would rather die than live with the lack of dignity that might result. If a person thinks that he or she ought to sacrifice for others, but doesn't have the will to carry out that choice, he or she may have trouble living with the resulting lack of dignity. On the other side, if one does not get the benefit of the victory of the political goal, why should one sacrifice life for that victory? Given the well-known ability of people to rationalize their own behavior, it may be expected that few will have trouble living with what we outsiders might call the resulting lack of dignity. Therefore, we may conclude that ordinarily individualism is an unreliable basis for producing heroes willing to die for a political idea. If individualism is morally supreme, desertion under fire is to be expected. From the standpoint of the nation, this is an obvious disadvantage. We should note here that the fact that there is so little desertion[19] becomes an argument against the idea that individualism is a dominant moral style.

In sum, the strength of individualism is its dignity, the heady virtue of self-reliance. The true individual is beholden to no one but him- or herself. The disadvantage of individualism is its unreliability for the community. The true individual is the servant of no one but him- or herself—and perhaps not even a good servant to that self.

We have considered all the prominent possible views that take humans, in some number, to be the proper moral object. These positions can be considered varieties of humanism, obviously. The final possibility is that nothing human is to be chosen as the beneficiary of sacrifice. That leaves us with a choice between the view that something nonhuman is the moral object and the skeptical attitude that there is no moral object. Religious positions take the first of these; something nonhuman, more than human, is the proper beneficiary.

Religious Foundations

The position of using a religious foundation, introduced earlier in this chapter, takes the moral object to be God or several gods.[20] Certain advantages of this view are fairly clear. If we have a specific and pertinent answer to the question of what God or the gods desire, we have the solution to moral problems. Act for God's benefit; help to achieve His desires. Things go smoothly with this premise as long as (1) we accept the *religious question*— What does God desire?—as basic; (2) we either have a sacred text or a source of revelation to answer that question; and (3) the text or revelation is pertinent and unambiguous.

The disadvantages of the religious basis include matters that are connected with each of the elements of the position. First, consider the status of the religious question. Why should the desire of God be taken as defining what is right and good? As Plato put the problem in the dialogue *Euthyphro* (somewhat restated): *Is something good because the gods desire it, or do the gods desire something because it is good?*[21] If we take the first alternative, we call something good because a great and fearsome power terrifies us into submission to its will. This action looks to be mere cowardice rather than an impressive and dignified position. If we take the second of Plato's alternatives, then certain things are themselves good due to some innate property that they possess. Using this assumption, we might hope to learn the criteria of good independently of the gods; we might discover that the gods are sometimes in error on the matter of a specific good or evil.

Whichever side of Plato's question we take, the status of God *as moral object* seems almost untenable. For a number of moralists, such as Kant, therefore, there are no *moral duties* to God but only to other kinds of entities (such as humans, or rational beings, or living beings). For many such authors, the problem is not the existence of God, but the question of whether His desires make something a moral obligation. *Should* we do whatever God desires, if such desires are known? An affirmative answer would seem to be mere individual opportunism: doing something because it will lead to personal benefit. We expected that response in the previous section about individualism, but not here, as religion.

If we can imagine good and bad religions, or good and bad gods, then we are using the second of Plato's criteria for our judgment. We are assuming that there is a basis for judgment that is independent of what a god desires.

The other side of Plato's question takes it that there are some *absolute criteria* for values and that these exist regardless of what the gods desire. Using this alternative, reason is a likely method for discovering the nature of value, of what is good and should be chosen. Of course, if we assume that such an absolute principle of moral value exists, we might treat that principle as a god and sacrifice for it. Giving a principle this status would count as a religious position, one that took its god to be a certain abstract concept. Political principles are sometimes given this status. We will return to this possibility after further consideration of traditional religious options.

Beyond the problems raised by Plato's question, the matter of the choice of sacred texts comes into play. Here we refer not merely to the choice between alternative religious texts, such as the Koran for Islam or the Old and the New Testaments for Jews and Christians, but also the matter of translations that purport to be the same text. For example, the Ten Commandments in the Hebrew Scriptures are not translated into English in the same way by all those concerned. "Thou shalt not murder" in the English version used by Jews in America[22] is translated as "Thou shalt not kill" in the King

James version.[23] These two translations are certainly not equivalent; "Thou shalt not kill" would seem to require strict pacificism, and there are those who understand it that way, refusing to serve in the armed forces of their countries. On the other hand, "Thou shalt not murder" does keep open the possibility of killing under circumstances that are not murder. What are called legitimate military engagements are ordinarily not taken to be murder, even when they result in killing.

Referring to different texts to show that God is jealous or that He is benevolent and merciful involves the matter of the relevance and the ambiguity of sacred writings. Suppose we are considering the question of whether or not to shoot a spy. Do sacred texts give an answer, even for those who accept the religious position? We must find a passage that either gives us a command that is directed to the problem or an example that has a clear principle for our action. It may take an army of interpreters to answer this, and we may never have an answer that is either free of doubt or available fast enough to be of practical use in connection with the spy. Do the texts rule on such issues as women participating in warfare, using gas warfare, napalm, poison on crops, area bombing, or taking hostages? Some stories can be interpreted as analogous to similar problems but certainly not without ambiguity. Some of these issues are as old as warfare (such as hostage taking), and some are technological novelties (such as the use of napalm). Where different passages in a sacred text can be quoted to support different answers to a question, we no longer have a clear decision basis. Of course, if a certain example and one line of interpretation are taken to be decisive, we may have grounds for a definite answer.

A modern author, James Turner Johnson, makes the point this way:

> What, precisely, was the message for later Christians in the rebuke Jesus gave Simon Peter after the latter had used a sword to cut off an ear of one of the men who had come to arrest Jesus in Gethsemane? (See John 18:10–11.) It is only broadly (and unhelpfully) true to say that Christian interpretations of this event have fallen into two groups, those that see it as a rejection of all violence and those that regard it as a rejection of a specified act of unjustified violence.[24]

Again, if we take a certain interpretation to be decisive, the example can become a clear guide. But, the interpretation comes from outside the sacred text.

Historically, religious positions have been central in answering the question, When is a war justified? When is a war "Holy"? Criteria for a justified war have been developed in a somewhat formal way by three groups of thinkers: Christian theologians, international lawyers, and military professionals.[25] The theologians' role in this, starting with St. Augustine, has been one of the major forces in Western thinking about what justifies going to war. At one extreme of "justification," there is the view that certain wars are an effort to carry out God's will; these are properly called "Holy Wars." Islam and ancient Judaism both claimed to fight holy wars. The Islamic claim of a "jihad" plays a role in contemporary political and military factors, and such a holy war may be considered a sacred duty by Muslims. Obviously, an enemy who considers it a sacred duty to kill you is a serious and formidable opponent.

The Golden Rule: Is Reciprocity the Test of Morality?

Consider what is known as the Golden Rule: "Do unto others as you would have them do unto you." Does it make distinctions relevant to military operations, and is it a rule that we ought to follow? We must pay attention to both of these questions.

The rule needs some qualification in order to be made operational. The obvious qualification is that it is to be applied to people in similar circumstances, although even this distinction is vague. May I shoot an enemy soldier who blocks my path? Before answering, according to the Golden Rule, I must decide what I would have the enemy do to me. I don't want him or her to shoot me, but I might agree that after the declaration of war between our countries, each of us has the same basis for attacking the other. Perhaps, I might think, if I were a citizen of his or her country, I would now be wearing his or her uniform, carrying his or her weapon, and pointing it just as he or she is. But this mental experiment of putting myself in that person's shoes is not quite what the Rule specifies. It orders us to treat the enemy just as we would have them treat us. Well, we would like to have them surrender immediately to us. Does this mean that we should surrender to them? Should we surrender at the earliest opportunity? If so, the Rule is hardly an ideal military principle. A less specific interpretation is called for.

If I would prefer that my enemy behave like a good soldier, then I must do so. But a good soldier tries to fire before being fired upon; where does this leave the Golden Rule? If I prefer that my enemy not be a good soldier, then I must not be one! Again, we have an unsatisfactory consequence. Of course, there are some matters to which the Rule applies. I would have the enemy obey the Geneva Conventions, and so I must. I would have the enemy keep his or her word, and so I must. I want the enemy to show a high regard for military honor, and so I must as well.

The Golden Rule asserts that my behavior should be founded on *symmetry*, on the notion that I must follow the same course of action that I desire my enemy to follow. For a certain number of questions, the Rule is morally quite appropriate: There are behavior patterns that we want both sides to follow. Essentially, we want both sides to follow the military codes, the Geneva and Hague Conventions. Of course, the essence of the military role is the intention to produce an unequal result. We want the enemy to surrender to us; we don't want to surrender to the enemy. The terms of the surrender are to be strictly followed by both sides, but the act of surrender and its consequences are not to be symmetrical.

Conclusion: The Golden Rule, the demand for symmetry, is morally impressive and desirable in some areas but not others. The Rule shares the idea of fairness that is the essence of universal fairness, discussed earlier. The same rules should apply to both sides; however, these rules need not lead to the same results. The analogy is with sport: The same rules are in effect for both sides in the game, but a fair game can produce winners and losers. The rules are the military code and the concept of honor, but the specific military operations and the goal of those operations can certainly differ. We want the enemy to follow the Conventions, but we don't want the enemy to be as successful as we intend to be. More significantly, we are to follow the Conventions not only for the prudential reason that our behavior may induce the enemy to do so but also because our own honor and the morality of fairness require us to do so. The Rule impresses us with this element. As we might expect, the Golden Rule has its advantages and limitations. This discussion has dealt with the rational rather than the religious foundations of the Rule.

Religion as Art

From a *purely rational* viewpoint, not one of the elements of the religious position seems to be a legitimate foundation for morality. Even if a position has no literal or objective status, however, it may be extremely useful and significant. Like literature, religious stories may be enjoyable and have great value even if they are not dependable as sources of morality. It is of great human importance to talk about and think about matters that are not verifiable, even if they do not contribute directly to specific moral problems.

Some aspects of this view of religious literature were developed in the work of American philosopher George Santayana.[26] Santayana's view is that religion is to be understood, enjoyed, and used just as great poetry should be understood, enjoyed, and used. But it is a very special kind of poetry: It provides images and symbols for "the Powers on which our destiny truly depends," as Santayana, with some rephrasing, put it.[27] For him, "religions will thus be better or worse, never true or false." What advantages does religion have in such a view? The advantages are the assertion of the limits of man and the hope of absolute good in the world. The ability to express these matters poetically may, on occasion, be a basis for maintaining sanity. According to this attitude, "We must thank religion for the sensibility, the reverence, the speculative insight which it has introduced into the world."[28] To have a way of referring to *a standard beyond that of one's government, or of any immediate human demand,* is to have something most valuable morally. It provides a context against which to consider the immediate and short-run goals.[29] That it is taken symbolically creates the disadvantage of not giving precise direction but also adds the advantage of applying its ideas broadly. There are, however, dangers to morality here, as the idea of absolute confidence in a holy war indicates.

What are the ways in which a religious moral position may enter military contexts? For some people, it never enters. For them, neither taking God as the moral object nor asking "What does God desire?" are serious ways of responding to moral problems. For others, religion may sanction particular military targets, as when the group who assassinated President Anwar Sadat of Egypt shouted, "Death to the unbeliever!" And, for many, when comrades are to be buried and their sacrifices need to be put into some meaningful framework, religious language seems the only and most relevant source of appropriate thought.

The constant danger in religious language is that it may be taken to be a basis for describing physical and moral reality; that would mistake the nature and role of great poetry. Religious poetry cannot tell us when to fight, who to fight, how to fight, or upon which terms to stop the fight. When we need rest and relief from the actual world, however, religious poetry—like all poetry—can produce the symbols and images of alternative worlds.

Whether religions provide clear moral guides or not, universal respect for the religious interest has led to special protections. The Geneva Conventions, as we see in Chapter 4, are very specific about religious freedom to worship and protection of buildings dedicated to religion. Why such special consideration for religious activities during war? Because it is so widely agreed that there is something more significant and more dignified in the world than the immediate political goals of a government. One of the purposes of military custom is to "safeguard certain fundamental human rights,"[30] and religious freedom is specified as one of them.

Nationalism as Religion

We have not yet defined *religion*. One of the most useful definitions was offered by Edgar A. Singer, Jr.[31] Where the term *religious* is an adjective, Singer took it to describe a view that (a) there is one highest goal in life, one heaven; and (b) everyone ought to seek that same heaven. In Singer's definition, there cannot be a pluralistic religion, one that accepts several goals as equally supreme. He took all religions to be essentially proselytizing, even if they were not actively so. This definition does not require belief in a supernatural being but instead focuses on the purposiveness of the attitude toward the highest goal. A full discussion of Singer's definition, and of various others, would go beyond our subject; however, there is one feature of Singer's idea that must be noted.

If the essential feature of a religious position is not a belief in a supernatural entity but rather the belief that there is one absolute and supreme goal in life, then *complete and dedicated patriotism* can be classified as religious. Such a patriot believes that the highest goal for one's life is the strengthening of the nation and that that goal is worth any sacrifice. He or she also believes that everyone ought to take the same view of this perfect nation. For such a patriot, the nation is god. In this sense, absolute nationalism is a religious position. When we consider the eager willingness of people to answer their nation's call, its battle call, in the last century or so, it can seem quite natural to describe nationalism as the religion of the age. When people are willing to sacrifice anything, including their lives, for their nation or their nation's principles, we must call their attitude religious. In this sense, we in the twentieth and the twenty-first centuries live in a great religious age, and we have already seen impressive holy wars. The decisions about whether to go to war and about how to fight those wars are now made by political leaders. These decisions are not made by the leaders of the traditional religions—the rabbis, priests, and ministers. Occasionally, as in Iran, the leaders are simultaneously the political and the traditional religious heads. But this is an anomaly, a case of cultural lag, from Western Enlightenment standards.

The moral advantages and disadvantages of the religious position hold whether the god is the nation, an absolute principle, or a supernatural entity. The advantages include the satisfying feeling that one is sacrificing for something more significant and enduring than a mere limited human goal. The disadvantages include the risk that there may be no such entity as the god for whom one sacrifices. If the god is supernatural, it can't be seen; if it is an absolute principle, that principle may not really have supreme value; and if it is a nation, that nation may actually be a collection of contemporary humans rather than an entity with a life and future of its own.[32]

Now we must put the advantages and disadvantages of all of the moral alternatives together as a group.

The Range and Limits of the Different Moral Styles

We would like, naturally, to gain all the advantages of the four positions without any of the disadvantages. Can they all hold simultaneously? Perhaps in some cases the goal of one of the beneficiaries is also the goal of each of the other three. If so, these are morally trivial (they provide no moral problem). Obviously, we can easily note cases in which choices must be made, in which we cannot satisfy both the community and the individual, both our community and the rest of humanity, both ourselves and our god. The four different moral principles produce six pairs of beneficiaries, six cases in which a choice between two may have to be made. (There are also four triples, groups of three, that may have to be ranked.) This section proposes a way of characterizing the choices.

The Two Kinds of Errors

Whenever there is more than one way of deciding something and when one of the ways is actually right, there is a risk of error in making the decision. Suppose we face a choice between A and B, when A is actually the right answer. Two different errors are possible. We might pick neither, which would be rejecting the right answer. Or, we might choose B, which is accepting the wrong answer (as well as rejecting the right one). These two different kinds of mistakes are called:

> Type I Error: *rejecting an alternative when it is right*
> Type II Error: *accepting an alternative when it is wrong*

Of course, for either kind of error to exist, there must be right and wrong answers. If we cannot be right or wrong, then we cannot make an error in choosing.

Let us assume that there are right and wrong answers to moral questions. (Assume that the moral skeptic is wrong.) We can then characterize each of the four moral positions in terms of the risk of error that its holder is willing to run. Of course, no one wants to make an error. However, humans are capable of mistakes, and one must *risk* an error in making any decision. The serious question, therefore, is this: If an error will occur, which error would the moral actor prefer to make?

A moral action is an act of sacrifice. Each of the four moral positions sacrifices at least some possible beneficiaries for the sake of others. To sacrifice certain beneficiaries runs the risk that the wrong beneficiary may be chosen. The universal fairness position takes all of humanity to be the right beneficiaries and so ignores the selfish desires of the individual. It may turn out that humanity is ungrateful, and moral actors may wish that they had put themselves above the abstraction called humanity. Still, they prefer to risk an error in this direction, rather than the other direction. On the other side, the egoistic moralists risk the error that ignoring humanity's interests, putting their own personal happiness above the concept of humanity, may leave them empty and contemptuous of themselves. Still, egoists would rather risk the possible error of future emptiness than the possible error of discovering that there is no such thing as humanity and of the future disgust at their own lack of respect for themselves.

Compare the religious position with one of the others—for instance, the utilitarian. The religious moralist prefers to risk the error that there may be no god rather than the error of choosing to live for the benefit of the majority when there really is a god and a heaven beyond the desires of the majority. The utilitarian prefers to risk the error of discovering that the majority is ungrateful, or is just a fiction, or is not a worthy beneficiary instead of risking the error of putting any other entity above the serious needs of the majority of his or her society.

As put earlier, every decision involves a balance of risks of the two kinds of error. A soldier's decision, which he or she makes at induction, to swear to obey the orders of the president and to defend the Constitution of the United States from all enemies, foreign and domestic, also involves a choice of risk of error. To accept induction into the armed forces risks the possible moral error of agreeing to follow orders that are immoral—for example, an order to kill innocents. Not to accept induction risks a different moral error—not to defend innocents against immoral enemies. We cannot know in advance which choice is actually the right one, so we must risk making a mistake. Whatever choice is made, including the choice not to make a choice, one risk of error is being maximized and another risk of error is being minimized. Where they are not pushed to maximum and minimum, they are given some balance—either one is somewhat larger than the other or they are chosen to be equally large. There is no avoiding the fact that every significant choice produces a *certain balance of risk of the possible errors.*

Style

A brief detour to the concept of style may be of use at this point. Contrast two officers: One demands regular saluting and no use of his or her first name by inferiors in rank. A second "fraternizes" with the troops. The formal officer who lives by the book prefers the risk that the lower ranks will hate him or her rather than the risk that they may not obey in a crucial situation. The friendly informal officer prefers to risk a lack of obedience rather than the risk that the troops will not like him or her personally. These different choices of which error to prefer, if an error is made, can be called *differences in style.* Of course, it could turn out that it is the informal officer who is obeyed under stress and the formal one who is not. Each chooses a style and then hopes that it produces either no error or what is taken to be the lesser error.

Other familiar examples should make the identification of style and risk of error obvious. Compare one person whose desk is always completely cluttered with another whose desk is clear and even dust free. The first prefers to avoid the error of wasting time on housekeeping incidentals; the second avoids the error of losing things under a pile of new arrivals—different styles, we say. Consider two student extremes: one who always raises a hand to answer the question and a second who never talks in class. For the first, the Type I error is a terrible thing: To know the answer and not tell the world would be a calamity. The risk of saying something false is a less serious error. For the second student, to accept and assert a falsehood would be devastating, people would laugh; so the student avoids the Type II error by never speaking.

Personal styles differ. The difference can be classified as different preferences for error, if an error is to occur. So, here the term *style* means a certain balance of the two risks of error. Given a problem—that is, a situation with more than just one possible act—there will always be more than one way of choosing that balance, more than one possible style.

Moral Style

It seems clear that we cannot speak without choosing to speak in some language. It is also held that we cannot be religious without choosing some religion. Similarly, we cannot be moral without choosing a particular moral style. Because being moral means acting for the benefit of one of the several different possible moral objects, one such object must be chosen. The choice that is made is a choice to balance the possible risks of error in a particular way. Therefore, being moral means choosing a certain style, a certain balance or pattern of risk of error.

We have already described the advantages and disadvantages of each moral theory. To restate these in the language of risk, of moral style, can easily be done. The rephrasing, however, will not tell us which style is perfect for all occasions. As mentioned earlier, moral monism is the position that looks for one view, one moral style, to answer every problem. Considering the disadvantages to be found in each of the four moralities, we are quickly led to pluralism; however, this leaves us with the question of when to follow which style. When should we put ourselves above the majority, and when not? If there were a logical or rational way of answering this, there would be a *science of morality*. Fortunately or not, no such science is available. Therefore, humans choose their moral styles by their own feelings of what is appropriate or fit. They get advice, and orders, from other humans, but the choice of whether or not to follow that advice is also a matter of personal style. Humans cannot avoid personal responsibility for their own moral styles.

Should all humans have the same moral style? Our attachment to freedom suggests that we mean to countenance differences. Are there styles so extreme that we cannot permit them to be called moral? Yes, there are limits to the range of style that deserves to be allowed as moral. Kant gave us a criterion for the term *morality* that we can use to limit moral style. Kant's "categorical imperative" is his rule that the principle of one's action must be capable of being universally followed.[33] Not the specific act but *the principle* of the act must be one that everyone can follow. Does this rule out any of our four alternatives? Not on a wholesale basis. The version within each must be examined to see if it meets Kant's imperative. For example, if a religion is one that some but not all people could in principle follow, it fails Kant's test. If all could equally be members of that religious community, it passes the test. If the variety of individualism is such that each of us could hold and follow it, the rule is satisfied. If some of us could not be such individualists, by the rule's theory, then it is not satisfied. Kant's rule does not tell us which moral style is the one and only one to take, but it does limit us to styles that theoretically everyone could choose.

Kant's rule sets the boundaries to acceptable styles but offers no method for picking the best or perfect moral style—and none exists. Individual dignity or freedom consists in the need and the ability to be responsible for one's own moral style. That does not mean that anything goes or that you can choose whatever you like. *Some choices violate the categorical imperative, the rule of universality, and are therefore not moral. That's the meaning of* moral. But this limit still leaves choices of styles to individual judgment.

The soldier who has sworn to or affirmed that he or she will obey the president and defend the Constitution must do so or violate the rule of universality. We cannot break promises and also seriously make promises: Promises would not exist under such principles. The soldier, however, must balance the risk of error in violating the promise to obey the president against the risk of error in violating the requirements of universal fairness if he or she obeys an unfair order.

The problem of choosing between the four moralities—and choosing a variety within any one of them—cannot be removed, nor would it be desirable. Human dignity, as described above, means that the choice of moral style is to be made by the individual alone. There are limits to the choice, however, and we do have an absolute rule that defines those limits. This rule is absolute because it defines the meaning of morality. Honesty turns out—no surprise—to be a requirement of any moral style. To do one's duty is to behave honestly, to do what one has promised. The reason for an induction ceremony is to formalize the soldier's promise to defend the Constitution. He or she then has accepted a duty. In each of the following sections of this book, we find that the acceptable range of styles falls within Kant's rule. The categorical imperative gives the parameters—the bounds—of styles that can be thought of as moral. Often, more than one action can qualify.

We have not properly responded to the skeptic. The skeptic listens to the discussion of these problems and laughs. "Can't find the solution," he or she thinks, "because there is no such thing as morality." We join the skeptic in smiling at those who look for morality itself, but we go on to explain that morality is not a thing or a single rule but a *certain relationship* between an actor and a beneficiary. That it is a relationship rather than an object does not make it less real or significant. After all, the relationship "west of" has reality, although there is no such thing as west. Likewise, to note that someone takes a certain entity to be a moral object has real significance. We have held that the moral relationship consists in a certain style or balance of the risks of error. And we can show the skeptic that he, also, displays a moral style in whatever decisions he makes. To make a decision is to choose a pattern of risk, and to choose a pattern of risk is to choose a moral style. Skeptics may insist that their own style is nicer, safer, more elegant than that of others, but they cannot argue that they have no moral style or that there are no differences among moral styles. If decisions cannot be escaped, moral style cannot be escaped. Just because we prefer to ignore our moral patterns does not mean that they do not exist. Pittsburgh is west of Philadelphia, whether Pittsburgh knows that or not. Certain relationships do exist, and moral relationships are among them.

Of course, the skeptic does have one final desperate retort: We are assuming that people make choices freely. If we were mechanical entities without freedom, we would have no responsibility for our styles. Let's grant that.

The problems of choosing specific moral styles or moral strategies must be dealt with in terms of examples. They come in later chapters. At this stage, we should look at available alternative theories.

The Professional Army Ethic

The language and special definitions developed in this chapter are closely related to the material presented in a prior edition of the well-known Army Field Manual, FM 100-1, *The Army* (here and below all references are to the August 1981 version).[34] We have shown relationships and distinctions between the parts of the traditional professional military ethic and have supplied some of the philosophical background, but we have not invented a new moral code. Rather, the above material provides some new ways of sorting out, thinking about, and using the traditional military values.

In a section on these problems, FM 100-1 states that "the Army ethic holds resolutely to four fundamental and enduring values: Loyalty to the Institution, Loyalty to the Unit, Personal Responsibility, Selfless Service." These four values can be interpreted in terms of the four moral "styles" already presented. By considering certain expansions of the official language, we can put philosophical meat on the military bones of Chapter 4 of the FM 100-1. This hypothesis requires a moral inflation of the four traditional values.

The first two of these values—loyalty to the institution and loyalty to the unit—may be distinguished by regarding the institution as the widest group of persons to whom we owe loyalty and the unit as a smaller group to which we also owe loyalty. Then, the widest group, morally, is the class of all humans; the next-widest group is the nation. Of course, this *generalizes* the terms *institution* and *unit* far beyond their ordinary meanings as well as beyond the clear way that they are used on page 24 of FM 100-1.

The motives for this broadening of the concepts (replacing *institution* with *humanity* and *unit* with *nation*) are threefold. First, the military code recognizes the humanity of the civilian and military personnel of all other nations and gives instructions on and limitations to dealing with them. Of course, the loyalty owed to them is not experienced as strongly as the loyalty to one's own side. Second, by introducing the new category, humanity, we add an additional basic moral style. Third, and unavoidably if we are to be guided by our basic historical traditions, this expansion of the term *institution* to mean "humanity" rather than simply "the nation" has its basis in the Declaration of Independence.

In its first sentence, the Declaration of Independence explains that the signers of that statement were addressing an audience different from the highest authorities of Great Britain. Up to that time, the signers had been loyal subjects of the king of Great Britain.[35] However, this document was written to justify themselves before *mankind*. They placed special and high value on "the opinions of mankind." Therefore, their declaration was an explanation required out of "a *decent respect to the opinions of mankind.*" Their statement explained in some detail why they no longer respected their king, but they said that they were required to respect this separate entity, mankind. Their loyalty to their nation did not last as long as their loyalty to mankind! Therefore, we have to understand mankind—humanity—to be worthy of a different and sometimes higher loyalty than that owed to the nation. So it was for the founding fathers of the United States.

For a certain narrow patriotism, the Declaration of Independence was and may still continue to be embarrassing. It simply explains that a value exists that may last longer than loyalty to one's nation. With the nervousness that the Declaration intrinsically produces, we can take the widest loyalty specified in the FM, that called "Loyalty to the Institution," to be loyalty to mankind. Thus, in terms of our four moral styles this produces mankind—humanity—as the moral beneficiary and universal fairness as the method.

The second value, "Loyalty to the Unit," can be understood as the morality of social utility, or loyalty to the nation. What the FM describes as the consequences of "Loyalty to the Institution" can be located here under social utility as loyalty to the nation.

The third value, "Personal Responsibility," fits quite easily into our category of individualism. It has all the features, strong and weak, that we faced in the earlier consideration of that style.

Finally, the FM's "Selfless Service" can be understood in the terms in which we have presented the religious style. The FM explains that this is to stand for selfless service *"to the nation in general"* (p. 24). This notion of the nation *"in general"* apparently denotes an abstract entity, a nonhuman entity that has absolute value. Of all four values, the FM calls this one "perhaps most important, of the fundamental ethical values" (p. 24). As a nonhuman yet highest value, this abstract entity fits the category of the religious style of sacrifice, for it is only in this one of the four that the FM uses the word *sacrifice*.

It may be of use to review this "interpretation" of the text description of the four values of the professional army ethic:

1. We take universal fairness as a broadening of the idea of loyalty to the institution.
2. Social utility is understood as "loyalty to the unit." "The welfare of one's comrades" in FM 100-1 is the notion of utilitarianism in the social utility position, the greatest good for the greatest number in one's community.
3. Individualism, in one of its senses, includes the personal responsibility concept of FM 100-1. If the individual is the essential moral actor, that individual must accept all credit and all blame, that is, all responsibility for significant actions. This responsibility, of course, includes responsibility for those under one's command.[36]
4. The religious position on values implies the need for absolute sacrifice, the concept of selfless service that FM 100-1 proposes as the fourth fundamental value.

On the face of it, the FM description merely underlines the potential need to sacrifice one's life in support of the first two values, loyalty to the nation and to the Army. The religious position holds that there is something more significant morally than any specific human beneficiaries and that one should be prepared to sacrifice in favor of this "something more." The emphasis in FM 100-1 on selfless sacrifice is derived from the idea that the nation and its army have the absolute value of a god, the value of that "something more" than the ordinary material objects around us.

What basis is offered in the FMs when a choice must be made involving these values? First, the easy one. When there is pressure to follow a value outside of these four, FM 22-100, *Military Leadership*,[37] calls on intuition: "You usually know in your heart the right thing to do. The real question is whether or not you have the character to live by professional values when under pressure."[38] Suppose things are complex; two or more values collide and intuition is not clear. The FM responds, "*You* must decide which value will lead to the highest moral good—that moral outcome which best helps the Army serve *the ideals of the nation*"[39] (emphasis mine). "You," the individual, must make the judgment, and "the ideals" of the nations are to be the beneficiary. That is what is to be served. What are the ideals? They are expressed in the Declaration of Independence and the U.S. Constitution.

FM 22-100 also proposes a useful thought experiment. Consider an ethical dilemma such as a question about mutiny. Suppose you think that the ideals of the nation might best be served by mutiny. (The novel, *The Caine Mutiny*, is an example.) Ask yourself this question: "Could you justify the morality of your actions before a group of your peers and seniors?" This is a reasonable thought experiment, but this may still produce more than one acceptable moral style.

Choosing Among the Four Moral Styles

Recall earlier conclusions about this critical matter. *First,* there is no science of morality, no perfectly dependable way of making moral judgments in all situations. We are personally responsible for our styles. *Second,* we must confine ourselves to styles that obey the categorical imperative. The meaning of morality demands that restriction. *Third,* the categorical imperative requires honesty. Promises must be kept, and these include the promise made at induction.

Within these three conclusions remains some moral flexibility—more than one way of behaving morally, more than one way of balancing the risks of moral error. But these variations in personal style cannot fall outside of the categorical imperative. All variations must follow rules that could be universalized to apply to everyone, meaning that when there is a conflict, universal fairness dominates.

Therefore, one can be an individualist, if doing this follows rules that anyone could follow. One can serve any god, if doing so is obeying rules that anyone could obey. One can take a social group as one's beneficiary, again, if the rules permit anyone to take a similar action. The range is wide, but universal fairness sets the limits.

To return briefly to a question that arose early in this chapter: If all people are equal moral objects, how should we think about war? The Declaration of Independence gives us significant guidance. After the list of charges against the British king, the Declaration criticizes the British people for being "deaf to the voice of justice." Then, in the last sentence of the paragraph, it says that we hold [our British brethren], "as we hold the rest of mankind, Enemies in War, in Peace Friends." All of mankind are considered to have two potential relationships to us: At one time we may be at war with them, at another time at peace. No humans are so depraved that they must always be enemies, and none are so close to us that they may never be enemies. This attitude toward human nature combines suspicion and generosity. Our current allies may oppose us in the future; our enemies of the moment may be our friends tomorrow.

One of the problems in a moral perspective toward the enemy is the need to combine the dual attitude of the Declaration of Independence with the military need to act as efficiently as possible, to kill as many of the enemy as possible. The Declaration reminds us that an enemy today is a human whom we hold to be capable of peace and friendship with us. But that peace and friendship is, in the words of St. Augustine, "not just yet."[40] An honest soldier can know that the enemy is human and also know that the enemy must be attacked ferociously. A dignified soldier has that dual knowledge, but a fanatic does not.

Respect for human dignity does not eliminate the need to fight. Each person may need protection from an enemy, and each person deserves the freedom to chose an enemy. That holds for our enemies—our temporary enemies—as well as our allies. All enemies must be considered temporary because the object of war is to win and make peace with them.

3

Military Honor and the Laws of Warfare

When Can I Lie to the Enemy?

In ideal terms, military honor is military persons' display of what Thomas Hobbes called *the relish of justice:* "That which gives to human actions the relish of justice, is a certain nobleness or gallantness of courage, rarely found, by which a man scorns to be beholden for the contentment of his life, to fraud, or breach of promise."[1] In other words, honor is honesty even when it hurts. If honor is desirable and if Hobbes is right that it is rarely found, can we teach it?

Military Education

When students in a civilian college are found to be cheating on an examination, it does not make a story in the national media—not even headlines in the local papers and probably not a story in the college newspaper. The students may have a hearing before a student/faculty disciplinary board, and a penalty may be imposed if the verdict is that the students are guilty. The penalty may be a failure in the course or a brief suspension from the institution; often it is less severe than either of these.

The West Point scandal of 1976 made front-page news across the country. Military students were cheating, which *violated the honor code*. That event, a most serious matter, was followed by student dismissals and lengthy editorial comment. In the junior class, 184 students were formally accused of cheating, and 152 of those were expelled.[2]

Similar cheating "scandals" at the Naval Academy in Annapolis and at the Air Force Academy in Colorado Springs have also been given the most serious attention.

Why is cheating by an officer candidate taken more seriously than cheating by a civilian student at the same educational level? The question almost answers itself. Civilian schools have honor codes, but moral education is usually not a conscious educational goal. The Military Academy at West Point has a well-known honor code requiring that "a Cadet will not lie, cheat or steal, nor tolerate anyone who does." The experience of living by such a code, we hope, will help produce officers who can be trusted to avoid moral individualism. They will have consciously practiced the reflex of honesty, of consistently doing what they promised to do, regardless of temptation. The thought and temptations of individualism are always in the mind, but we assume that people can be found who consciously adopt another moral style.

Can candidates for military service *be educated* to consistently carry out their duties? Or, is honesty either innate or not the sort of thing that can be instilled in people? This is an old question in moral theory, and the answer is far from clear. In *The Republic*, Plato considered the problem of selecting and training the guardians of his community:

> We must find out who are the best guardians of this inward conviction that they must always do what they believe to be best for the commonwealth. We have to watch them from earliest childhood and set them tasks in which they would be most likely to forget or to be beguiled out of this duty. We then choose only those whose memory holds firm and who are proof against delusion.[3]

Plato proposes to test in order to find those who behave honorably, who put duty to their community above all else. If we are lucky, we find them in adequate numbers. If we do not find them, we are not at all certain that educational devices like an honor code can manufacture them. Are there actually persons who follow duty rather than the selfish style? Strangely enough, on occasion, there seem to be. However, if they are free humans, we can never be certain of the next style that they will adopt.

Recruiting Scandal

How morally successful are the graduates of our military programs? Measuring is difficult, and the occasional scandal is hard to evaluate. One must consider not only the matter of individual integrity but also the question of collective or institutional style. A headline in a minor story makes the point: "Navy Admits that Its Recruiters Helped Cheaters in Vermont Test."[4] The story involved testing recruits at a high school in Middlebury, Vermont. The newspaper story makes the Navy itself the dubious moral actor:

The Navy previously denied that the recruiters had been involved in any cheating, despite sworn statements from a State Education Department investigator that she had seen recruiters passing out test answers and changing wrong answers on the recruits' tests.

The change in the Navy's position occurred one day after Senator Patrick J. Leahy, Democrat of Vermont, asked to see a Navy report that cleared the three recruiters of the charges. Navy officials said last month that the recruiters had admitted violating military guidelines and had been fined $75 each, but that there was "absolutely no evidence" that there had been any cheating.[5]

The moral style of the Navy was dubious: That is, (1) it first apparently preferred to increase the risk that the individuals involved (both recruiters and recruits) might take cheating to be an acceptable style in an effort to diminish the risk of not having enough recruits—or, at least, enough from Vermont. Then, (2) the Navy preferred to risk some disclosure rather than admit that its recruiters (officers?) had been cheating and thus risk lower public esteem. Finally, (3) when Senator Leahy asked for their report, they admitted that their recruiters had "helped" cheaters. Their final moral style was to prefer the risks of the bad publicity about the truth than risk further lying and its even worse public perception. (It is not known if the recruiters suffered any change in their punishment—the $75 fine.)

Several questions are raised by this little bit of history. One wonders how typical it was. Is this the ordinary military pattern? Plato would hope not. Then there is the issue of institutional versus individual morality. Was it Navy policy to cheat in order to get more recruits, or were the individuals doing it for their own benefit? They may have had quotas that were difficult to meet honestly. The cover-up was apparently a Navy, rather than an individual, moral decision. This chapter is largely concerned with individual honor: Whatever we conclude about this, the matter of institutional honor still remains.

Respect Means Fear

We may find a lesson in the Navy recruiting story. Start with a basic assumption about human motivation. Respect means fear: To respect something is to fear that it may cause you pain.[6] Plato came upon this relationship when he considered the matter of respect for the gods. He took it that we respect the gods because we fear their power to cause us harm—no fear, no respect. We use the term *respect* this way in many and perhaps all contexts, in and out of the military. We respect the barrel of a gun, a charging lion, a policeman, and another human being because each of these can cause us pain. To have contempt for an enemy is to have no fear of him or her, To respect the enemy is to believe that he or she is capable of inflicting harm.

People can be expected to do their duty only when they have a greater fear of not doing it. What might such a greater fear be? It might be fear of discovery by peers or other ranks. It might be fear of punishment by the gods—fear of not gaining heaven.

Other examples of the definition of respect are easily found. Respect for command is fear of punishment for disobedience. Respect for senior officers is fear of punishment. Respect for the inspector general is fear of being caught at something. The idea of respect for the dead may date from the period when it was thought that they could return to cause pain. What, one wonders, were the fears or dangers that the Navy recruiters balanced?

Let us suppose that the Navy specified very high quotas for the number of recruits who were expected to be accepted. Let us also suppose that the Navy had managed to produce an atmosphere of victory, an expectation that no one in the Navy will ever fail to carry out a mission—or, horrors, ever surrender. If failing to carry out a mission perfectly is an absolute fear, then dishonesty becomes a lesser danger. Of course, this is speculation. The speculation, however, leads to the idea that military education must emphasize the need *to balance the goal of winning with the goal of honor*. The recruiters' problem was a peacetime situation, and they failed; the point of military education is to prepare for battlefield problems, where moral failure is critical.

A variety of works have studied the problems of military education in recent years. The point of the recruiters situation has been found to be pervasive "in the entire military system."[7] At West Point, "we seem to have the cadet model of the 'up or out' pattern characteristic of the larger Army, complete with concern for short-range performance goals. Perhaps it is here that the concept of career as an overriding imperative originates and is continually reinforced."[8]

Honor: Dual Duties

Why care about honor?[9] Is the notion of honor a fraud to dupe the infantile, the stupid, or the romantic? Or is it, as some insist, "the ultimate protection of societies"?[10] Totalitarian governments have taken their concept of national honor most seriously, democratic market-economy societies hold the honoring of business contracts to be a basic feature of their civilization, and no society seems able to give up some application of honor. This discussion will be but a brief comment on some military aspects of the subject.

In a general way, *military honor* refers to courage and fidelity. The role of courage is clear enough, as is willingness to do one's duty (e.g., to follow orders regardless of danger—no desertion under fire). The notion of fidelity is more complicated. *Fidelity* means careful and exact performance of duties, but the term leaves open the matter of just what duties require this special role. For the military tradition, *the duties are dual: to king or government and to the military code.* We must consider both, starting with the code.

Duty to the Military Code

The military code, or law of warfare, is explicitly and formally stated in the Hague and Geneva Conventions, and almost every nation has agreed to be bound by it (140 nations had signed it by April 1976, and it is about 170 as of this writing). The code also consists of unwritten law, what FM 27-10 calls "the body of unwritten or customary law firmly established by the custom of nations."[11] The relationship between treaties or conventions and the unwritten code is like the relationship between legislative enactments and the unwritten common law in the Anglo-American legal framework. Both the written and unwritten parts are most serious elements.

The Three Purposes of the Code

The U.S. Army and the British War Office put the three purposes for the law of war in identical phrases. In order to diminish the evils of war, the law of war requires:

a. Protecting both combatants and noncombatants from *unnecessary suffering;*
b. Safeguarding certain *fundamental human rights* of persons who fall into the hands of the enemy, particularly prisoners of war, the wounded and sick, and civilians; and
c. *Facilitating the restoration of peace.*[12]

Each of these is a basic part of the military code and deserves special attention.

Protecting Combatants and Noncombatants: The distinction between combatants and noncombatants is intended to maintain a line between those who announce themselves as ready and willing to fight and those who sympathize with them but who do not take part in combat. Why this distinction? It is an unequal fight if a prepared, trained, and willing individual attacks someone who is weak, unwilling, and unprepared. An unequal fight is immoral by the standard of universal fairness. The principle—attack those who are unwilling to fight—cannot be used by each party against the other. There is nothing to boast about when a fully armed and powerful warrior kills a defenseless child or elderly person. Philosopher Friedrich Nietzsche pointed to the old idea that members of the noble class take their revenge only within the circle of equals. Morality, and therefore honor, requires a fair fight against a worthy, prepared opponent. So, the military code distinguishes between soldiers who are ready for combat and those who are not prepared to fight. In the next chapter, we find that we are not to choose noncombatants as acceptable targets.

The term *unnecessary suffering* turns out to be less precise than one would wish. The intent is that only that amount of force or pain be inflicted that is necessary to achieve the military objective. If the city can be captured, the enemy forced to surrender, and the post taken with just a certain level of pain, then any pain beyond that is unnecessary. The Hague Convention specifies, "It is especially forbidden . . . to employ arms, projectiles, or material calculated to cause unnecessary suffering."[13] The FM explains that: "Usage has, however, established the illegality of the use of lances with barbed heads, irregular-shaped bullets, and projectiles filled with glass, the use of any substance on bullets that would tend unnecessarily to inflame a wound inflicted by them, and the scoring of the surface or the filing off of the ends of the hard cases of bullets."[14] A dum-dum bullet[15] that stops a soldier no more effectively than an ordinary bullet can cause more pain; therefore, such bullets, and "projectiles filled with glass," are forbidden by the Convention. Honorable soldiers are to obey the Convention and not use these bullets, even if they would cause additional terror among the enemy and thus speed up the mission.

If glass-filled shells are forbidden on the grounds of unnecessary suffering what about flamethrowers, napalm, and gas and chemical weapons? The next chapter discusses the special convention forbidding gas. The FM tells us that the question of what is unnecessary for the military objective—what is "unnecessary injury"—is to be decided "in light of the practice of States in refraining from the use of a given weapon because it is believed to have that effect" (p. 18). The practices change, and so the classification of weapons that cause unnecessary suffering changes. However, the general principle remains: It is forbidden to cause more injury than necessary to achieve the military goal.

Given that principle, how are atomic and nuclear weapons to be classified? Because they cause more injury than that involved in the immediate military activity (they have radiation effects that go on for years after a war), they would seem to be in the same category as glass-filled shells—forbidden! In addition to the unnecessary suffering inflicted on military personnel, they attack noncombatants—an ideal combination for the Hague Convention's "especially forbidden" category. This question is much too serious for an automatic classification.

The Hague Convention (18 October 1907) is more than 100 years old, Hence, it does not tell us that nuclear weapons are forbidden; rather, it says that weapons that do what they do are to be forbidden. However, such weapons abound today. Is the old Convention still a serious demand on military honor? Despite the Convention's age, we must note that the Constitution is still older and that the Hague Treaty is specified in FM 27-10 as having "a force equal to that of laws enacted by the Congress . . . [to be observed] with the same strict regard for both the letter and spirit of the law which is required with respect to the Constitution and the statutes enacted in pursuance thereof" (para. 7.b., p. 7). Chapter 11 considers nuclear devices in more detail, but the overlay with matters of honor should be obvious. If the use of these devices is to be construed as a violation of the laws of warfare, then honorable personnel—those strictly following the professional military ethic—have the obligation to explain this to all parties involved. Those parties include the political leaders. We will return to the relationships between military honor and political honor below.

Safeguarding Fundamental Human Rights: The second purpose of the military code comes from the idea that there are *fundamental human rights* that persons retain even when they surrender and become prisoners of war, even when they are wounded or sick and unable to defend themselves, and, of course, even when they are civilians who are not fighting. The laws of war are called a *natural law* theory; that is, they are based on the assumption that all humans have certain rights just because they are human. This assumption sometimes has a purely rational basis, sometimes a religious basis.

What are those rights? The special Geneva Conventions on the treatment of prisoners and the sick and wounded give some specifications for these categories. In gross terms, the point is to eliminate torture and sadism, which are or should be gratuitous to the military goals. Cutting off the ears of a few POWs and sending them back to terrify the enemy may well cause terror among the enemy and reduce enthusiasm for fighting; however, it violates the assumed natural rights of the individual to be free of such "unnatural" abuse. Is it unnatural? Consider a comment by Francis Jennings on the wars between Indians and Europeans in the history of the United States:

> Plenty of sadism was evident in both cultures. Indians vented it directly upon the person of their victim, hacking and slashing at his body democratically with their own hands. Even old women would satisfy some horrid lust by thrusting firebrands at his genitals or chewing off the joints of his fingers.[16]

According to Jennings, the term *democratically* here means that they did it themselves rather than have it done by the officers of the government, as would have happened in "civilized" white Europe. What is and is not to be considered a natural or fundamental human right depends on custom, and the custom or practice is now to take it as a fundamental right that the individual not have to suffer dismemberment or torture by firebrands. Why is this practice more moral than the earlier one? It is more moral because it follows the universal fairness criterion.[17]

Certain other fundamental rights, such as the right to practice one's religion, are also assumed and protected for POWs and others, as we will see.

These and other "fundamental rights" are taken to exist by the natural law theory and are denied by alternative theories. A different theory, a "positivist" view of law, assumes that the term *law* refers to specific acts of a government and only to those acts. On such a basis, people have only the rights that governmental decisions give them. No rights exist before or outside the jurisdiction of a legitimate government. The law of war certainly rejects the positivist view: It bows to unwritten law, and it assumes fundamental human rights, as we have seen.

Facilitating the Restoration of Peace: The third purpose of the law of war was mentioned in Chapter 1. Facilitating the restoration of peace is one of the purposes of anything but a war of complete extermination of the enemy. Could there seriously be a war with the purpose of extermination? There could be extermination of all of the soldiers, yes, but their families would hardly forget and may well plan further defiance. Exterminate all soldiers and their families? The distant relatives and friends remain to cause trouble. Exterminate anyone who is involved even distantly, plus all those who may have heard about the extermination? The risk would always remain that someone may discover the evidence of the extermination. Destroy all possible ways of reconstructing the evidence of the extermination? The ambition of exterminating the enemy hardly seems serious, to say nothing of its being a violation of the universal fairness morality. In addition to its other risks, this kind of war risks the outrage and contempt of one's own forces. To eliminate an enemy and then have one's own army revolt—overturn the command and the government—is hardly to gain the fruit of victory.

While historical matters are not really the subject of concern in this book, two points in American military history ought to be mentioned in connection with this question of extermination or annihilation of an enemy. In 1785, Benjamin Franklin, acting on behalf of the recently formed United States, negotiated and concluded the first modern world treaty that specified rules for the protection of the wounded and prisoners of war. This was "The Treaty of Friendship and Trade" between Prussia and the United States. Students of the much-later Geneva Conventions acknowledge that this treaty produced by Benjamin Franklin and Frederick II of Prussia "laid down rules . . . which very closely foreshadowed the provisions of the Geneva Convention."[18] While Franklin (and Frederick II as well) is better known for other accomplishments, this one gives the United States the pride of an early claim to concern with internationalizing the laws of warfare. On the other side of the matter, however, is the argument made by Russell Weigley in *The American Way of War: A History of United States Military Strategy and Policy.*[19] Our history shows that "the strategy of annihilation became characteristically the American way in war."[20] Of course, these are different matters; treatment of the wounded and prisoners is not the same as strategy, but they both involve honor.

As argued earlier, the purpose of a war is to win. But to win is to have the enemy surrender—that is, first, to accept the conditions of the surrender and, next, to stay surrendered. The war, therefore, must be conducted with certain restraints so as to maintain the respect of the enemy for the honesty, the trustworthiness, of their opponents. *Military honor is a military weapon as well as a moral duty!* The enemy must believe, must trust, that duties will be carried out scrupulously and that the duty to obey the law of war is the cardinal duty for military honor.

For the soldier, there are dual duties: to his commander and to the military code. What of a conflict between them—an order by the commander to violate the demands of military honor, perhaps to kill innocent civilians? The military code is quite clear. As, FM 27-10 phrases it, "Members of the armed forces are bound to obey only lawful orders."[21] *Only* lawful orders: An order to violate the Hague or Geneva Conventions is *not a* lawful order. In Chapter 8, we return to this matter of illegal orders.

An Example of Choosing Honor over Victory: Admiral Wilhelm Canaris
One wonders, do soldiers ever actually put the military code above the victory of their own side? The history of warfare is not filled with such moral heroes. However, there are many examples on both sides.

It has come to light that Admiral Wilhelm Canaris, the head of the Abwehr—the German military intelligence organization—faced just such a choice: obedience to his commander, Hitler, or obedience to honor. In 1983, the U.S. House of Representatives released previously secret testimony on the history of the Central Intelligence Agency by Allen Dulles, its first head. Dulles said that Admiral Canaris "furnished information to me . . . about the German development of the guided missiles, and some of the first clues that led to the bombing of Peenemunde. . . . The top five men in the German intelligence were all executed as traitors. . . . They became disgusted with Hitler's tactics."[22] Writing in the *New York Times,* a commentator on Admiral Canaris's decision said, "Here was a man who placed his honor as a German officer, his duty to his fatherland and his responsibility as a human being ahead of his loyalty to a mad leader. With courage and clarity of purpose, Admiral Canaris deliberately dared to commit the crime of high treason."[23]

We may assume that when the head of the Abwehr chose honor over obedience to Hitler, he understood the balance of risks that he chose. As the head of military intelligence for his nation, he would understand that better than anyone else. Apparently, he preferred the risk of being caught to the risk that Hitler's Germany might win. As we found in the last chapter, within the bounds set by the categorical imperative there is nothing in the nature or history of logic, reason, and moral theory that tells us when to obey the king and when to obey the apparent commands of one of the other choices of beneficiary. Both the king and the other moral objects always want to be the beneficiary of every choice. That choice is a personal preference for a certain moral style.

For his moral style, his balance of risks of error, the admiral was caught and executed. He honored the military code—the demand for respect for the fundamental rights of everyone—above the political leadership of his nation. Does honor mean anything? It is not always successful, but it is always morally impressive. We respect it because it shows a standard that we fear that we ourselves should be able to but may not manage to attain and because it is sometimes successful.

Robbery vs. Honor: One of the purposes of the law of war is to distinguish between criminal acts of armed robbers and the actions of honorable soldiers who are members of a militia. Both armed robbers and soldiers carry weapons and do what they want; however, actions of the latter sort satisfy four conditions. The soldiers

1. Are commanded by someone responsible for subordinates
2. Have a fixed, distinctive sign recognizable at a distance
3. Carry arms openly
4. Conduct operations in accordance with the laws and customs of war

Each of these conditions is important. The distinction shown by the first is that a criminal acts for his or her own selfish goals; soldiers act for the sake of someone other than themselves—for commander and country. Because soldiers are not ashamed of what they do, they wear a sign, a uniform, to proclaim their loyalty and to openly warn their enemies, as the second condition above requires. To be "out of uniform" is to pretend to be something other than what they are. The third condition shows that they hope to win by open, honest, proud effort, not by deviousness or lying to the enemy. The fourth condition, the requirement that the laws *and customs* of war not be violated, has its complications—but continues in the same spirit. The difference between a sneaky, selfish thief and a proud soldier lies in the open, honest willingness to sacrifice for the sake of others and to do so without violating the agreements and precepts of the military code. (Certain specifications of the code involving hostilities are the subject of the next chapter.) It should be obvious that the moral style of the soldier is the complete rejection of individualism: His immediate beneficiary is certainly not himself.

Duty to the King or Commander and the Code of Conduct

The oath taken by an officer of the Army of the United States is to "Support and defend the Constitution of the United States against all enemies, foreign and domestic . . . and to well and faithfully discharge the duties of the office." The officer's commission by the president charges and requires the officer "to render such obedience as is due to the president, the future president of the United States, or other superior officers." The oath and commission are well known to the general public; however, the Code of Conduct for the Armed Forces of the United States is probably not well known, but it deserves our attention. It runs as follows:

> Code of Conduct for Members of the Armed Forces of the United States (Executive order, 15 August 1975, amended April 1988)[24]
>
> I. I am an American, I serve in the forces which guard my country and our way of life. I am prepared to give my life in their defense.
>
> II. I will never surrender of my own free will. If in command I will never surrender the members of my command while they still have the means to resist.
>
> III. If I am captured I will continue to resist by all means available. I will make every effort to escape and aid others to escape. I will accept neither parole nor special favors from the enemy.
>
> IV. If I become a prisoner of war, I will keep faith with my fellow prisoners. I will give no information nor take part in any action which might be harmful to my comrades, If I am senior I will take command, If not, I will obey the lawful orders of those appointed over me and will back them up in every way.
>
> V. When questioned, should I become a prisoner of war, I am bound to give only my name, rank, service number, and date of birth, I will evade answering further questions to the utmost of my ability. I will make no oral or written statements disloyal to my country and its allies or harmful to their cause.
>
> VI. I will never forget that I am an American, responsible for my actions, and dedicated to the principles which made my country free. I will trust in my God and in the United States of America.

The Code is presented to personnel in training with an explanation of each of the six parts. The reasons for the update in the Code go back to the behavior of American POWs during the Korean War when it became clear that more training was needed about the proper limits of cooperation with the enemy. POWs are constantly tempted to accept small favors and privileges in exchange for helping the enemy, and they must be prepared against that temptation.

The First Declaration: Willingness to Die for My Country: The first statement in the Code asserts two of the elements of the soldier's framework. The moral object is "my country and our way of life"; the method is complete loyalty: "I am prepared to give my life." Political theorists differ over the meaning of "our way of life" and explain that we do not all live the same "way." The induction oath, however, directs us to the Constitution, which defines the way of life for which the recruit has sworn, or affirmed, to be prepared to give his or her own life. Having a political ideology as a moral object is a new feature in the history of warfare.

In *A Study of War,* Quincy Wright discusses this feature of history. Civilized war, he insists, is distinguished "by ideological conflict, a struggle for values beyond the immediate interest of the participants—values *which may be achieved even though all the combatants die*" (emphasis mine).[25]

> Primitive people . . . have not tolerated wars so severe as to assure the death of the participants, to threaten the existence of the group, and to destroy intergroup relations. *But when war is for an idea,* especially a very broad one deemed fundamental in the civilization, *the necessary limits to destructiveness have not been evident.* If one fights for democracy, it may be appropriate to destroy all the states and most of the individuals so that a clear field will remain in which democracy can grow. If it is Christianity against Islam, each may be prepared to destroy all the adversaries if only a few of its side can remain to perpetuate the true faith.[26] (emphasis mine)

Someone has been quoted as saying that if a nuclear war ends with three of their people left and ten of ours, we win!

If the ideology "the true faith" is more important than life, an individual may have no trouble accepting the first proposition in the U.S. Code. The morning after the attack on Pearl Harbor, the lines at the recruiting centers seemed to show the impressive size of this population. Obviously, many people prefer the dignity of death in combat to the indignity of life without a certain, most desirable, set of ideas.[27] This phenomenon, taken by itself, would be a superficial explanation of the success of recruiting efforts. People volunteer for military service for many more reasons than ideology, which when compared to group pressures of various sorts may be the least significant element.

The ideological elements in warfare may be more significant to civilians than to the military forces of a nation. In his study of combat soldiers in Vietnam, Charles C. Moskos, Jr., reports that

> when left to themselves, the soldiers rarely discussed the reasons for America's military intervention in Vietnam, the nature of communist systems, or other political issues. . . . The American combat soldier displays a profound skepticism of political and ideological appeals. . . . They dismiss patriotic slogans or exhortations to defend democracy with, "What a crock." "Be serious, man," or "Who's kidding who?"[28]

Moskos does go on to give a theory of the "latent ideology" of the combat soldier and of its "concrete consequences for combat motivation." (p. 147)

The Second Declaration: No Surrender The second declaration of the Code, no surrender while there are means to resist, has some ambiguity. Must the "means to resist" be enough to avoid capture, or not? Suppose a company can resist only by taking great losses followed by the capture of the remaining 1 percent. Suppose the means are such that the company will all be killed. This situation might have military significance in overall terms, and so the declaration of no surrender is to be taken literally. Where there are no means of resistance, however, the surrender is not voluntary.

Why not surrender when further resistance will probably lead to one's death? Is this just the coward's question, or is it also a reasonable question for everyone? We cannot escape personal moral style in our response. The hero prefers to risk the loss of life to the loss of social and private standing as a person of honor. The coward balances the risk of loss the other way. Must we be either heroes or cowards by these definitions? Unfortunately, there sometimes are such choices: There are commands that we either follow or disobey. And, the names for our choices are well known. Not every decision is so crucial, although politicians always talk as if each is, but not every decision is trivial. There are decisive moments.[29]

The Third Declaration: No Parole Will Be Accepted The third declaration has a special history behind it. Whether or not to give *parole,* one's word not to escape, is a serious decision. The Geneva POW Convention specifies that "prisoners of war who are paroled or who have given their promise . . . are bound on their personal honour scrupulously to fulfill . . . the engagements of their paroles or promises."[30] The FM warns that violation of parole may be punished under Article 134 of the Uniform Code of Military Justice; soldiers must stick to their word. If they agreed not to escape, then they must not . . . If they agreed not to commit sabotage, then they must not.

There is one qualification to the order that parole not be asked for or accepted. A "temporary parole" may be used in special situations. Suppose a POW has an extremely painful toothache or requires the removal of an appendix, and suppose that the only medical or dental service is a few kilometers away from the POW camp. The senior commander *of the POWs* may authorize the soldier's acceptance of a temporary parole for the specific purpose of getting medical care. If all these qualifications are met and the senior commander of the POWs authorizes it, a POW can give his or her word—parole—not to escape. Then, even if the soldier has the opportunity, that person is bound on "personal honour" not to escape but to return to the POW camp as promised. Why obey this formal requirement? Both sides gain because it makes possible the parole of others in need and it maintains respect for the honor of both sides. Because parole is not to be violated, the U.S. Code tells all personnel not to accept parole from the enemy. Temporary parole is not mentioned here in the Code. If prisoners did accept any form of parole, they would have to stick "scrupulously" to their promises.

The Fourth and Fifth Declarations: POW Commander and Personal Responsibility The fourth and fifth declarations in the U.S. Code are very important and partly obvious. Again, both can have unforeseen complications. In a POW situation, nothing should be done that may harm fellow prisoners. The choice of a U.S. commander for U.S. prisoners follows a pattern of rank, if this is possible. The fifth declaration allows the Geneva Convention requirement of giving name, rank, service number, and date of birth but warns against disclosing information or making statements harmful to the United States or its allies or other soldiers.

The Sixth Declaration: Personal Responsibility and Trust in God and Country The last declaration of the Code reminds military personnel that they are *personally* "responsible" for their actions. This declaration starts with "*I will never forget that I.* . . . " The individual cannot evade personal responsibility for illegal or dishonorable actions. This covers actions before, during, or after a term as a POW. The intent of the U.S. Code may have been to stress personal responsibility during a term as a POW; however, this responsibility of the individual soldier holds during his or her entire period in the service, whether captured or not.

One part of this last declaration comes close to being a violation of the First Amendment to the Constitution. To declare trust in "my God" does not directly involve a "law respecting an establishment" of religion; however, it is hardly clear what this trust means to those of Western as well as non-Western religious heritage. The president, as commander-in-chief of the Armed Forces of the United States, has ordered (on 15 August 1975) all members of the Armed Forces to "trust" in their own God. One wonders what would count as a violation of this trust. If nothing would, it appears to be an empty command. (An empty command is one in which nothing can be a clear act of obedience or disobedience to it.) The government, the United States, shares top-level status with God; the sentence that starts with "I will trust" has God and the United States as joint members of the predicate conjunction. Apparently they are co-equal moral objects, unlikely to have different goals. The serious point of this part of the fifth declaration is to remind potential POWs that survival under difficult circumstances may depend on psychological factors such as the strength of trust in God and country and the hope of victory. A dramatic example of the power of this factor—minus the trust in a Western God—has recently turned up in the case of the last Japanese soldier to surrender in World War II.

Corporal Yokoi: The Most Loyal Soldier of the Emperor On 25 January 1972, Lance Corporal Shoichi Yokoi was found living in the jungle on Guam,[31] about twenty-seven years after the end of the war and twelve years after two Japanese soldiers had been discovered in the Guam jungle (Bunzo Minagawa and Tadashi Ito) and assumed to be the last surviving soldiers. Corporal Yokoi was described as "a peaceful tailor . . . who was obliged to endure unimaginable solitude for 28 years as a faithful soldier of the Emperor."[32] Trust, hope, and loyalty can have obvious operational consequences. When a faithful soldier of the emperor was told not to surrender, he held out in the jungle for twenty-seven years. Of course, he is hardly typical, but he represents an impressive human capacity for loyalty, for sacrificing for a beneficiary other than one's self.

This ability of humans to sacrifice themselves for the community may well have been a significant factor in the evolution of the species up to this stage. From here on, given the power of modern weapons and delivery systems, this habit of political loyalty could be counterproductive for the future history of the human species. Where the need is for an international government, loyalty to the existing nations becomes cultural lag. Loyalty to an emperor, or to some existing political arrangement, is sometimes—but not always—a morally desirable pattern. While we respect and are impressed by Corporal Yokoi's sense of honor, his fantastic dependability and loyalty to the emperor, we must also pity him for the unnecessary waste of so many years of his life. He is an inspiring example of honor, as well as an example of the stupidity of such a conception of honor. There is a point at which devotion to honor becomes fanaticism. Twenty-seven years playing hide-and-seek is hardly a rational and dignified way to live.

The official explanation of the sixth affirmation of the U.S. Code includes this statement: "A member of the Armed Forces who is forcibly detained by a foreign state or entity *must never give up hope*. He must resist all attempts at indoctrination and remain loyal to his country, his service, and his unit" (emphasis mine).[33] Corporal Yokoi never gave up hope, but one wishes that he had tempered his honor with a bit of Aristotelian moderation.

Aristotle called our attention to three possibilities: "For it is possible to desire honour as one ought, and more than one ought, and less."[34] While Aristotle is talking here about honors that others may give us, and they are not the same as personal internal honor (self-respect), we still find merit in *the idea of a mean between extremes*. Neither we nor Aristotle want moderation in truth telling and honesty, but loyalty to the emperor or the government might well be taken with some moderation—some effort to avoid the extreme of fanaticism.[35] Because humans so easily and regularly make errors in judgment, the judgment that absolute loyalty should *never be reconsidered* is a dubious decision. When to maintain loyalty and when to reconsider it is the question: The response marks the moral style of a soldier. Moral style, as developed in the previous chapter, is the balance chosen between the two risks of error. Whatever the behavior, it cannot avoid the display of some moral style.

Honor and Personal Risk: Hero or Coward?

Suppose that I am walking down the street with my best friend. A group of town bullies appear and attack my friend. I can either come to my friend's defense, at great risk to my own safety, or run away. If I run away, I lose my sense of dignity, of honor. If I run away, I give up the assumption between friends that each may be depended upon by the other, that each is willing to sacrifice for the sake of the other. If this assumption of friendship be called personal dignity, can I live without it? Can I stand the thought of life with the knowledge that I deserted my friend? With this knowledge in my community? If I would rather risk the loss of my life than the loss of my dignity, I fight. If I prefer the loss of personal dignity, if I think that either I don't need my old friends, that I don't need any friends if they cost so much, or that I can make new friends, then I run rather than fight. The labels *hero* and *coward* are available for these choices of risk pattern. The question becomes: Is it stupid to be a hero? (Of course, *hero* is reserved for something more than an expected defense of one's friend.)

Ideology as Moral Object

In the example above, consider sacrifice for the sake of a good friend. One thinks of protecting a wife, a husband, a parent, a sister or brother, a lifelong buddy. Suppose, as Quincy Wright has noted, we are asked for heroism in defense of an idea. Is there an idea or an ideology that is worth one's life, worth heroism? Assume that one would die to protect his or her family: Is there a civilized ideology that equals the value level of family as a moral object? The coward may think that to fight and run away allows one to live to fight another day. For the coward, it is never exactly the right time to die. The good fight can be better fought another day. Is the coward right, with regard to political ideas? Are they worth a life? Think of the centuries of religious wars, and a parallel question arises: Is the difference between one religion and another, or between one religion and no religion, worth one's life? Religious wars have not completely ended; consider the Middle East, Northern Ireland (perhaps this is no longer an example of religious wars), Pakistan, and Iraq. But, we now can easily imagine a period in which religious wars are past, not because one of them has defeated all the others but because the Western world no longer takes them so seriously and has become tolerant of the differences. Perhaps we can imagine a comparable period for the end of political wars.

Political wars might end in one of two ways. Either one political system will have defeated the others, or the world will produce so much economic abundance that there will be no scarcity to fight about and little else. Neither of these two results seems likely in the near future; therefore, we find all national entities preparing to fight political wars, wars to protect or to extend their "way of life." We may, however, expect that two ideas will eventually come to be obvious. *First,* that *with moderate prosperity,* almost any system can provide a good, and even an exciting, life. Is there a difference between political systems *A, B,* and *C* such that we would rather be poor under *A* than live well under *B* or *C?* When put to the test, our individual selfishness might move us toward the prosperous life, and we would rationalize the system under which that life could be led. The *second* notion that may come to be commonly accepted is that as they grow industrially, nations resemble each other more and more. The differences between powerful industrial nations may become so small that old political principles will become fussy, trivial details. Because of the force of these two notions, we must expect that it will make sense to think of the enemy armed forces as composed of fellow human beings, humans with whom we may eventually live in peace.

Does awareness of the factors that make for the hope of peace produce less of a will to fight and, therefore, a less-effective army? In the short run, it would seem that the answer is "Yes." Such an army is less fanatical or single-minded. However, because the goal of war is to have the enemy make peace on our terms, the enemy must be dealt with in a fashion that makes surrender possible. As argued regularly in this book, to make it possible for the enemy to surrender and to accept the terms of surrender with trust, we must behave with the honor that the laws of warfare require. Therefore, to be somewhat ambivalent about the right to kill the enemy, to think of the enemy as humans who are not evil in every way, is to avoid fanaticism. A fanatical soldier is neither intelligent enough nor honest enough to be trusted with the dangerous weapons of modern warfare.

Does this conclusion support the coward over the hero? No, it does not. It argues that we think carefully about the goals for which life is to be risked and lost. My understanding of a bully's personal motives does not excuse me from defending my family. Dignity requires it. Likewise, my understanding of the political motivations of the enemy does not excuse me from defending my own political system if I really desire it. The strength of my desire for a political pattern might be measured by my willingness to sacrifice for it. I say "might be measured" because I might desire a goal highly but only if someone else makes the sacrifice to get it. To offer to hold your coat while you fight for me is not the peak of bravery: There are politicians who make this offer, indeed who make it not merely an offer but a demand. Dignity requires more than this. If I want something, *I* ought to be willing to make the sacrifice. That is the moral cost of individual dignity or honor.

Desertion

Given the apparent strength of individualism, of selfish motives, it must seem surprising that there is so little desertion from military duty. We might expect a large amount of desertion under fire or "combat refusals"—not so. We find that desertion rates are higher in peacetime than during a war. Russell Weigley, the distinguished American military historian, has reported that late nineteenth-century desertion rates were exceedingly high—during periods of peace. There has been no desertion rate anywhere near those levels during a war.[36] Apparently it is boredom and not danger that leads to desertion. The strength of the individualist style of morality seems to be balanced with the other styles; otherwise, the desertion rates during war would have to be higher. Desertion in Vietnam will be considered separately below.

Comments on desertion must be tempered by the thought that we do not seem to have much reliable information. The war departments (or defense departments) of every country are rather shy about calling attention to their own desertion rates. Professor Russell Weigley, however, has pointed out that facts can be obtained indirectly. The history of the British Air Forces during World War II mentions the number of "navigational errors" made by U.S. aircraft (bombers) that forced them to land in such neutral places as Sweden and Switzerland. Likewise, the history of World War II written by the U.S. Air Force notes the number of "navigational errors" that the British Strategic Air Force made that unfortunately forced them to land in the safety of Sweden and Switzerland. I gather that there were about one hundred or so on each side. Were these desertions under fire, or were they errors? Only the participants know. Perhaps even the navigators were ambivalent and not quite sure what was a conscious and what was an unconscious decision. We do know (and so did they) that during certain periods the risk to the Strategic Air Forces of being shot down over Germany was quite high.

With the qualifications mentioned above, we must still be impressed by the success of military training in producing forces that behave honorably. When personnel are taught the difference *and when their leaders are observed to take great risks themselves,* it may be easier to find honorable than dishonorable behavior. This characteristic seems to be a general human rather than a particular nationalistic trait and can be noted throughout the history of warfare. There are, however, embarrassments.

Honor and the U.S. Officer Corps in Vietnam

According to some commentators, the behavior of U.S. forces during the Vietnam War was a dramatic exception to much of the material above. The final analysis may not yet be in, but there are arguments that have to be met. The most serious charges can be found in *Crisis in Command* by Richard A.

Gabriel and Paul L. Savage, who deliver a severe indictment of the morality of the U.S. officer corps. The officers showed more interest in their own careers than in anything else; there were more officers and more high-ranking officers than necessary; there were unearned medals; and there was a rotation system that was unfair to enlisted men. (Officers served six months in front-line units while enlisted men served twelve months.) The Vietnam desertion rates

> exceeded those of World War II by over ten per thousand, at their height, and by over forty-one per thousand when measured against the Korean War's maximum desertion rate. Indeed, the annual rates of increase in desertions during Vietnam exceed anything in U.S. combat experience despite the fact that the Vietnam conflict, when seen in historical perspective, demanded comparatively low levels of sacrifice.[37]

Gabriel and Savage also give some data on what they call "a peculiar characteristic of the war. . . . This was the practice of 'fragging,' defined as attempts to kill with an 'explosive device,' ordinarily a hand grenade."[38] Fragging was the attempt to kill "leadership elements," officers or noncoms. The idea can hardly be ignored that there are, crudely put, just two leadership commands. One is "Follow me," and the other is "Go that way." The moral difference is obvious. After analyzing the number of fraggings plus "combat refusals" and desertions, Gabriel and Savage contrast the U.S. pattern in Vietnam with various other examples in military history, including the British ability to produce successful forces out of a wide variety of colonial enlistees. "We suspect that successful military socialization is linked intimately to the conduct and leadership of the British officers and NCOs, who always led their men at the front and very often died leading them."[39] To say that they merely "suspect" is a bit of British understatement by the two former American officers. (Savage is retired and Gabriel is in the Reserve.) Their book is a serious challenge to the honor of the U.S. Army Officer Corps. In a later article, they offered an equally contemptuous challenge to what they call the "American elite"—the most established group in the country, but a group that does not itself run the risks of battle.

According to Gabriel and Savage, American officers did not die in the expected numbers in Vietnam. Their judgment is based on comparisons with the relationship between the number of enlisted men and officers who died in other wars. It must be noted, however, that the data (as always) can be classified in more than one way. If you count only combat officers, you get one answer; if you count all officers in Vietnam, you get another. For some purposes, we might compare losses of officers of different rank. On the surface, it would be easy to compare the French and the American military performances in Vietnam because both groups faced somewhat similar problems. "French officers lost in action constituted some 29 percent of the French officer corps in Indochina. Of total French Army casualties, 11.3 percent were officers. . . . By comparison. . . . U.S. Army officer deaths due to hostile action amounted to approximately 2 percent of [its total] strength."[40] Amazing. For explanations we look to luck, skill, or dereliction of duty. We must distinguish, however, between combat officers and those involved in other duties such as logistics and the advisors programs. Taking data from Gabriel and Savage's own study, we find that in the category of "deaths among battle casualties," officer deaths were 10.7 percent of total losses, which is not far from the French record (if the French data on casualties are comparable to these data on deaths). This figure, however, includes warrant officers, and they are a rather anomalous category (what Aristotle might have called "nature's mistakes," the term that he used for those who were not clearly qualified to be masters or slaves: Warrant officers are not line officers or enlisted personnel). Because warrant officers did not lead ground combat units, including them gives a misleading impression. Without warrant officers (who often were helicopter pilots), the officer death rate turned out to be 8.4 percent of total battle deaths.[41]

Are figures on the ratio of battle deaths of officers to enlisted men an indication of the honor of the officer corps? If the point of the military establishment is preparation for battle and not for parades, the answer must be "Yes." Of course, the case in Vietnam as in other wars still needs careful analysis. Reliable data do not just appear: Their sources must be understood or they are meaningless or worse. Because the previous chapter on moral styles has made the notion of sacrifice the central relationship, the questions of who makes the sacrifices and what those sacrifices are become the basic moral issue. If the ratio of battle deaths is not a moral question, nothing is.

Gabriel and Savage have certainly shown that much of the establishment in Vietnam was essentially not involved in combat; however, the case against the honor of combat officers is not so damaging as it would appear if these officers were just included in the total number of officers who could be found in Vietnam. (The size and composition of the military establishment in Vietnam is not the present subject.) The purpose of Gabriel and Savage's book is the analysis of leadership styles that developed in Vietnam, and the number of officers involved in combat cannot be avoided.

What is the result of leadership from the rear?

Eventually the enlisted men's contempt for officers and the system they symbolized was revealed in the number of officer and NCO assassinations, acts of insubordination, and mutinous actions, all of which are clear symptoms of a loss of military self-respect, unit pride, and unit cohesion. The result was disintegration at the small-unit level.[42]

Gabriel and Savage locate the poor military result in Vietnam in the low level of professionalism and of honor in the officer corps—not in the antiwar protests, the "permissive society," or the other familiar excuses. If they are wrong, the refutation has yet to appear.

Conclusions

We have considered a few but certainly not all the aspects of the concept of honor. We have emphasized the idea that military honor requires dual duties, duties to the government and to the laws of warfare—the military code. In a conflict between the two, we have held that obedience to the limitations of the laws of warfare should take precedence over the duty to obey commands of the government. There are situations in which the style of Nathan Hale[43] ought to be chosen over that of Admiral Canaris and other situations in which their styles ought to be exchanged. All governments present a Nathan Hale as the ideal for their own forces and an Admiral Canaris as the ideal for their enemies. There is no escape from the personal responsibility to decide whether the situation is such that honor requires us to imitate Hale or Canaris, the spy or the traitor.

We have held that military honor is both a weapon and a moral duty. Of course, to say that is to speak from one and against another of the moral styles. The pure individualist wants to *appear* honorable, not necessarily to *be* honorable. Honor is a matter of the intentions of the person, and the outer world knows only the consequences.[44] So, the pure individualist has a fair chance of having his or her behavior taken, now and again, for the intention to behave honorably. Ordinarily, the world will not know.

Political Honor

Candor requires that we at least mention an embarrassing subject. Military literature often makes reference to "the wisdom of Karl von Clausewitz regarding the preeminence of politics in the role of war."[45] The "wisdom" of Clausewitz in pointing to the connections between politics and war (could those connections possibly be missed?) must not lead us to confuse these very different but related areas and professions. Political questions and military questions have certain things in common, but they also have impressive differences. Political morality and military morality, in particular, are different. This idea is poorly phrased because while morality is the same, typical examples in politics and in warfare are different. While taking off the uniform and carrying out a military action may seem to be an excellent political decision, it is a very dubious military matter. There is a code, a set of laws, of warfare: There seems not to be any code of political honor. We can teach something about military honor by using the Hague and Geneva

Conventions as texts: To teach political honor, we have our students read Machiavelli.

Politicians ordinarily show little sense of military honor and the restrictions that it puts on acceptable missions. I would gladly retract this statement if I could. We return to this matter in Chapter 11, but the problem may be put in terms of honor. Relations between the military and civilian branches of the U.S. government are not problematic; the Constitution makes the military subservient to the commander-in-chief, the political leader. The military, however, must have the moral courage to say *no* to politicians when they ask for violations of the international conventions that define military honor. One example is General Eisenhower's response to Churchill when that great British political leader suggested something that made no moral and only questionable military sense to the general. According to the report,

> In July 1944, when Allied bombing failed to knock out the German V-2 missile sites then nearing completion, Winston Churchill was so agitated by the impending threat that he urged an attack with poison gas. General Eisenhower dismissed the idea out of hand. "Let's, for God's sake, keep our eyes on the ball and use some sense," he replied.[46]

The ball on which General Eisenhower had to focus was the total mission and not just certain missile sites and targets. In such conflicts between political and military leaders, it is quite clear that the political leaders do and should set the framework in a democracy. But, illegal orders call for soldiers to have the moral courage to explain the matter. There seems to be no nice rule that can resolve all such conflicts, but at a minimum, the issues must be called to the attention of all parties concerned. Responsible officers must have the guts to say, as General Eisenhower did, "Let's, for God's sake, keep our eyes on the ball and use some sense." When the laws of war are clear, honor insists that they be obeyed. Unfortunately, they are not always clear.

In the case of Corporal Yokoi, we should first consider whether he intended to evade capture or just remained in the jungle accidentally. Quickly we reject the latter. Yokoi's behavior qualifies him as a hero, up to a certain point. He followed his duty to his emperor at impressive cost, but as outside spectators who knew that the war was over and that the emperor had surrendered all his fighting forces, we move from considering Yokoi as hero to pitying him for playing an empty role and pointlessly wasting his life, The choice of style for honor cannot be made abstractly; we must make assumptions about the actual world as well as about moral theories. One lesson from Corporal Yokoi is that honor requires more than just obedience to command; it also requires attention to the changing facts of the world.

Hachiko, the Loyal Dog

Examples of loyalty and honor range from the sublime to the stupid—and degrees in between. Consider the famous dog, Hachiko. In a busy public area of Tokyo, just outside the west exit of the Shibuya Station, stands a bronze statue of a dog. This dog, Hachiko, walked with his master to the station to work every day and came back to the station to meet him in the early evening. In 1925, his master died while away, and Hachiko waited at the station for him to return for the next ten years. His loyalty became well known (concerned people fed him), and after his death a statue of him was set up on the spot of his vigil.

Was Hachiko's ten-year wait an example of the loyalty—the dedication— that we would like to inspire in the military? As soon as we ask the question, we feel that we have been insulting and rush to make distinctions. A human who behaved like Hachiko, whose knowledge of the facts of the world was as limited, would be classified as retarded. Suppose someone did know that his or her most valued beneficiary was dead but still waited, "out of respect," still serving a nonexistent master? After a decent interval of mourning, we would call that person mentally ill. Suppose that someone served one and only one master for all or most of his or her life? Would that behavior be beautiful, or would it be doglike? Slavelike?

One conclusion that the questions about Hachiko-like behavior lead to is the idea that healthy people are not dedicated to one style or one benefici- ary alone. Buildings can be "dedicated," but not healthy people. Aristotle's advice, applied to a somewhat different subject, points the way. We expect healthy humans to have a moderate interest in each of the moral styles. The emphasis here should be on *moderate* and on *each*. To have only one bene- ficiary, to be "single-minded," is not to be a complete or a healthy person. We know that each of the four styles has certain attractions as well as lim- its. On some occasions each of them is appropriate; on others, they are not. Hachiko had only one beneficiary and only one style of sacrifice. Therefore, he had no ambivalence (as far as we know) about his choice of style. We ex- pect a human to have more than one beneficiary and, therefore, to have at least some ambivalence about his or her sacrifice. *A human can display honor by having more than one beneficiary and then unselfishly choosing to favor one.* Hachiko displayed no honor in choosing the unselfish goal be- cause we do not think that he understood the attractions of more than one goal.

The point is that a "value-healthy" person is not merely aware of one and only one possible beneficiary. Such a person vacillates between self and service to the unit or to someone or something else but, despite the vacilla- tion, still behaves unselfishly. That is what we mean by honor. Hachiko sug- gests honor by analogy if and only if we interpret him as desiring both his master's return and his own comfort. If he cared only about his master's return and nothing else, we would have to judge his behavior as consistent, not honorable. No temptation, no honor.

Back to the Aristotle remark: We can assume a "value-healthy" person to have some interest in each of the four moral styles. What, then, is the mark of honor for such a "healthy" human? Honor is displayed by overcoming temptation, by following the categorical imperative even when it hurts. Again—no temptation, no honor. For Hachiko to be a symbol of honor, of human loyalty, we must interpret his world as multivalued. If an autopsy showed him to be brain damaged and thus unable to perceive ambivalence or conflict, we would lose him as an example of loyalty. In that case, Hachiko would be seen essentially as a consistent machine, not an attractive symbol of a desirable display of loyalty.

The Tyranny of "The Mission"

One of the lessons of Hachiko is the need to rethink the meaning of the term *the mission*. Certainly a combat unit must focus on its mission, its target. The need to concentrate on just one mission at a time can easily, too easily, be supported by examples from history and analogies from sports. The problem is that there is always more than one mission—or, in a sense, an explicit order, written or not, and an implicit order. The explicit order may be "Take that position"; the implicit order is "And remain an American soldier while doing it." It's not completely implicit; it is point I of the Code of Conduct cited above. The mission, therefore, has a dual character: to gain a certain objective and at *the same time* to obey the laws of warfare. Therefore, there is always more than *one* mission underway.

This comment on the tyranny of thinking in terms of just one mission may be taken as another way of saying something that a former company commander in Vietnam emphasized. In a paper on "Human Values in War," he wrote, "Fourth, and possibly most destructive of values, is the imperative of immediate success—that modern, myopic societal expediency that excuses the sacrifice of values and standards as long as the outcome is superficially successful."[47] To think in terms of just one mission is to aim for immediate, short-run success. Where there are actually two missions, to ignore one of them is to fail. The same article, discussing rules of engagement, insists that "first the rule must be tactically valid, and, second, it must be morally valid." Where these two missions are consistent, we have no problem. Where they conflict, we look for honor.

Now we must face the question with which this chapter opened. Can we teach honor? We can train butterfingered recruits to field-strip an M-16 rifle blindfolded; how hard can it be to train them to be honorable? We can teach the history of military honor, giving examples of honorable and dishonorable conduct. We can teach the theory behind honor, explaining the differences between sacrifice for one and for another possible moral object. We can give inspirational talks on the subject. We can threaten a dishonorable discharge. But, at the end of all our efforts, the apparent free will of the individual defies a precise prediction of human activity. Suppose we agree that we cannot eliminate the chance of dishonorable conduct, can we at least teach people how to make the honorable judgment?

As soon as we phrase this question, several problems become apparent. First, there may be more than one honorable judgment. Which style do we teach? Ah, we teach the limits of the acceptable styles, in terms of the universal fairness criterion. Yes, we can do that. However, the second problem remains. A *theory* can be taught, a *history* of examples can be taught, matters of fact and *law* can be taught, but *judgment* cannot.[48] A judgment is a decision that a particular case, all risks considered, falls under a certain class of cases. Although computers, and people, can be taught to make that decision if we program them with a certain moral style, a certain balance of risks of error, we do not seem to be able to program for the decision of *when* to take *which* balance of risks in a new situation.[49]

Because this programming does not seem possible, we may take comfort in the notion that it may *not* be desirable to program people for one and only one moral style for all situations. Military education can teach honor by producing the atmosphere of honor. The history, theory, facts, and laws involved in military honor can be given large attention. Examples of heroic and cowardly behavior on both sides of the hard cases can be given. The problem of when honor points to obedience and when it points to disobedience can be regularly studied. And yet, after all this, there still remains the necessity of teaching by example.

Socrates himself, the most effective teacher in the history of philosophy, could teach only by the example of his own life. He had an opportunity either to escape from the laws of his city or to obey the laws at the cost of his life. He discussed the question with his students, considered it from several standpoints, and then took the honorable course of obeying the laws. Although he thought that the law had made a mistake in his case, honor required that even such laws be obeyed.[50] Unfortunately, no easy tricks exist: Teaching honor requires the example of honor in the leadership. Even then, judgment may not be teachable.

The critical judgment, for military honor, is judgment in applying the laws of war during hostilities. We turn to that in the next chapter.

4

Hostilities

All Is Not Fair

T he laws of war will allow the enemy's water supply to be bombed, or the enemy to be drowned in it, but they will not allow putting poison into that water. The enemy can be made to die of thirst or drowned but cannot be killed by an undetectable poison. Odd though it may seem, there is a reasonable basis for this distinction. Here we consider this and related limitations on hostilities.

Protecting Powers

Before studying the specific details of international law that affect hostilities, we must note the role of "protecting powers." The Geneva Conventions (1949) clarified the status of a nation or organization designated a "protecting power" as ordinarily a neutral nation "whose duty it is to safeguard the interests of the Parties to the conflict."[1] If the belligerents want to communicate with each other about reported violations of the Conventions or such matters as the status of POWs, civilians, religious leaders, and buildings of general cultural importance, they can ask the protecting power to assist. Although the protecting power is usually a nation, the International Committee of the Red Cross (ICRC) has accepted some aspects of this role and carried out various humanitarian functions, including visiting and inspecting and delivering mail and food packages to POW camps. The officials of the ICRC are (always, it seems) Swiss citizens and have an impressive record of neutrality. There is some expectation that the ability of the ICRC or another protecting power to inspect POW camps will help keep the camps running on a humanitarian basis.

Respect for the ICRC is based on *the fear that they will publish* an embarrassing report on conditions in a POW camp. Is fear of publicity a serious fear? Apparently it is, based on the reported efforts to clean up problems before such visits. Every nation seems to care about being regarded positively by the rest of the world and seems to have "a decent respect for the opinion of mankind" (as our Declaration of Independence put it). This is fortunate because the power of publicity is one of the main forces that keep nations respectful—fearful—of the agreements that they have signed. We turn to some of the details of these agreements.

The Hague Rules and Some History

The Hague Convention (18 October 1907) is the international textbook on how to fight a war. Schoolteachers, of course, have noticed that textbooks are not always read, or understood, or believed. However, what are known as "The Hague Rules" (in the "Annex to the Convention" of 1907) consist of fifty-six "Articles" that are generally taken to be the written codification of the "Laws and Customs of War on Land."[2] The Hague Rules did not just suddenly appear, waiting to be signed by the original forty-two states. The 1907 Convention was preceded by two earlier major "International Declarations" in the nineteenth century, and those also followed earlier efforts.

The United States was rather prominent among the participants in those earlier movements. As mentioned earlier, a Treaty of Friendship and Trade was concluded in 1785 between Prussia and the United States. Benjamin Franklin, for the United States, and Frederick II, for Prussia, used it to lay down rules for the protection of the wounded and prisoners. Although written in a time of peace between the two countries, the treaty was an effort to set up rules to be followed during war, It was a groundbreaking statement, said to have "very closely foreshadowed the provisions of the Geneva Conventions," as mentioned earlier.[3] At this stage, however, it was only a treaty between two nations and not an international law expected to apply to all nations.

The next development, and one of the most significant in this brief history, was the Lieber Code. As noted earlier, Francis Lieber produced, and President Lincoln ordered the Army to follow, the most impressive code that had guided any military force up to that time.

At the initiative of "the Imperial Cabinet of Russia" in 1868, an international military commission assembled in St. Petersburg and signed a declaration "Renouncing the Use, in Time of War, of Explosive Projectiles Under 400 Grammes Weight." The agreement is printed on less than one page. It declared:

That the only legitimate object which States should endeavour to accomplish during war is to weaken the military forces of the enemy;

That for this purpose it is sufficient to disable the greatest possible number of men;

That this object would be exceeded by the employment of arms which uselessly aggravate the sufferings of disabled men, or render their deaths inevitable;

That the employment of such arms would, therefore, be contrary to the laws of humanity;

The Contracting Parties engage mutually to renounce, in case of war among themselves, the employment by their military or naval troops of any projectile of a weight below 400 grammes, which is either explosive or charged with fulminating or inflammable substances. . . .

The Contracting or Acceding Parties reserve to themselves to come hereafter to an understanding whenever a precise proposition shall be drawn up in view of future improvements which science may effect in the armament of troops, in order to maintain the principles which they have established, and to conciliate the necessities of war with the laws of humanity.[4]

The point was that an ordinary bullet stops a soldier as well as a small explosive bullet and does not cause the additional pain and damage. Because the additional pain gives no immediate military advantage, the small explosive bullet was outlawed on the grounds of humaneness. Large exploding shells were not affected by this declaration.

This agreement set the precedent for a series of international treaties on limitations on weapons and the conduct of war, a series of treaties that continues to the present. Agreements on weapons testing and weapons reduction are regularly matters of current debate. The St. Petersburg Declaration was followed by the 1899 Hague "International Declaration Respecting Asphyxiating Gases" and, on the same date, by a declaration "Respecting Expanding Bullets." Their titles essentially explain them. The St. Petersburg Declaration was signed—or acceded to—by twenty nations, and the first two Hague Declarations by twenty-seven; the United States signed neither.

Of course, the United States did sign the basic and more complete Hague Conventions of 1907. The Hague Conventions of 1907 produced the international textbook, the treaties that are regularly referred to as specifying the laws of warfare. They deal with (1) the opening of hostilities; (2) the laws and customs of war on land, the annex to which is referred to as "The Hague Rules"; (3) the rights and duties of neutral powers and persons in war on land; (4) bombardments by naval forces; and (5) a declaration prohibiting the discharge of projectiles and explosives from balloons. Not all states signed each of these separate declarations but many, including the

United States, did. These 1907 Hague Treaties remain in force except for the one on balloons that was specified to hold just for a period up to a certain (the third) peace conference.

Both the Hague and the Geneva Conventions are efforts to use humanitarian principles and traditions to restrain violence. Their difference is that the Hague Conventions deal particularly with rules and relations among nations, while the Geneva Conventions concern the protection of the individual. Nations declare war and determine policy on such issues as bombardments and use of gas, but individuals become wounded, sick, shipwrecked, imprisoned, or dead, or they have the status of civilians.

A Declaration of War

Why warn the enemy? Why not just attack without advance notice? The Hague Convention gives two reasons. First, that "it is important, in order *to ensure the maintenance of pacific relations,* that hostilities should not commence without previous warning" (emphasis mine). To be constantly on guard against attack is to be inefficient in many ways. To gain the advantages of "pacific relations," a nation must have some assurance that it will not suddenly be attacked without time to prepare its defense. The second reason states that "it is equally important that the existence of a state of war should be notified without delay to neutral Powers." Neutral countries have interests that are at risk during a war, and it is unfair to them to increase their hazards without warning.

In addition to these two specified purposes, consider the point made in Chapter 3: To attack without warning violates the morality of universal fairness. To unexpectedly stab someone in the back is to follow a rule that the victim cannot also follow. The rule that one individual may be the first to attack without warning is not a rule that both parties can follow. Only one can be the first, and if the rule cannot apply equally to all parties, it is immoral.

Therefore, Article I of the Hague Convention states: "The Contracting Powers recognize that hostilities between themselves must not commence without previous and explicit warning, in the form either of a reasoned declaration of war or of an ultimatum with conditional declaration of war."

The FM immediately follows the text above with the remark that surprise is still possible. "Nothing in the foregoing rule requires that any particular length of time shall elapse between a declaration of war and the commencement of hostilities." The suggestion is that a nation might declare war and, without waiting for the study of the reasoning in the "reasoned declaration," attack as soon as the declaration is delivered. The interpretation in the British Manual agrees that there is nothing to impose any period of delay between notification and attack and adds, "For this reason, sudden and unexpected declarations of war for the purpose of surprising an unprepared enemy would not seem to be incompatible *with the letter of the Convention.*"[5] However, they seem to understand that this would certainly violate the spirit of it.

What has the practice been? The Japanese attack on Pearl Harbor, 7 December 1941, was "a date which will live in infamy," as President Roosevelt phrased it, because it was a surprise, a violation of this Convention. (That an ambassador was on his way to deliver the declaration but was delayed does not change the fact of the violation.) In 1939, Germany began war against Poland by crossing the frontier and bombarding military objectives from the air. A declaration of war was issued *simultaneously* with these acts. Of course, the treaty requires a "previous," not a simultaneous, warning. In June 1941, Germany invaded the Soviet Union without any declaration of war. After the war, the International Military Tribune judged this act a war crime, and the persons responsible for it were punished.

At this point, perhaps the reader should be warned that the emotional level is about to rise somewhat over the next topic.

In a number of situations since World War II, we have seen military action, and sometimes major military action, without any party bothering with what has almost become a fussy little detail, a declaration of war. Current discussion of possible ICBM attacks never, or almost never, includes any attention to the point at which a war declaration must be made. Rather, the discussion is in terms of such issues as the minutes between launch and strike or launch and interception, questions of a second strike, targets that are military force or civilian, and hardening of sites. The "legalism" of a declaration may be a preoccupation of a Judge Advocate General (JAG) desk somewhere, but the outer world hears nothing of it. Is this the result of technological progress or moral regress? On the face of it, the latter.

This new "casualness" about combat without a declaration is cause for alarm wherever it occurs and is particularly surprising when the United States is the actor. Korea and Vietnam seemed, to the Congress and the public, not to require declarations of war, and minor legal details about the status of veterans of those undeclared wars have arisen. More recently, the United States attacked Nicaragua by mining a harbor without a declaration of war. Although the International Court at The Hague decided that the U.S. acts in that case were violations of international law, not all cases of military action require a declaration of war. The Convention permits defensive actions, police actions, and warnings that retaliation will follow if certain acts occur. The U.S. air attack on Libya in the spring of 1986 was a military action that followed some warnings, and perhaps those warnings might have been construed as a conditional declaration. However, the action is surprising on the part of the nation whose president called Pearl Harbor Day "a date which will live in infamy." Any attack without a declaration of war is a matter of infamy. If we have abandoned that "old" requirement of military honor, we should say so. Otherwise it is still the law. Undeclared wars—attacks without warning—are one of the marks of terrorism.

Obviously the War Powers Act and the constitutional requirement that Congress declare war are relevant here, but they are outside the scope of this book.

The Nature of Law

The historical details in the paragraph above raise a question: What is the point of a convention dealing with war if it is often violated? Why pretend that there is international law if nations break the law when they find it convenient? A brief excursion into the nature of law should produce a pertinent response.

The point of having a law is *not* that it will prevent the action that it calls illegal. Many cities have a law against parking in front of fire hydrants; yet the law does not stop the practice. Laws against murder do not seem to stop that activity. The fact that laws do not totally deter crime does not mean that we should repeal them. The point of having laws was expressed nicely by Professor Roger Fisher of Yale Law School:

> The essential talent of the law lies not in producing perfect order but in coping with disorder in an orderly way. Contract law, negligence law and criminal law "work" not in the sense of producing a society with no broken contracts, no negligence and no crimes, but by telling us how society should respond when things go wrong.[6]

We are not born knowing what to be shocked at and what is acceptable. We learn this from many sources, and the law is one of the clearest expressions of where a society intends its line to be. The law tells us two things: *what to be shocked at* and *what to do about it*. When the law specifies the range of punishment, we know what can be done in response to a violation. Does the existence of law ever prevent a crime? Perhaps, and that might be considered a nice fringe benefit of the law, although hardly dependable, as the laws against murder show. The essential talent, as Fisher put it, is to specify just what we want to be outraged at and what we expect to do about it. Of course, law is not the only agency that society uses. Custom, tradition, family, and other informal pressures are basic parts of civilization as well, but we can hardly imagine the history of civilization without the history of law. To repeat, law tells us what to be disturbed at and what to do about punishment.

A reader persuaded by this view of law can still point to a dramatic difference between domestic and so-called international law. The domestic variety has enforcement power, a police department. The international community has no power, no police or military agency, to enforce its law.

The International Court at The Hague does not have a sheriff or chief of police armed and capable of carrying out its decisions. Instead, it has the power of publicity and the weight of public opinion. The United Nations has raised and still does raise military forces to patrol borders and to ensure that certain decisions are respected. The United Nations did respond to President Harry Truman's request by participating in military action in Korea. However, the criticism stands—at this stage of world history, international law depends on voluntary compliance and that depends on sensitivity to world opinion.

If the only function of law were to guide the police in their enforcement, international law without enforcement would be trivial. The role of law as a guide to civilized behavior, however, does not depend on enforcement alone. International law, like domestic law, shows us what to be upset about, and that is extremely significant. It also serves to tell us what machinery to use in response to violations. For example, war crimes (see Chapter 8) are to be punished by court-martial or international tribunal.

Another question arises. Victors may court-martial the vanquished. Does one side ever punish its own soldiers for war crimes that they commit? For the crimes at My Lai in 1968, Lieutenant William L. Calley, Jr., was tried and convicted *by his own side!* (He was sentenced to life imprisonment. The sentence was later reduced, and the case had a number of odd legal turns.) One of the problems with breaking the law is that not only the enemy but also your own side may come to have contempt for you. Nevertheless, it is quite clear that a country is reluctant to admit that its side has violated the law and, therefore, is reluctant to punish its own personnel. In part, this is a sign of the force of world opinion.

Let us return to the features of the Hague Conventions with the assumption that international law has some clear roles as well as weaknesses.

Status of Civilians

When war is declared between two or more nations, does this declaration involve only their military personnel, or are their civilians also expected to fight and become targets? The British Manual gives an extended response to this problem:

> One of the consequences of the existence of a condition of war between two States is that *every subject of the one State becomes an enemy to every subject of the other.* It is impossible to sever the subjects from their State, and the outbreak of war between two States cannot but make their subjects enemies. Before the First World War the tendency was to regard hostilities as being restricted to the armed forces of the belligerents, and to differentiate between them and the ordinary citizens of the contending States who did not take

up arms. As the result, however, of *the practice followed by the belligerents in the two world wars,* it is no longer possible to say that international law protects the civilian population from injury which is incidental to attack upon legitimate military objectives. Nevertheless, notwithstanding these developments, it is a generally recognized rule of international law that *civilians must not be made the object of attack directed exclusively against them.* The view that war is a relation not only between State and State but also between individuals must be read subject to that important qualification.[7] (emphasis mine)

Several ideas in that passage are of significance. When a nation declares war on another nation, what does it mean to hold that the civilians of each are at war with the others? They are not to carry and use arms; if captured, they are not to have prisoner-of-war status. Can they be at war without acting in some special way? That they sympathize with their nation is granted. That their labor and taxes go to support their nation is basic to a critical part of the war effort.

The Hague Convention does distinguish between a neutral state and its citizens. *The state, as such,* is not to trade with a belligerent; but the citizens of that state are permitted to do so. The distinction between the state and its citizens is to be maintained and was formally maintained before World War II. This policy held for citizens of belligerent as well as neutral nations. The property of the state may be seized, but the private property of individuals may not. (Property can be requisitioned under certain circumstances; however, records and receipts must be maintained and return or compensation made as soon as possible.)

Why do the British countenance giving up the distinction between the state and its citizens? Perhaps they do so because they themselves gave it up by their area bombing of German cities in World War II. An unflattering explanation comes to mind from FM 22-100: "People tend to develop values to justify their behavior."[8] The matter is more complicated then this comment suggests; there were reprisals for reprisals for reprisals. (See Chapter 8.)

In a paragraph titled "Enemy Status of Civilians," the U.S. Field Manual seems to have taken directly from the British Manual.[9] Of course, the United States also carried out area bombing against civilian cities in Europe and in Japan. Hiroshima and Nagasaki were of little military significance; that is why they were still standing at that late date in the war. The question remains: Are civilians to be considered at war when their nation is at war? If they are, do they become acceptable targets, either directly or indirectly, in the course of an attack against something else nearby?

No army can exist without food. In addition, a modern army uses the products of the most sophisticated technology that its industry can provide. Where once it was easy to distinguish between the civilian economy and the war economy, at this stage the line between the two economies is far from clear. A citizen who works in a munitions factory is certainly involved in war production. The waitress or waiter who serves lunch to this person is also involved, although less directly. The dentist who takes care of the teeth of the waiter is involved, still less directly, as are the grandparents who babysit for the dentist's children, and so forth. Does this make a case for indiscriminate bombing of cities? Certainly not!

The Uniform Code of Military Justice (hereinafter, the UCMJ) makes "aid to the enemy" a crime that may be punished by death, a ruling that applies to all persons. However, it covers only areas under U.S. control. Before capture of an enemy city, for example, citizens who obey their government by paying taxes and the like are not under the jurisdiction of our UCMJ.

The Hague Rules simply forbid an attack on an undefended civilian city. "The attack or bombardment, by whatever means, of towns, villages, dwellings, or buildings which are undefended is prohibited" (Article 25). (U.S. respect for this article was reaffirmed in the 15 July 1976 update of FM 27-10, in which the interpretation of "an undefended place" was given added detail.) If an area has legitimate military targets as well as civilians, Article 26 requires that "the officer in command of an attacking force must, before commencing a bombardment, except in cases of assault, do all in his power to warn the authorities." Warning can be given by dropping leaflets in advance, for example.

The argument on the side of abandoning the Hague Rule and targeting enemy civilians is sometimes made in this way. Morale is a fact of military consequence, and by attacking civilians the morale of "the home front" can be destroyed. This kind of attack, however, would give up too much of the concept of military honor and of morality. Even where such an argument is adopted and carried out, it leaves a sense of shame and guilt, as Walzer points out in his discussion of the British terror bombing carried out by Air Marshall Arthur Harris during World War II.[10]

Another argument on the side of making civilians acceptable targets is the view that they are responsible for their military forces, who are their employees. From this viewpoint, not the underlings but the civilians responsible should be the proper targets; however, the honorable demand is for an open statement of the matter, and the public law that still pertains formally denies most of this view. Of course, new international conventions will no doubt take place, and the British view described above may become the general view. Until that happens—and it may never—civilians are not honorable targets.

The Principle of Double Effect

The phrase "directed exclusively against them" raises the matter of what is called "the principle of double effect." If an individual performs an act in order to reach a certain goal and the act has more than one consequence, he or she has a double effect. In a well-known example, "If I go to prison rather than perform some action, no reasonable person will call the incidental consequences of my refusal—the loss of my job, for example—intentional just because I knew they must happen."[11] In this instance, we may distinguish between the *intended* goal and the other effects that may well be *foreseen* but are only accidental accompaniments of the essential goal. We now have the phrase "incidental fallout" to make the same point.

Can obliteration bombing of cities be justified if the direct intention is a military target and the civilians merely foreseen but unintended targets? We have already noted the clear Hague Rules—not only cities but undefended *"dwellings or buildings"* are "prohibited" targets. *Prohibited!* The effort to use the principle of double effect as an excuse was anticipated by Hague Rule 26; hence, that effort must meet the requirement of the rule to give advance notice with time for the civilians to leave the area.

One more argument is used in an effort to justify attacking noncombatant enemy citizens. The restrictions of the laws of war change and have changed over time. Custom, the practice of all parties for an extended time, can be a basis for reinterpreting or changing those laws. The advance of technology may also call for changes. The St. Petersburg Declaration noted the effect that advancing technology would have and mentioned that "future improvements which science may effect" will be a reason for new agreements. Obviously, in World War II, the Allies used new technology to carry out terror bombing of enemy cities. So, an argument goes, the custom of "area bombing" has been established by usage and has replaced the Hague Rules against it. In other words, commit a crime often enough, and it is no longer a crime!

We must agree that new customs and new scientific developments call for reconsiderations but not of the moral foundations of the issue. Killing the innocent is not to be reconsidered for approval. Where "noncombatants" are not innocent, that needs to be established openly. If we lose the prohibition against killing the innocent, there is no line between legitimate acts of war and simple murder.

Hostilities: The General Principle

The Hague section on hostilities begins with a general principle that should be familiar: *"Belligerents have not got an unlimited right as to the choice of means for injuring the enemy"* (Article 22). All is not fair in war. The most solemn international conventions and the customs of military honor and human decency are the foundation of this principle. It is a basic principle that the military must often reteach to the politicians. For example, there is the report about the German V-2 missile, quoted in the previous chapter, that, "Winston Churchill was so agitated by the impending threat that he urged an attack with poison gas. General Eisenhower dismissed the idea out of hand. 'Let's, for God's sake, keep our eyes on the ball and use some sense,' he replied."[12]

The Hague Rules, Article 23

It seems easier to understand why the enemy should be limited in the right to choose means of injury than that we should. The question of just what the limitations are is sometimes difficult and technical; however, the Hague Article 23 was and remains a firm set of boundaries. We reproduce it here:

> In addition to the prohibitions provided by special Conventions, it is particularly forbidden:
> (a) To employ poison or poisoned weapons;
> (b) To kill or wound by treachery individuals belonging to the hostile nation or army;
> (c) To kill or wound an enemy who, having laid down his arms, or no longer having means of defence, has surrendered at discretion;
> (d) To declare that no quarter will be given;
> (e) To employ arms, projectiles, or material calculated to cause unnecessary suffering;
> (f) To make improper use of a flag of truce, or the national flag, or of the military insignia and uniform of the enemy, as well as of the distinctive signs of the Geneva Convention;
> (g) To destroy or seize enemy property, unless such destruction or seizure be imperatively demanded by the necessities of war;
> (h) To declare abolished, suspended, or inadmissible the right of the subjects of the hostile party to institute legal proceedings.

A belligerent is likewise forbidden to compel the subjects of the hostile party to take part in the operations of war directed against their own country.

Poisonous Gases and Bacteriological Weapons

Paragraph (a) on poison has been supplemented by the Geneva Protocol of 1925, which prohibits gases and bacteriological warfare. The United States did not sign this protocol until 1975—fifty years later.[13] (Forty nations originally ratified or acceded to it.) We are now bound by it, but we have accepted the prohibition only of *the first use* of "chemical weapons." Chemical weapons are "asphyxiating, poisonous or other gases, and . . . all analogous liquids, materials or devices." We also have renounced first use of chemical herbicides in war, except as we use them domestically. Because we accept only the prohibition against first use of poison gases and other chemicals, we may—and do—build and stockpile such weapons in preparation for possible retaliation with them.[14] We also reserve the right to use chemical weapons in "riot control" and to use such chemical weapons as produce "merely transient effects that disappear within minutes after exposure to the agent."[15]

The Geneva Protocol of 1925 also prohibits "bacteriological methods of warfare," and on this matter the United States has agreed to the ban *without any reservations*. We will not retaliate with bacteriological methods even if another state uses them. What are such methods? An example was mentioned in a chemistry journal report on testing in the Soviet Union of a technique by which rats are infected with bubonic plague and then dropped over enemy territory. To readers who think that bacteriological warfare is so inhuman as to be unlikely, we might mention that the British Manual reports:

> In December, 1949, a number of Japanese nationals were tried and convicted by a Russian Military Tribunal at Khabarovsk on a charge of preparing and using on repeated occasions in 1939, bacteriological weapons against the Mongolian People's Republic, and in 1940–1942, against China where a campaign of bacterial contamination organised by the Japanese Army caused epidemics of plague and typhus.[16]

An exact specification of these methods may be difficult and somewhat vague. As the FM states:

> The United States considers bacteriological methods of warfare to include not only biological weapons but also toxins, which, although not living organisms and therefore susceptible of being characterized as chemical agents, are generally produced from biological agents. All toxins, however, regardless of the manner of production, are regarded by the United States as bacteriological methods of warfare within the meaning of the proscription of the Geneva Protocol of 1925.[17]

Why we reserve the right to retaliate against chemical but not biological weapons is unclear.

Treachery

Paragraph (b) of Hague Article 23 prohibits a treacherous attack—that is, an attack by someone who pretends not to be a soldier, not to be fighting. The U.S. Field Manual explains, "This article is construed as prohibiting *assassination,* proscription or outlawry of an enemy, or putting a price upon an enemy's head, as well as offering a reward for an enemy 'dead or alive'" (emphasis mine).[18]

If assassination is forbidden to military personnel by international law, what of civilians? Can civilians do what is forbidden to soldiers? One thinks of the effort by the United States, apparently admitted, to assassinate the Cuban leader, Prime Minister Fidel Castro. Military morality was higher than civilian morality in this regard—and others—until Congress passed special legislation forbidding assassination by any agent of the government. Why not remove the uniform, dress as a native farmer, get within close range of the enemy commanding officer (or anyone else), and kill him? Or why not become his cook and poison him? As an earlier chapter explained, it would be dishonorable; it would be unfair because it is essentially lying, pretending to be something other than what you are. An honorable act is an act that one is not ashamed of and performs openly. It would also be treachery for a soldier to pretend to be wounded or dead and then to attack an enemy who approached without hostile intent or to surrender and afterward to open fire upon an enemy who was treating him or her as a victim of combat or a prisoner. (These last examples are mentioned in the British Manual. Of course, this section applies only to treacherous killing.)

Strange that one may kill or wound an enemy but not use treachery to do it. Recall, once again, the purpose of war: to have the enemy surrender and remain surrendered. Because treachery weakens that purpose, it is both dishonorable and inefficient in the long run. A soldier is just as dead whether killed by open attack or by treachery. The difference is a matter of morality, and the Hague Rules forbid the low road.

Respecting Surrender

Paragraph (c) serves the purpose of warfare as well as being humanitarian. Because the object is to have the enemy surrender, a guarantee of safety after surrender is an obvious inducement. Suppose that some enemy soldiers surrender, but the situation is such that your own safety and that of your patrol will be at great risk unless those prisoners are shot and left. Can they be shot to defend your own security? No. If the choice is between shooting them or becoming a prisoner yourself, then you must become a prisoner. It would be a war crime to shoot them. (See Chapter 8.) Suppose the choice is to either shoot them or be killed yourself. The answer is the same. It is a war crime to shoot prisoners. Each of the actions in Article 23 is "particularly forbidden," the strongest prohibition of the military code. There are a number of special aspects of the prisoner-of-war status, and they are considered below.

As an example of the violation of paragraph (c), "A German S.S. officer was convicted for the shooting carried out by his troops, on his orders, of 100 men of the Royal Norfolk Regiment who had surrendered at Wormhout near Dunkirk in 1940: *The Case of Fritz Knochlein.*"[19]

Accepting Surrender

Paragraph (d), the refusal to give quarter—for example the refusal to take prisoners—is obviously a violation of the laws of warfare. Kurt Mayer, the commander of a German unit, was convicted of having incited his troops to deny quarter to Allied troops (the Abbaye Ardenne Case). In the Jaluit Atoll Case, the accused was convicted of the shooting of unarmed prisoners of war. In the Ruchteschell Trial, the accused was found guilty on the charge of continuing to fire on a British merchant vessel after it had indicated surrender.[20] Unfortunately, examples are found on all sides; however, there are also examples of obedience found on all sides.

Unnecessary Suffering

Paragraph (e) forbids *unnecessary suffering*. Exactly what is *unnecessary?* We considered some aspects of this issue in the discussion of the St. Petersburg Declaration. Suffering is unnecessary if the immediate military objective can be reached without it. Whether that can be done may depend on the weapons used by the other side; therefore, the FM explains, "What weapons cause 'unnecessary suffering' can only be determined in light of *the practice* of States in refraining from the use of a given weapon because it is believed to have that effect"[21] (emphasis mine). The practice, or the usage, is the basis for knowing whether a weapon is considered to cause unnecessary suffering. The FM goes on to say that "Usage has, however, established the illegality of the use of lances with barbed heads, irregular-shaped bullets, and projectiles filled with glass." But usage permits what the St. Petersburg Declaration seems to forbid, explosives in small mines and hand grenades.

The use of flame throwers and napalm bombs "when directed against military targets is lawful. However, their use against personnel is contrary to the law of war in so far as it is calculated to cause unnecessary suffering."[22] And, the British Manual adds, "Flame throwers were used extensively during the Second World War and napalm bombs were used during the Korean conflict."

Two criteria can be employed for determining whether a weapon causes unnecessary suffering: a specific international agreement and the practice of States. When these conflict, the unwritten military code or law of warfare *might* be a guide. The British say, "In the absence of any rule of international law dealing expressly with it, the use which may be made of a particular weapon . . . will involve merely the application of the recognized principle of international law."[23] In the case of napalm, international law—the Hague Rule under discussion—forbids its use, but the practice by at least one side (the United States during the Vietnam War) seemed to accept the weapon.

How does the rule against unnecessary suffering apply to nuclear or atomic weapons? If lances with barbed heads, irregularly shaped bullets, and projectiles filled with glass are forbidden, it's hard to imagine that nuclear and atomic weapons are not. They certainly cause more unnecessary suffering than projectiles filled with glass! Both the U.S. and the British Manuals are coy about the matter. The FM says "The use of 'atomic weapons' whether by air, sea, or land forces, cannot as such be regarded as violative of international law in the absence of any customary rule of international law or international convention restricting their employment."[24] Of course, it is an empty tautology to hold that if no specific law exists, then no specific law can be violated. The British Manual goes somewhat further. It says, "There is no rule of international law dealing specifically with the use of nuclear weapons. Their use, therefore, is governed by the general principles laid down in this chapter."[25] The chapter covers the Hague Rules on hostilities, and the general principles involve unnecessary suffering and poison or poisoned weapons.

To mention just one other aspect of nuclear weapons: Radiation poisoning *is* poisoning and therefore might well make nuclear weapons forbidden under the Convention. Neither the FM nor the British Manual draws this conclusion, however. (Nuclear weapons have features beyond this, and they are considered in several other connections in this study, particularly in Chapter 11.)

Enemy Uniforms and the Red Cross Emblem

Paragraph (f) involves issues that seem to be an effort to make war into an athletic contest between two schools. Some of the motives for sportsmanship are the same as the motives for military honor. Needless to say, more is at stake in one than in the other. A *flag* of truce is like a time-out in a basketball game: You can't score points during that interval in the game, nor can you use a flag of truce as a cover for gaining military advantage. The FM warns that flags of truce "must not be used surreptitiously to obtain military information or merely to obtain time to effect a retreat or secure reinforcements or to feign surrender in order to surprise an enemy."[26] But the statement quickly adds that an officer receiving a party under a flag of truce still has the duty of "exercising proper precautions with regard to them."

The flag, insignia, or uniforms of the enemy are not to be used. These are excellent devices to hide movements; yet, the game would be unclear if played that way. In football, if a few players on one side changed into the uniforms of the other, they might well catch a ball not intended for them. An unsportsmanlike way to gain the ball, it is dishonorable in sport and dishonorable in war. Another aspect of the matter is that, if you are found in the uniform of the enemy, and therefore out of your own, you can be considered a spy and shot rather than being taken as an ordinary POW. Clothes consciousness can make the difference between life and death.

The FM notes that this Geneva Rule prohibits the *improper use,* not every use, of the enemy's flags, uniforms, and insignia. The Manual explains that using them during combat "is certainly forbidden," while using them at other times is not. What other times might there be? Perhaps the authors of the FM had in mind use in a theatrical production. Actually there are non-combat uses that have been accepted, although the matter is not clearly established. During World War II, the German intelligence service in Belgium located an organized network that helped Allied airmen who were forced to land. They used German soldiers disguised in British uniforms. The British Manual reports this incident and adds, "It would seem that this use of enemy uniform outside of battle operations is a legitimate ruse."[27]

The Convention is an agreement on *definitions* of what can and cannot be done by civilized nations during war. Of course, as with most *definitions in ordinary rather than formal language,* some cases are clearly acceptable, some are clearly forbidden, and some remain in a vague area in which things are not obviously one or the other. The essential point of this paragraph of the Convention is clear: To use the enemy flag and other symbols during combat would be to misrepresent, to be dishonest—something that the military code forbids.

This paragraph also forbids improper use of the Red Cross (called the distinctive sign of the Geneva Convention). What is proper and what is improper here? First, some comments about the emblem may be of interest. The emblem of the Red Cross was chosen as a compliment to Switzerland. Formed by reversing the Swiss Federal colors, this heraldic device of a red cross on a white ground is the emblem and distinctive sign of medical services. However, certain alternative emblems (as mentioned in an earlier note) are also used: Turkey, Pakistan, and certain other Moslem states use a red crescent on a white background; Iran (Persia until 1935), a red lion and sun on a white background; Israel uses a red shield (Star) of David on white. (Syria has objected to the Israeli emblem.) The following section uses the term *Red Cross* to stand for these alternatives as well.

The proper use of the Red Cross emblem is to mark hospitals, ambulances, hospital ships (or aircraft or trains), and medical supplies and equipment. The International Red Cross organization, the ICRC and its personnel, may also use the symbol. The purpose, obviously, is to protect personnel, buildings, and so forth when they are used *exclusively* for medical assistance and treatment. Permanent medical personnel carry a special identity disk in addition to the usual military tags. So much for the proper uses.

It has occurred to certain parties that using a truck marked with the Red Cross is a very secure way to bring ammunition up to the front. To prevent ammunition from being blown up, it might be stored in a hospital or a building with a Red Cross on its roof. Observation posts and communications buildings might be more reliable when marked with a Red Cross. Firing from an ambulance can take the enemy by surprise. Of course, these uses of the symbol are forbidden. And, on the other side, anything properly marked with the Red Cross is a forbidden target. Violations in either direction are war crimes.

Protected Property

Paragraph (g) deals with the treatment of enemy property. Recalling a point made earlier, we know that among the things upon which military honor depends is the distinction between a legitimate act of war and plain armed robbery. War is not taken to be an effort to steal property. As a requirement for a military objective, such property can be seized and destroyed only if it is "imperatively demanded by the necessities of war." We have already noted the distinction made between public and private property. Public moveable property that is captured on a battlefield may be retained by the State, but private property is considered differently. (Individual soldiers have long used the phrase "to liberate" where the owner or an impartial observer might say "to steal.")

Paragraph (h) on the legal rights of enemy citizens is fairly clear and certainly important. Legal rights can produce difficult cases, but we will not raise them here.

Protected Buildings

In addition to installations properly marked with a Red Cross because they are medical or belong to the ICRC, the Hague Rules protect other buildings: "In sieges and bombardments all necessary measures must be taken to spare, as far as possible, buildings dedicated to *religion, art, science, or charitable purposes,* historic monuments . . . provided they are not being used at the time for military purposes" (Hague Convention, Article 27). Of course, these buildings must be marked by suitable signs and the enemy notified of their location and nature. Why? Because civilization is a common possession. The morality of universal fairness takes humankind to be the proper moral object, forming the moral basis of the laws of warfare. Therefore, historic monuments and buildings dedicated to religion, art, science, or charity are to be protected. Each of these has special features that should be obvious.

Buildings Dedicated to Religion

The bombing of churches has a history of its own. Despite the fact that it is a war crime to do so, these "incidents" are found on all sides. In almost all cases, when public attention turns to the event, an apology or explanation has been issued. Let us look to three such bombings from World War II: Cassino, Coventry, and Nagasaki.

The town of Cassino, in central Italy, is at the foot of a mountain. In the process of forcing the German Army out of Italy, the Allies completely obliterated Cassino by bombs and shelling.[28] The famous church at the top of Monte Cassino was shelled very heavily. The explanation given was that we had reports that ammunition was being stored there. The reports turned out not to be true; however, the church, on a dramatic mountain top, *may have been* used as an observation post.

Coventry, England, had a famous historic cathedral that was completely obliterated by German bombing. The cathedral was no military target, of course, but the city of Coventry had a very important factory that built lorries. The factory was not far from the cathedral. *Perhaps* the cathedral was hit by error. To hit it in an effort to destroy public morale would, as it turned out, have been an error: Public will became firmer than ever after the bombing. (The remains of the cathedral were left as a monument, and a new cathedral was built alongside it.)

The third example of direct bombing of a church happened in Nagasaki. As everyone knows, this Japanese city was hit on 9 August 1945, three days after the bombing of Hiroshima, by the second atomic bomb dropped by the U.S. Air Force. The Air Force map of the city, unclassified after 1 May 1950, shows the target area and concentric circles around it.[29] *The major institution directly under the hypocenter of the atomic bomb,* actually 600 meters northeast of the hypocenter, was the largest Catholic cathedral in the Far East, *the Urakami Roman Catholic Cathedral.* The cathedral was completely destroyed, along with a part of the city. Also within two thousand feet of ground zero were the Mitsubishi Hospital (Urakami Branch), the Chinzei High School, the Shiroyama School, the Nagasaki prison, the Blind and Dumb School, and "miscellaneous small industries." None of these, with the possible exception of the small industries, was a legitimate target. The major industries were all outside this immediate area.

There has never been any evidence of military use of the Urakami Cathedral. Making it the target was clearly a war crime. Of the three religious institutions, the cathedral at Coventry, the church on Monte Cassino, and the Urakami Cathedral in Nagasaki, the first two received a great deal of public attention, but the destruction of the cathedral in Nagasaki has been just about ignored in the West.

Of course, the novelty of the atomic bomb was the major news event. However, we might expect that targeting the major Catholic cathedral in the Far East would at least be noticed or mentioned in Western stories, studies, and analyses of the bombing. There are reports of the human targets in this community; for example, "Of the City's 20,000 Catholics, some 15,000 are said to have been concentrated in this area [Urakami]. About 10,000 of them are thought to have been sacrificed to the atomic bomb."[30] In addition, this

Japanese Catholic community was quite well known: For some generations, they had had to live underground as secret Catholics because their religion was banned, and they could only live openly when religious toleration returned. (Historians sometimes call this a *heroic* community.) Compared to the destruction of people, the destruction of a building, the cathedral, is trivial and was, to the best of my knowledge, ignored even by the Catholic press.

Buildings Dedicated to Art, Science, and Charity

Art is of general human interest, and the interest in protecting buildings of significance is obvious. This covers both buildings that house collections and buildings that are themselves of importance to the history of art. Of course, art is a feature of human civilization and so of international concern. No nation contains all of the values of civilization within itself. There is a story about an Englishwoman who passed a young man of military age on the streets of Cambridge during World War II and asked, "Young man, why aren't you fighting for civilization?" He quickly responded, "Madam, I *am* civilization." (British overstatement?)

The concern with charitable institutions is akin to the humanitarian interest in protecting medical facilities. The case for scientific institutions, however, is not so clear. During a war, can there be scientific pursuits that are not of military significance, not of use to the enemy? At this stage in the history of science, it hardly seems likely except, possibly, in a very short war.

The scientific community, however, has shown that it is international in some ways. Robert Oppenheimer, the head of the Los Alamos project that produced the first atom bombs, reported that among the first messages of congratulations on the scientific breakthrough in producing a successful atomic bomb was a telegram from the Japanese Physicists Association![31] It is amazing that citizens of the target nation could think of it in scientific terms at that time. Yet science, like religion and art, has no essential nationalistic bias and can be respected by both sides at war. *Respected* in this context means that one fears that the destruction of a scientific, religious, or art work would be a greater loss than preserving it, more damaging to our side in the long run than to the enemy in the short run.

The moral object behind each of these protections of cultural buildings is not winning the war in the shortest time possible. The moral object for which these sacrifices are made is the progress of civilization, the goal of humankind.

Pillage

We have remarked several times that a legitimate act of war is clearly distinguished from robbery. Hague Article 28 makes the point succinctly: "The pillage of a town or place, even when taken by assault, is prohibited."

Legitimate and Illegitimate Strategy

With all of these restrictions on the conduct of war, what *is* allowed? The Hague Rules draw a line between what is and what is not acceptable in terms of custom and the concept of treachery considered above. First, as Hague Article 24 puts it, "ruses of war and the employment of measures necessary for obtaining information about the enemy and the country are considered permissible." However, some lies are acceptable under this article, and some are not. The FM and British Manual give examples of each, but they preface their examples with a paragraph on the importance of "good faith." In the U.S. manual, we find:

Good Faith

Absolute good faith with the enemy must be observed as a rule of conduct; but this does not prevent measures such as using spies and secret agents, encouraging defection or insurrection among the enemy civilian population, corrupting enemy civilians or soldiers by bribes, or inducing the enemy's soldiers to desert, surrender, or rebel. *In general a belligerent may resort to those measures for mystifying or misleading the enemy against which the enemy ought to take measures to protect himself* (para. 49, p. 22; emphasis mine)

Treachery or Perfidy

Ruses of war are legitimate so long as they do not involve treachery or perfidy on the part of the belligerent resorting to them. They are, however, forbidden if they contravene any generally accepted rule.

The line of demarcation between legitimate ruses and forbidden acts of perfidy is sometimes indistinct, but the following examples indicate the correct principles. It would be an improper practice to secure an advantage of the enemy by deliberate lying or misleading conduct which involves a breach of faith, or when there is *a moral obligation* to speak the truth, For example, it is improper to feign surrender so as to secure an advantage over the opposing belligerent thereby. So similarly, to broadcast to the enemy that an armistice had been agreed upon when such is not the case would be treacherous. On the other hand, it is a perfectly proper ruse to summon a force to surrender on the ground that it is surrounded and thereby induce surrender with a small force.

Treacherous or perfidious conduct in war is forbidden because it destroys the basis for a restoration of peace short of the complete annihilation of one belligerent by the other. (U.S. FM 27-10, para. 50, p. 22; emphasis mine)

A number of comments are relevant to these paragraphs. Some authors dispute the question of bribing the enemy. An example is the case of the reward paid by the United States in 1953 to a North Korean fighter pilot who flew a new MIG fighter plane over to the United Nations command lines in response to an offer of a reward. After mentioning this incident, the British Manual says, "Although many writers dissent, military practice has always sanctioned such acts."[32] The idea of corrupting the military honor of the enemy is apparently distasteful to some commentators; it undercuts the macho idea that victory should come by force of arms alone. Psychological warfare would be in the same category; however, as the British point out, practice has always allowed these activities.

The line between "disinformation," or lying, that is and is not acceptable depends on what the FM calls "a moral obligation to speak the truth." When does this obligation come into play? We have a principle in the "Good Faith" paragraph above. We can "mislead" the enemy by activities that the enemy ought to be intelligent enough to anticipate and protect against. We do not have to restrict ourselves because of the stupidity or inefficiency of the enemy. On the other hand, if the enemy has no way to protect against our lies, we are not to lie. In the case of our announcing that the enemy is surrounded, the enemy ought to have read enough military history and have the imagination to guard against such a deception. An announcement that the war is over or that an armistice has been declared, however, is more difficult to analyze in the field. To lie about this even once is to become untrustworthy should the event actually occur. For another example, the enemy ought to have thought about the possibility that the water supply might be diverted, but an undetectable poison in that water supply would be something that the enemy could not take protective measures against. Although the line is indistinct, as the FM says, there are clear cases on each side.

We are still left with the expected variety of tricks, such as pretended attacks, retreats, false radio messages, false orders from the enemy command, use of the enemy's codes, dummy guns, dummy landmarks. All of these are acceptable.

This chapter on the "textbook" set of rules for warfare should not give the impression that merely "going by the book" will make all decisions simple. The real world is full of situations that the laws do not quite predict. Examples come at us from all sides. Can a military convoy be hit after it leaves the open road and hides in an occupied village? Can we attack a child carrying a covered object, a child whose brother threw a grenade yesterday? Sometimes we can and sometimes we cannot wait for a carefully composed answer. The best preparation includes just about everything.

Ideally, the perfect commander would have three kinds of knowledge, dual motivation, and the judgment to balance all four military values when weighing the risks of error. The three kinds of knowledge are the knowledge of (1) the laws of war, (2) the basic principles behind them, and (3) the customs in that theater. The motivation ought to be dual: to behave honorably as well as to succeed with the mission. And, as if this wish list were not enough, that commander should have the ability to balance the four moral values and come up with an honorable style.

The basic questions remain: Are the laws of warfare still pertinent? Do they need repairs, and if so, where? We return to some of these in Appendix 1. The answer that this study proposes is that *the problem is not to make the laws fit the military but to make the military fit the laws.* The laws of war define an honorable military. These laws will always need new protocols, new amendments, but a world without them would be absolutely barbaric. Our problem is how to encourage respect for and obedience to them.

A good deal of the content of the war conventions concerns various aspects relating to *prisoners of war,* the subject of the next chapter. A number of life-and-death questions, such as who is and who is not a spy, depend on the agreements about prisoners of war.

5
Prisoners of War

Earlier chapters made regular reference to the modern conception of *prisoner of war* (POW) and used the concept in various ways. However, the subject is so important that it calls for special consideration. In the Army's FM 27-10, the chapter on POWs is by far the longest. Here, we will give merely an outline of a few of the many aspects of the POW status.

A History of the POW

The British Manual on Military Law gives a helpful bit of history:

> Few of the customs of war have undergone greater changes than those relating to the treatment of prisoners. In ancient times captured soldiers were killed, mutilated or enslaved. In the Middle Ages they were imprisoned or held to ransom. It was only in the 17th century that they began to be regarded as prisoners of the State and not the property of the individual captors. Even during the wars of the 19th century they were often subject to cruel neglect, unnecessary suffering and unjustifiable indignities. After the Second World War a great number of German and Japanese officers were tried and convicted for the murder or maltreatment of prisoners of war. (Examples: The Dachau Concentration Camp Trial was concerned with the murder or ill-treatment

of prisoners of war on a large scale, . . . and the Belsen Trial where the charges against the accused specifically referred to a British prisoner of war who was murdered in Belsen concentration camp. Other British and many thousands of Russian prisoners of war were murdered in Sachsenhausen concentration camp, the staff of which were tried and convicted by the Russians at Oranienburg in 1948, for these and other war crimes.)[1]

The modern rules for dealing with POWs were formulated in the Geneva Prisoner of War Convention in 1929 and then reformulated in 1949. We start with the generally accepted definition of *prisoner of war* given in the Geneva Convention on POWs.

Defining the POW

The question of who is and is not a POW can be a matter of life and death. Someone caught at hostile action can be shot as a spy (after a trial), unless that person is accepted as a POW. Those who are POWs must be given a certain minimum level of food, clothing, and safe shelter and have other privileges, as we will see. Their impressive privileges or rights are that they may not be attacked after they have surrendered and that they may not be wounded or killed after being captured. So, the matter of membership in the class of POWs is hardly trivial.

Article 4 of the "Geneva Convention Relative to the Treatment of Prisoners of War, 12 August 1949" (GPW), reads as follows:

Prisoners of war . . . are persons belonging to one of the following categories, who have fallen into the power of the enemy:

1. Members of the armed forces of a Party to the conflict, as well as members of militias or volunteer corps forming part of such armed forces.

2. Members of other militias and members of other volunteer corps, including those of organized resistance movements, belonging to a Party to the conflict and operating inside or outside their own territory . . provided that such militias or volunteer corps fulfill the following conditions:

    a. that of being commanded by a person responsible for his subordinates;

    b. that of having a fixed distinctive sign recognizable at a distance;

    c. that of carrying arms openly;

    d. that of conducting their operations in accordance with the laws and customs of war.

3. Members of regular armed forces who profess allegiance to a government or an authority not recognized by the Detaining Power.

4. Persons who accompany the armed forces without actually being members thereof, such as civilian members of military aircraft crews, war correspondents, supply contractors, members of labour units or of services responsible for the welfare of the armed forces, provided that they have received authorization from the armed forces which they accompany, who shall provide them for that purpose with an identity card. . . .

5. Members of crews . . . of the merchant marine . . . and civil aircraft of the Parties to the conflict, who do not benefit by more favourable treatment under any other provision of international law.

6. Inhabitants of a nonoccupied territory, who on the approach of the enemy spontaneously take up arms to resist the invading forces, without having had time to form themselves into regular armed units, *provided they carry arms openly and respect the laws and customs of war.* (emphasis mine)

The groups listed above are the main groups; the following are also given the status of POWs: (a) former members of the enemy power, particularly when they have tried to rejoin their former armed forces; and (b) persons who qualify as POWs but who are in the power of a neutral when that neutral has diplomatic relations with one of the belligerents.

As mentioned in an earlier chapter, the primary basis for POW status is membership in a militia, meaning that the individual carries arms openly and wears a uniform or a part of one with a distinctive sign to show the world that that person is a soldier under a specific command. Being soldiers means that those individuals "respect the laws and customs of war" and have identification establishing that "they are not persons acting on their own responsibility," as FM 27-10 puts it.

This statement makes explicit the distinction between armed robbery, for example, and a legitimate military action. Robbers act for their own personal goals; military personnel act for the goals of someone or something else. Also, the responsibility for the military action is not the personal decision of the individual but the decision of that person's commander. Soldiers, therefore, "are not persons acting on their own responsibility," as the Convention puts it. Of course, a commander-in-chief does act on personal responsibility but does so for the benefit of the political entity to which loyalty is owed.

This location of the overall responsibility for military operations does not relieve the individual soldier of personal responsibility for the earlier requirement that he or she "respects the laws and customs of war." Individuals are not able to commit a war crime and evade responsibility by claiming that their commander so ordered them. We consider this more carefully in Chapter 8.

Being "clothes conscious" in the military is more than a matter of personal ego satisfaction, group cohesion, or easy identification, although it can certainly be all of these. Wearing a uniform, or an obvious part of one, is a matter of protecting the status of a potential POW, as well as a matter of honor in refusing to conceal one's identity.

A point to be noted in the definition above is that both combatants and certain noncombatants have a right to be treated as POWs. However, both must have identification that establishes their connection to the "Parties to the conflict," as section (5) above, puts it.

Treatment of POWs

POWs are not the property or possession of those who have captured them. Just as a soldier is not acting for personal gain, what or whoever is captured by that soldier is also not to be disposed of as a personal possession. As noted earlier, this concept is a restriction of the modern world. Historians chill some of the great respect for ancient heroes by the reminder, "War began with plunder. [Quoting Thucydides's *Peloponnesian War*], 'Both Hellenes and Barbarians . . . were commanded by powerful chiefs, who took this means of increasing their wealth and providing for their poorer followers.' The Romans managed the most efficient city-smashing, land-grabbing, slave-catching machine of antiquity."[2] The modern protection for POWs is an obvious mark of moral progress, and this progress is measured by the scope of the universal fairness criterion.

General Protection

A discussion about POWs must start with Article 12 of the Geneva POW Convention:

> Prisoners of war are in the hands of the enemy Power, but not of the individuals or military units who have captured them. Irrespective of the individual responsibilities that may exist, the Detaining Power is responsible for the treatment given them.[3]

Article 12 also requires that the Power that has taken POWs must not transfer the captives to any other Power unless that Power has signed the POW Convention or agreed to follow it.[4]

Killing Prisoners

Very specific protections and rights have been developed and agreed to in the POW Convention because of the clear dangers to POWs. A POW who may have just killed and wounded a large number of the enemy may, a moment later, become a prisoner completely at the mercy of the comrades of those he or she has killed. Why not immediately kill the prisoner who seconds earlier was trying to kill you and did manage to kill some of your company? This situation is an enormous test of military honor.

Why not kill that prisoner? You could have legitimately killed him a moment earlier, but if he has been captured or surrendered, he is no longer able to fight. When he accepts capture or signals surrender, he essentially says that he will no longer fight. Someone who is no longer able or willing to fight is not an honorably acceptable opponent; therefore, the Code and the Convention protect such persons from attack. The morality behind this protection is quite clear: Undefended persons must not be attacked. A prisoner is such a person, although he was something quite different a few moments earlier. The same point may be heard in a school playground fight, "Pick on someone your size!" After capture, without his weapons, the enemy is "not your size." We, therefore, are not surprised to find the Convention insisting, "Measures of reprisal against prisoners of war are prohibited."[5]

Suppose that unless the POWs are killed, your own unit will be greatly weakened, perhaps disclosed and captured. Suppose that your POWs will shortly be freed by their own forces unless you kill them. FM 27-10 gives a clear response:

> A commander may not put his prisoners to death because their presence retards his movements or diminishes his power of resistance by necessitating a large guard, or by reason of their consuming supplies, or because it appears certain that they will regain their liberty through the impending success of their forces.[6]

Suppose that it is a matter of self-preservation—either you kill your POWs or your unit will be destroyed. Remember they are not your POWs to dispose of as you wish. The U.S. Army directive still takes the high road with the statement, "It is likewise unlawful for a commander to kill his prisoners on grounds of self-preservation."[7]

The last two quotations are not the language of the Geneva Convention but the explanations given by the U.S. Army, which are identical to those in the British Manual (p. 53). Of course, as we have had to note earlier, making something unlawful does not prevent it from happening. Making an act unlawful sends the message that the act should not occur and that it is a crime when it does occur. How should we react to a crime? We should: (1) be shocked, (2) take steps to stop the act, and (3) seek punishment for those responsible. When violations occur, the purpose of law is to produce these three responses.

Killing prisoners is hardly unknown or, in certain circumstances, unlikely (e.g., by poorly trained troops under pressure). The British Manual reports, "The last authenticated case [?] prior to the Second World War of the killing of prisoners in cold blood occurred in 1799, at Jaffa, when 3,563 Arabs were shot down or bayonetted on the sea shore by order of Napoleon, as he was unable to spare an escort to conduct the prisoners to Egypt without wasting his small army."[8] Note the date of Napoleon's order—1799—and the fact that we now have international conventions that forbid such orders.

Acceptable Treatment

So much for what cannot be done to POWs. How *are* they to be dealt with? It is still convenient to phrase matters negatively, in terms of what cannot be done. They must "at all times be humanely treated."[9] Does this allow them to be tied and left outdoors in tropical rain or sun, for example? Obviously not. A few years ago an embarrassing photo was printed on the front page of the *New York Times*. It appeared to show that POWs, who had been taken in the Grenada action, had been tied and left for a day or so. A protest against this action, based on the Geneva POW Convention, apparently caused a quick change in the way the prisoners were being held.[10] This is an example of the enforcement mechanism that the Conventions depend upon: publicity. Although this was hardly the most serious violation of the Convention that could be documented—it was not rape, arson, or fiendish torture—the point should be clear. For violations great or small, publicity or the fear of publicity can provide protection. We return to this theme in later chapters.

Tying Hands

The matter of tying prisoners' hands has had an instructive history. Consider the following from the British Manual:

> Before the raid on Dieppe by a Canadian division in August, 1942, an order was issued without authority [sic] that whenever possible the hands of prisoners of war will be bound so that they cannot destroy their papers." This order was captured by the Germans during the raid. On complaint being made by Germany the order was countermanded and the German allegation that prisoners had had their hands tied was denied by the War Office. Shortly afterwards, in a raid on Sark in October, 1942, five captured Germans had their hands tied so that they could be linked to their captors whilst being escorted to the boats of the raiding party. In a statement made in the House of Commons on 13th October, 1942, the Prime Minister said: "His Majesty's Government had never countenanced any general order for the tying up of prisoners of war on the field of battle.

Such a process might, however, be necessary from time to time under stress of circumstances and might indeed be in the best interest of the safety of the prisoners themselves." As a result of this raid the Germans ordered the fettering of British prisoners of war in camps in Germany. Such shackling, far from the battlefield, purported to be an act of reprisal. As such it was clearly prohibited by the 1929 Convention, Art. 2 (iii) forbidding reprisals against prisoners of war.[11]

The British Manual then adds that the raid on Sark produced evidence of slave labor deportations to Germany, and also that the "German Commando Order" was issued a few days after these incidents, on 18 October, 1942.

Several things may be particularly noted in this history. That the order to tie hands in the Dieppe raid was issued "without authority" might mean that the authority involved knew that it was an illegal order. A second point is that the authorities were not only aware that tying hands was a violation but they also did not want to admit that they had done it and denied that it had been done. And finally, publicity worked: Hand tying was stopped, at least temporarily, in one sector. Respect for the military conventions was a serious part of the conduct of that war. Such a remark hardly means that the Conventions were always absolutely obeyed. History shows otherwise. Morality is one of the weapons of war, but—like all weapons—it cannot always be depended upon to operate perfectly. And, not merely a weapon of war, it is also an independent civilized requirement.

Reprisals

Reprisals against POWs are clearly unfair. Because they are defenseless after surrender or capture, POWs must be protected. The responsibility for their protection and treatment falls to the "Detaining Power," the power that has captured them. They can be transferred only to other powers that are parties to the POW Convention. Should such other powers fail to take proper care of the POWs, the original "detaining" power must "take effective measures to correct the situation or . . . request the return of the POWs."[12]

At a point in the early stages of the Vietnam War, the U.S. forces apparently—according to accounts in the *New York Times*—took prisoners and turned them over to the government of South Vietnam. The prisoners were reportedly held in unacceptable conditions. At first, the U.S. forces denied responsibility, insisting that since the United States was not at war, it could hardly be involved with POWs. If the United States merely provided advisors and equipment to South Vietnam, POWs could not be its responsibility. Publicity and international pressure apparently produced a change: The United States accepted responsibility for the prisoners that it had captured and improved their living conditions. This account shows the power of the war conventions. No country wishes to have it known that its respect for human rights stops at its borders and is limited to its own citizens.

Humane Treatment

The Geneva Convention specifies that treatment is to be "humane" and adds that this prohibits, among other things, "causing death or seriously endangering the health" of a POW.[13]

Medical Experiments

The use of prisoners for medical experiments by the Germans during World War II, and by the Japanese in their germ warfare section, has been widely reported. The knowledge of these violations of a prisoner's human rights has produced an obvious revulsion; therefore, it is not surprising to find that the Convention's paragraph dealing with this issue insists that "no prisoner of war be subjected to physical mutilation or to medical or scientific experiments of any kind" that are not justified by that individual prisoner's own interest. Military medicine has always had, and continues to have, special concern with finding the best therapy for the wide variety of wounds and disabling problems that military action can cause. However, this propensity is clearly no excuse for using prisoners as laboratory animals to study such things as skin grafts. In this case, the morality of social utility is absolutely denied. The moral individualism of the prisoner must be respected, regardless of community or social benefit.

Even after accepting the principle that prisoners must not be used for experiments against their interests, there remains a question that must occasionally be considered. We have civilian situations in which prisoners are asked to "volunteer" for medical experiments.

There is sometimes a need for civilian trials of new drugs on human subjects, although the drugs are expected to be perfectly safe. Civilian prisoners are given complete and truthful descriptions of the drugs and their probable consequences. They are also paid for their risk, and it is sometimes suggested that they may have their parole chances improved if they "volunteer." (We return to the matter of experiments on prisoners in Chapter 8.)

If civilian prisoners may be used in this way, may POWs also be asked to "volunteer" for such experiments—with such things as truthful descriptions of the risks and with extra pay? Participating in an experiment may be in their interest, even if it is not in their medical interest. The spirit of the Geneva Convention would seem to forbid it. The coercion under which a prisoner lives limits the meaning of "volunteer." However, it is obvious that the bounds on volunteering by POWs are not absolutely clear in every case.

Protection against Civilian Attack

The notion of humane treatment is also designed to protect POWs against "acts of violence or intimidation and against insults and public curiosity." Civilians must not be allowed to attack POWs or to "insult" them. This is the tradition of the honored foe. POWs "are entitled in all circumstances to respect for their persons and their honor."[14]

After World War II, the matter of protecting POWs from civilians, from the general public, led to a number of convictions as well as formal condemnations. The cases go all the way from insulting POWs, to violence against them, to causing their deaths. The International Military Tribunal (Tokyo) condemned "the Japanese practice of parading prisoners of war through cities and exposing them to ridicule and insults."[15]

History records that more than mere ridicule and insult have been aimed at POWs. In the trial of General Macher, the German Military Commander in Rome, the accused was convicted of exposing POWs in his custody to acts of violence, in addition to insults and public curiosity.[16]

As a further example, consider the case of General Schmidt, a German Air Force Commander. As the British Manual reports it, General Schmidt "was convicted for ordering that escorts provided by the armed forces should not use their weapons to protect captured Allied airmen from the fury of the civilian populace. This prohibition was of general application throughout the Reich in 1944 and was known as "the Terror Fliers Order." As a result, many airmen were lynched by the civilian population while their escorts were passive spectators.[17]

This obligation to protect POWs is a basic part of the Code, of course, and the convictions mentioned above are no surprise; unfortunately, neither are the crimes. After all, the POW may have been the one who killed someone's family and closest friends just a few moments before. It takes tremendous restraint to switch abruptly from complete focus on protecting your own life by killing a legitimate target to—suddenly—protecting the antagonist. Therefore, one of the accomplishments of the war conventions is to formalize and to legalize the need to respect POWs—their humanity, if not their bravery—and thereby avoid unnecessary suffering.

This last point, respect for POWs, runs against certain cultural patterns. In many situations, a POW is assumed to be someone who surrendered rather than obeyed the duty to fight. As we have seen, the U.S. Army Code forbids surrender while the means to resist remains. It certainly was, and still may be, the Japanese assumption that a prisoner is someone who has surrendered rather than performed his or her duty to fight. From this point of view, POWs deserve contempt rather than respect, because they are individuals who have obviously not done their duty. Of course, POWs can be produced by capture rather than voluntary surrender, and prisoners may or may not have fought well. These questions are irrelevant to the Geneva

Convention's requirements for providing POWs with minimum food, clothing, shelter, medical care, and general protection.

Fact vs. Fiction

Now, three final conclusions: First, it should be obvious that the existence of the POW Convention as a part of international and U.S. law means that *there is no such thing as unconditional surrender*. The conditions are specified in the Convention, and no captive is allowed to forfeit them. If understood literally, "unconditional surrender" is an empty romantic phrase.

Second, the command to "take no prisoners" is illegal. Under the Convention, soldiers have the right to surrender and become prisoners.

Third, there are cases of POWs being treated decently, although this chapter has offered examples of the opposite. There was an impressive POW camp in WWII that is reported in the *New York Times* in an obituary for the philosopher, Paul Ricoeur; "Serving in the French Army during World War II, Dr. Ricoeur was captured and spent five years in a German prison camp. There, he managed to continue his work translating the German phenomenologist Edmund Husserl into French in tiny handwriting in the margins of the book. The camp was a place of such intellectual ferment—the many French scholars there organized lectures, classes and even examinations—that the Vichy government eventually accredited it as a degree-granting institution. "[18]

Getting a degree from that POW camp was an impressive achievement, something to be proud of, because it had a very eminent faculty. All POW camps were not in violation of the Convention.

6
Spies

Defining a Spy

According to the Hague Rules, "a person can only be considered a spy when, acting clandestinely or on false pretences, he obtains or endeavors to obtain information in the zone of operations of a belligerent, with the intention of communicating it to the hostile party."[1]

Suppose the two countries involved are at peace. Does this definition apply to the case of obtaining restricted (confidential, secret, or other classified)[2] information from one's own country with the intention of giving it to a foreign power when the two countries are not at war? While such an act may be most serious and damaging to the nation, it is not "spying" within the strict sense of the Hague Rules. The Rules specify a "belligerent" and therefore seem to require that there be active hostilities. However, the term *spy* is usually used for such cases whether two countries are at war or not. As Thomas Hobbes explained in his classic study, *Leviathan,* Sovereign nations are always potential belligerents, enemies of all other sovereign nations.[3]

The Hague Rules, or the part of them quoted above, have been broadened by the Uniform Code of Military justice, as follows:

> Any person who in time of war is found lurking as a spy or acting as a spy in or about any place, vessel, or aircraft, within the control or jurisdiction of any of the armed forces of the United

States, or in or about any shipyard, any manufacturing or industrial plant, or any other place or institution engaged in work in aid of the prosecution of the war by the United States, or elsewhere, shall be tried by a general court-martial or by a military commission and on conviction shall be punished by death.[4]

Therefore, the "zone of operations" is enlarged to include manufacturing, storage, supply, and all military facilities, as well as active combat zones of operation. The phrases "lurking as a spy" and "acting as a spy" may be argued before and interpreted by the court-martial; however, the UCMJ also has a definition of "aiding the enemy" that carries the same punishment as spying. The definition of "aiding the enemy" includes not only helping or attempting to aid with such obvious hardware as arms and ammunition but also covers

Any person who, without proper authority, knowingly harbors or protects or gives intelligence to, or communicates or corresponds with or holds any intercourse with the enemy, either directly or indirectly; shall suffer death or such other punishment as a court-martial or military commission may direct.[5]

Clearly, this article covers both direct and indirect unauthorized contact with the enemy. Presumably, an enemy exists only during a war; while at peace, the problem is that of giving information to "foreign governments." The term *spying* has been broadened in general usage, as suggested above, to apply when the nation is at peace. Perhaps the word now gets this wide interpretation because the military strength of a nation so clearly depends on its industrial and scientific institutions: What was once merely "commercial espionage" now has obvious military consequences.

The overlap between industrial morality and military morality is an almost daily newspaper subject. The Toshiba case (a 1987 discovery) is a notorious example; it was a case in which a Japanese firm that understood perfectly well the agreements to restrict certain equipment from the U.S.S.R. secretly violated the agreements. The equipment that it supplied to the U.S.S.R. made Soviet submarines much quieter and more difficult to track. The moral questions include the matter of just what punishment is proper in a case like the Toshiba action, who gives it, and exactly who gets it. A few Toshiba executives did resign, with apologies and pensions intact. The matter of industrial spying is significant for our subject but outside our immediate scope.

To spy literally refers to entering an opponent's zone under false pretenses to get information. Those are still the essential elements. All foreign nations are potential opponents, and the "zone" may include an indefinite amount of a nation's scientific and industrial base. Therefore, beyond the classical situation of purely military spying during warfare, we have to deal with the morality of somewhat different but related cases in which our citizens violate a national security law by giving information to a foreign government. In the last few years, a number of individuals in or discharged from military service have been tried and convicted of passing information to agents of a foreign power.

Treason

Cases of treason, the betrayal of one's own country and covert action on behalf of a foreign nation, are immoral on two counts: the betrayal[6] and the covert action. Unfortunately, we have recent examples. Retired Lt. Commander Arthur James Walker was found guilty of participating in a Soviet spy ring that has been called the most damaging to the United States in decades. Walker was convicted (9 August 1985, Federal District Court, Norfolk, Virginia) of stealing classified documents for his brother, John A. Walker, Jr., a retired U.S. Navy chief warrant officer. The retired warrant officer had been arrested earlier and charged with espionage, as had his son, Seaman Michael Lance Walker, while Seaman Walker was serving aboard the aircraft carrier *Nimitz*. Our interest here is not in the details of the espionage, the damage to U.S. security, or the punishment meted out, but in the basis for moral judgments.

While we consider the moral framework of these agents, we cannot help speculating about their intentions. Note that these cases are not restricted to the uniformed services. An ex-CIA employee, Karl F. Koecher, is also a case (arrested on 27 November 1984) of a citizen charged with delivering classified national security information to, in this case, the Czechoslovakian intelligence service. Still more recently, a former U.S. Navy civilian intelligence analyst, Jonathan Jay Pollard, was sentenced on 4 March 1987 to life imprisonment for selling secret U.S. military documents to Israel.[7] Every nation seems to have had the same problem in recent history, including Great Britain, India, Israel, Syria, West Germany, and others.[8]

Civilians without military attachments have also been convicted of similar things. Perhaps the most widely discussed of these was the Rosenberg case, in which a man and his wife were found guilty of passing diagrams of parts of the construction of the atom bomb to the Soviet government. They were convicted in March 1951, sentenced to death, and later executed.[9]

The history of civilization shows a fair number of people changing their loyalties. To drop citizenship (or membership) in one nation and adopt the citizenship of another can be perfectly straightforward. (The biblical story of Ruth comes under that heading.) The moral issue involved here is the matter of secrecy. To publicly renounce one loyalty and adopt another is quite acceptable: To lie about the change in loyalty or conceal it is not acceptable.

In the Hague Rules the definition of spying is followed by a statement that soldiers who are not disguised are not considered spies, even if they have entered the zone of the hostile army for the purpose of obtaining information. Also, a spy who has managed to rejoin his or her army is no longer to be treated as a spy if captured afterward. The spying mission is considered over after the spy's return to his or her own forces; a previous history of spying is not a basis for the charge of espionage.

Punishment for Spying

The punishment for spying can range up to death; however, the punishment—even the death penalty—cannot be administered on the spot. Article 30 of the Hague Rules reads, "A spy taken in the act shall not be punished without previous trial." There is no quick informal execution in the field; a proper trial must be held. For example, after World War II, in the trial of Richard Rhode and others, the British Manual mentions that "the accused were found guilty of executing, without trial, four British women who had been sent to France in plain clothes to assist British liaison officers attached to the French Resistance movement."[10] Executions without trial are clearly forbidden, and we expect to find and do find trials held for those who order such executions. Of course, we might suspect that these "four British women" may well have been members of the armed forces because it was noted that they were in "plain clothes." (The British Manual does not use "plain" as a fashion comment.) In any event, whether they were military or civilian personnel, they should not have been executed without a trial.

The Morality of Spying

Unique moral issues are involved in spying. The spy undertakes to lie, lie directly, to the enemy. Military honor forbids removing all traces of one's uniform and undertaking a mission while pretending to be a civilian. Some obvious questions arise. Is it a violation of military honor to accept a spying mission? Even stronger, is it a war crime?

History and practice must be considered before responding, and history is full of examples of spying. The British Manual comments, "Many writers disagree but military custom has always sanctioned it [spying]."[11] The British Manual also cites, with apparent agreement, FM 27-10, which holds that spying is not a war crime and that "spies are punished not as violators of the law of war, but to render that method of obtaining information as dangerous, difficult and ineffective as possible for the enemy."[12] Apparently, it was necessary to insert that remark because of the *prima facie* assumption that there is something immoral about spying.

Despite the official positions that we have noted above and despite the long history of spying by military personnel, a moral question remains. Is it morally acceptable for a professional soldier to spy? First, is it lying to the enemy—acting a lie—if one says nothing about the subject but merely replaces the uniform with other clothing? Second, even if it is lying, is it an acceptable military ruse? Of course, it misleads the enemy if a soldier wears civilian clothing or the uniform of the enemy. A Hague Rule (art. 23, para. f) specifies, "It is especially forbidden . . . to make improper use of . . . the military insignia and uniform of the enemy."[13] In FM 27-10, a few lines below this Hague Rule, we find the U.S. interpretation: "In practice, it has been authorized to make use of national flags, insignia, and uniforms as a ruse. The foregoing rule does not prohibit such employment, but does prohibit their improper use. It is certainly forbidden to employ them during combat, but their use at other times is not forbidden."[14] The "use of spies," however, is mentioned as one of the "legitimate ruses" that may be used. What can we say of this interpretation? Clearly, it has been accepted and practiced by all sides; to go further and publish it as openly as the FM does is to make the pattern clear to potential enemies. Because spying by one side does not prevent others from undertaking the same activity, this interpretation appears to satisfy a part of the requirement for universality, for a compound reason. The nations and institutions involved can each do what the other does: They can employ spies. On an individual basis, however, things are a bit different. The individual spy effectively lies to other individuals, pretending something that is not true, hiding something that those around him or her do not know. The spy's intention is not to have all parties follow the same rule. So, institutional spying can follow the same rules, but individual spying cannot—not if it is to be successful.

How are we to judge an activity that is collectively acceptable but distributively—individually—not? Another way to say this is that institutions, by using individuals to do their dirty work, gain their goals without qualms, a point that has been noted more than once in human history. The requirement is to find individuals (and apparently there is no shortage) who are willing to make the sacrifice of their morality and take the risk of being caught.

As we found in Chapter 4, certain tricks or ruses are acceptable; others are not. There we noted the Field Manual's insistence that on certain matters there is an obligation to tell the truth, to keep good faith with the enemy. In a great many other cases, however, confusing and deceiving the enemy are perfectly acceptable. Some clear examples as well as some vague matters are found on each side of the line. To distinguish between *actively* and *passively* lying is sometimes of use. To accept parole and then break parole would be actively misrepresenting your intentions. To lie about a surrender would be an active lie. However, to appear to go in one direction while the bulk of a company goes in another is not actively misrepresenting: No one speaks falsely. To paint dummy weapons is likewise not an active lie, nor are planting bogus orders and a dozen other efforts that are designed to mislead. The distinction between an active and a passive misrepresentation does not always mark the line, but that distinction can help make a rough sorting between the two categories. Can spying count as "passive" and therefore an acceptable misrepresentation?

The objection to spying is muted if the individual gathers information without having to lie directly (for example, to say that he or she is a civilian). This example can be classified as "passive lying." The soldier who presents him- or herself as a civilian, making friends and using their trust in his or her statements, however, is an active liar.

All spy missions are not the same. We may distinguish between a passive observer–reporter of information and an active spy who ingratiates him- or herself as one of them (the enemy community). The line between active and passive is rough and can stand only limited scrutiny, but it does give us a way of thinking in terms of degrees of honor. The passive spy misrepresents in a way that is weaker than that of the active spy.

Is it acceptable to lie to a civilian on matters that would not be acceptable as lies to an enemy soldier? The tradition that an officer's word is his or her bond, in or out of uniform, suggests that the answer is *no*. If we understand officers to be leadership examples for enlisted personnel rather than a different kind of human, the answer for all military personnel must be the same.

We can easily imagine the response of several institutional as well as individual moral styles here. Suppose that a mythical nation holds to a strict construction of the basic concept of military honor: Its citizens insist that military honor requires that they not use spies either in civilian clothing or in the uniform of the enemy. Suppose all of the other nations followed the usual interpretation of the British and American military stated above, that spying is not a violation of the laws of war or of military morality. Could the strict constructionist nation be expected to fight effectively, if it had to fight? It would lose the information that could be gained by spies, but it might gain substantial respect from the enemy, respect that might result in desertions from the other side and other benefits. Possible, but unlikely. Not relying on espionage might force that nation to develop more formidable weapons and more impressive strategies. The risk in choosing such a moral style, however, would be enormous; the obvious assumption is that such a style of strict construction would be an unbearable loss of military efficiency. Of course, the question about fighting effectively is not the only thing to consider. The long-established custom, from the earliest Western records,[15] makes spying quite expected and, therefore, essentially acceptable. In most forms, this custom appears to satisfy the criterion mentioned in Chapter 4: The enemy ought to have expected it and taken protective steps against it.

From each of the four moral viewpoints, some actions are so wrong that they should not be taken even if the cost is loss of the battle or loss of the war. Killing large numbers of innocent people is an example for universal fairness. Is the use of spies such an action? At this point the different moral styles give different responses. Universal fairness would ask that the same patterns be available to all sides: Spying meets this test, at least institutionally. Then, universal fairness would also ask whether the same risk of sacrifices are required of all participants on the side using spies. The matter of equality of sacrifice is significant enough to be worth a diversion from our main question.

We can distinguish a group and an individual answer. As a group, each side can take the same risk as the other side—the risk of losing some of their personnel, who might be captured, tried, and shot as spies. Within each side, however, the situation is somewhat different. The spy mission is, ordinarily, a much more dangerous activity than another duty, and, if a spy is caught and convicted, he or she essentially agrees to give up some of the protection offered by POW status. So, the sacrifices within each army are not equal, a situation that may exist, even without considering spying. By definition, if there is a "front line," those on that line will be the first to face enemy action. Therefore, a commanding officer might ask for volunteers for something as uniquely dangerous as espionage. One could also imagine a commander using a lottery to choose personnel for dangerous missions. That anyone in a company might volunteer[16] or be selected gives the pattern some sort of equality of sacrifice, but the equal opportunity to volunteer is not the same as an equal risk actually undertaken. The relationship between the volunteer for espionage and other soldiers is similar to the relationship between the soldier and the civilian (mentioned in Chapter 1). One clearly risks more than the other.

These greater sacrifices are traditionally given military recognition through the presentation of awards, medals, stars on theater ribbons, ceremonies, and privileges. The civilian world recognizes these special military sacrifices by such means as bonuses to veterans, additional points for veterans on civil service waiting lists, and parades and ceremonies to welcome returning veterans.[17] One way to honor the sacrifices made by a spy, therefore, is to give special awards and honors. However, the continued usefulness of a spy or of particular techniques may be lost if special recognition is made public. Thus, the spy may have to sacrifice public recognition, among other things.

From the moral standpoint of social utility, spying may be an obviously desirable activity. The benefits to the majority might well justify the cost, even to the individual who takes the risk. Despite first impressions, even the morality of individualism may lead someone to risk the dangers of spying for the potential personal glory and excitement. As both literature and reality suggest, individualism may also lead someone to become a double agent for the sake of even more excitement and (perhaps) personal income. (Commentators have noted that some of the recent cases of selling information to foreign nations have involved relatively small amounts of money: Apparently the excitement of being so clever at fooling one's colleagues partly explains the motives involved.) For individualism, of course, the decision to take the risk of spying is to be left to the individual.

The final version of our question inquires about the religious position on the decision to use spies. If the moral object is something more sacred than or different from any human, then humans ought to be sacrificed for the benefit of this proper god. The sacrifice of an individual spy is most easily defended from this moral viewpoint.

We can conclude the following about the moral framework of espionage: The Hague Rules make it clear that a soldier is not to remove his or her uniform and pretend to be other than what he or she is. Like any law, these rules specify unacceptable behavior and explain what the punishment may be when the law or rule is broken. A law against an action does not stop that action from occurring; rather, it tells the world what to be shocked at and how to respond. Someone who breaks this rule is subject to trial and execution. A convicted spy is a POW but has forfeited some of the POW's basic protections.

Using this interpretation, may an honorable soldier accept a spy mission? Can we imagine Generals George Washington, Omar Bradley, or George C. Marshall acting as spies? Something in the personal moral styles of those officers (as presented in the usual accounts) makes it almost impossible to picture any one of them as good, successful liars; and a spy may have to be a convincing liar. As soon as we put the question this way, it should become obvious that individuals have different personal styles. Some may and others may not be able or willing to lie for their country. It seems odd that someone might agree to give up life to protect the nation but not be willing to give up personal honor. Fortunately or not, there appears to be no shortage of those willing to lie. Many of us with less ability than Washington, Bradley, or Marshall might claim to be better than any one of them at lying.

Chapter 3 presented the problems of (1) keeping good faith with the enemy, required by the laws of war (FM 27-10), and (2) using ruses of warfare that are acceptable under the same laws and Code. The requirement that one keep good faith with the enemy by not lying, for example, binds one while in uniform. Does removal of the uniform relieve a soldier of this part of the Code?

Morality out of Uniform

"But, Sir, I was out of uniform at the time!" How much of an excuse is this? Does it excuse one from the Hague Rules? From conduct becoming an officer? While there may be some precedent for the view that removing the uniform cancels certain obligations, this position cannot withstand scrutiny.

Of course, to take off the uniform with the announced intention of deserting is a different matter. We are not considering the desertion case here. A proper discharge from military service also certainly cancels the essential military requirements, but removing one's uniform is hardly the equivalent of holding a signed discharge paper. To sleep without a uniform may bring release from the day's tensions but not release from military service.

Suppose a war crime is committed—for instance, torture of a prisoner to get information—but it is committed by troops who have completely removed their uniforms. Even if they also remove their dog tags and underwear and carry out the torture while nude, they remain soldiers and their act remains a war crime. Whether they claim pay for the days out of uniform is irrelevant. If they were not properly discharged, they remain under military command; they remain soldiers under the Hague Rules.[18] Neither entering nor leaving service is a casual matter. The nation and the world must know who is and who is not a soldier. Why? Because enormous power is given to the soldier, and it cannot be given or abandoned lightly.

The uniform is a necessary symbol, and it can be used deceitfully in two ways. A person can impersonate a soldier by wearing a uniform without authority; a person can impersonate a civilian by not wearing a uniform under conditions that require it. Both impersonations are dishonorable. Obviously, under the Hague Rules, we must reject the argument that being out of uniform is an excuse for unmilitary behavior.

Conclusions

How does consideration of the out-of-uniform argument affect the major questions involved in spying? After all, there is an enormous difference between being out of uniform in order to spy and being out of uniform for the sake of an assassination. Although spying is a violation of the Hague Rules that require that the uniform be worn in combat, it is far from a major war crime. (We look at war crimes more carefully in Chapter 8.) The essential point is that the spy mission need not be considered combat, even though, in some very broad sense of combat, perhaps it is. The Rules make clear the procedures and punishments that are acceptable when a spy is captured. We have noted the difference between varieties of spying, between active and passive misrepresentation. All things considered, we must conclude that although spying is a violation of personal honor in the sense considered above, it is not a violation of military honor. Spying carries even greater risks than action in uniform.

The British Manual mentions the view that "the law of war [the Hague interpretation] in respect of spying, in particular with regard to the severity of punishment, may be obsolete."[19] We have already noted the fact that the British did not punish their part of the Rosenberg spy network, Klaus Fuchs, as severely as the United States punished the Rosenbergs. The British point may be that the usual practice has been to keep spies alive for the purpose of exchange. The possibility of execution does not seem to deter others from the practice.

Despite the conclusion drawn earlier, that the employment of spies is so customary that it has become acceptable, we must still respect the individual moral style that refuses to remove the uniform on the grounds that impersonating a civilian is lying. Impersonating a civilian violates the point of the Thomas Hobbes quotation that opened Chapter 3: It is contemptible to those who refuse to enjoy the benefits of "fraud, or breach of promise." Spying must count as some sort of fraud. In this sense, for certain people, it comes under the heading of "dirty hands," a subject that we consider in more detail in Chapter 9.

As in the other sorts of "dirty-hands operations," a nation may ask people to do things that are completely or partly dishonorable, enjoy the benefit of that action, and then deny that the action occurred or disown responsibility for it. When a spy is caught, it seems almost routine to say, whether true or false, "That person was not working for us." Why not admit that he or she is in our employ? For one thing, to do so may endanger the spy even more. Or it may not; each case is a bit different. One major reason for the immediate denial that person X was spying for a certain nation is that spying is lying, and to the universal fairness position, lying is immoral and remains distasteful despite its universal practice. Obviously, lying about a matter because it is distasteful to admit to a lie is still lying!

Military intelligence can be gathered in a wide variety of ways; using soldiers out of uniform is just one of them. This chapter has considered only the use of human spies. Although general practice has made spying acceptable as a military ruse, we can understand and respect those who might refuse to do it. While we can distinguish between those who remove their uniforms to gather intelligence and those who remove them in order to safely carry out any other military action, they both give up a certain amount of military honor. The spy sacrifices the respect due the ordinary soldier for openness, directness, and honesty.

A naive reader should be warned that the spirit of this chapter on spying is out of step with most military thinking and practice, both ancient and modern. It is generally held that spying is absolutely necessary and proper. Readers, however, are invited to consider the foundation for the loathing that democracies have for governments that make heavy use of a secret police. The police and the military are not identical—one has domestic and the other foreign scope—but some of the features of honor are involved in an essential way in both institutions.

7

Nonhostile Relations
with the Enemy

What dealings, other than hostilities, does a military unit have with its enemy? In addition to the responsibility for POWs, several kinds are to be expected. An armistice period, a period in which fighting ceases, may have to be arranged and carefully monitored. A surrender may be agreed upon and carried out. These activities, along with travel within occupied territory, must be regulated. Occupation of a territory may require all or most of the machinery of the ordinary government.

Parlementaires

In order to make the arrangements for an armistice, a surrender, or a safeguard for persons such as diplomats, the wounded, and civilians, it is necessary to communicate with the enemy. The term *parlementaires* (speakers) refers to persons who are used to speak or negotiate with the enemy commander. FM 27-10 notes that, in the past, negotiations were customarily started by displaying a white flag; however, in modern military operations, a white flag might be a very slow or useless way of getting the enemy's attention. Although the white flag still retains its meaning, messages sent by radio or dropped by aircraft are now more efficient. The symbolic white flag can mean either that the party (or the individual) wishes to surrender or that the commander wants to send a parlementaire for a discussion.

The person carrying the white flag "has a right to inviolability," according to the Hague Rules, Article 32. That protection also covers the party accompanying that person, specified in the Hague Rules as "the trumpeter, bugler or drummer, the flag bearer and the interpreter." Of course the musical accompaniment is not just aesthetic; it calls attention to the idea of the special protection that is to be given to the parlementaire.

While the parlementaire is not to be attacked while advancing toward the enemy, discussing the business at hand, or returning to his or her own side, this protection holds only if that person does not take advantage of the position "to provoke or commit an act of treachery."[1] The white flag, or "flag of truce," is not to be abused. It is an abuse of the flag to continue an attack while the parlementaire is still conducting business; to use the flag to halt the opponent's attack without any intention of sending a parlementaire; and, of course, to use the flag to signal surrender as a trick to continue or to launch an attack.

Armistices

An armistice or truce is a period during which the belligerents have agreed to stop hostilities. Far from a peace, it is merely a halting of active hostilities, based on an agreement between the opponents. That agreement might cover just one section of the conflict or all hostilities by all forces; it might be a brief suspension to collect and bury the dead, care for the wounded, and exchange POWs.

Two essentials are usually stressed when considering armistices. First, the precise details of the agreement should be presented in writing, if possible: the exact start and end, the exact area covered, and what is and is not prohibited during the period. Second, these details are to be precisely carried out. FM 27-10 adds its own language to the Hague Rules, and in Paragraph 493 states, "An armistice, like other formal agreements between belligerents, engages the honor of both parties for the exact and complete fulfillment of every obligation thereby imposed. It would be an outrageous act of perfidy for either party, without warning, to resume hostilities during the period of an armistice"—unless, of course, there is clear proof of violation by the other side. The Field Manual adds that an armistice is no excuse for lack of vigilance.

Surrenders

A formal surrender is based on an agreement about the exact conditions to be followed by both sides. Such an agreement is called a *capitulation,* and it can be either oral or written. Of course, a surrender can take place without a formal capitulation statement.

As one might expect, the Hague Rules insist on strict honesty in the matter: "Capitulations agreed upon between the contracting parties must

take into account the rules of military honour. Once settled, they must be scrupulously observed by both parties."[2] This rule requires that there be no capitulation that agrees to anything that military honor forbids, such as rape and torture.

The obvious questions about a capitulation are: Who has the authority to make such an agreement? and When is that individual justified in doing so? Ordinarily the answer to the first question is clear: Whoever commands a body of troops is the person "presumed to be duly authorized to enter into capitulations."[3] Of course, a commanding officer's authority to surrender covers only the forces, territory, and equipment under his or her command. A commander cannot agree to matters outside the scope of his or her immediate command, unless the government has given that additional authority. The British Manual mentions that "small detached parties, or even individual soldiers [may be in a situation in which they] are left to their own discretion, and the senior of the party or the individual, so far as concerns the parry or his own person, may do everything which a command might do with respect to himself and the troops under his command" (para. 471, p. 135).

The U.S. material on the subject is not as liberal as that of the British concerning individual discretion about surrender. The U.S. Code of Conduct, Second Declaration, is a no-surrender pledge, as noted in Chapter 3. The U.S. no-surrender pledge has two qualifications: I will never surrender of my own free will nor will I surrender my troops while they have means to resist. A surrender must be involuntary—no free choice and no means to resist, if the two differ.

The second question concerns the matter of when to surrender. The U.S. Field Manual puts the problem this way: "In the case of a commander of a military force of the United States, if continued battle has become impossible and he cannot communicate with his superiors, these facts will constitute proper authority to surrender."[4] This guideline is followed immediately by the warning, "If a commander of military forces of the United States surrenders unnecessarily and shamefully or in violation of orders from higher authority, he is liable to trial and punishment [under the UCMJ]." However, to maintain the trust of the enemy in military agreements, even a commander who surrenders in violation of orders "does not impair the validity of the surrender."[5] A rather impressive feature! Because of the need to maintain trust in the word of an officer or enlisted personnel wearing the uniform of the country, even a surrender in violation of orders will be respected. The military honor of the armed forces is understood to be more important than the immediate loss involved.

"With the Honours of War"

The British Manual mentions that in the past capitulations were sometime arranged in which the expression "with the honours of war" was used. Th

statement usually included "the right to march out with colours displayed, bayonets fixed, etc." Why give such rights to the side that has been overcome? The British Manual gives this historical example:

> In the Franco-German War very favorable terms were granted to the garrison of Belfort under Colonel Denfett-Rocheteau who surrendered under instructions from his government: "In recognition of their brave defence the garrison are allowed free withdrawal with the honours of war. They will take away the eagles, colours, arms, horses, carriages, and the military telegraph apparatus, as also the baggage of the officers and kits of the men and the archives of the fortress."[6]

Respect for a brave defense dominated any need to punish or embarrass the enemy. Respect for the accomplishments of the enemy was more significant than their sins as followers of a different command or believers in a different ideology. To talk of ideology is anachronistic; only in recent times has political ideology had the status of a religious cause (as mentioned in Chapter 3 in the quotation from Wright's *A Study of War*).

The point in calling attention to the notion of a capitulation "with the honours of war" is to emphasize the attitude of respect for the enemy as humans. Humans may behave well or not; they may show courage or the opposite. It is, or was, possible to fight and defeat an enemy without thinking of them as less than human. Now that we are living in the age of propaganda, this possibility seems less likely. Psychological warfare must also be considered. Such "warfare" is sometimes directed to the enemy and sometimes to one's own forces. In the latter case, where the object may be to have one's own side think of the enemy as less than human, such psychological warfare goes against the morality of the military tradition. (I am, of course, referring to my own preferred examples.)

Unconditional Surrender

Is there such a thing as a surrender with no restrictions or conditions, no limitations on what may be done with the captured forces? The earlier remarks on this matter may be extended. The U.S. FM gives the boundary that cannot be ignored, even in a so-called unconditional surrender: Such a surrender is still "subject to the restrictions of the law of war" (para, 478). This means, among other things, that the status and rights of POWs cannot be waived by any surrender document. The British Manual comes to the point: Even in an unconditional surrender, "the victor has nowadays no longer the power of life and death over his prisoners, and is not absolved from observing the laws of war toward them" (para. 476).

Why require an unconditional surrender, if it is not really unconditional? The capitulations at the end of World War II held a definite political

significance. An ordinary capitulation is an agreement with the forces of a particular government. Because one of the purposes of World War II was to abolish the governments that had, as the British Manual puts it, been "responsible for the initiation and lawless conduct of the war of aggression" (para. 461), an ordinary surrender would have essentially been an agreement with those governments and would have helped to perpetuate them. The unconditional surrenders nominally avoided that. One is forced to say "nominally" because the agreement to surrender—the capitulation—does, of course, require two parties. The capitulation of Germany in World War II was technically avoided by having the instrument of surrender signed (at Rheims) on behalf of the German High Command on one side and by no one on the other, but rather "in the presence of representatives of the allied forces," as the British Manual and the histories report the event.

Is there a difference between a capitulation signed by both sides and one signed by only one side *in the presence* of the other? No clear military difference exists, but perhaps a hair of difference in international law does. When the ceremony of signing a capitulation is conducted in the presence and under the control of the victors, it carries the sense of an agreement by the victors. The agreement is understood to be an expression of contempt for the enemy rather than refusal to agree to the capitulation terms.

Safeguards

A *safeguard* is, literally, a guard posted to protect the "persons, places or property of the enemy, or of a neutral."[7] The term may also refer to a written order covering such protection. The effect of either the written safeguard or the personnel posted as guard, as put in the U.S. FM, "is to pledge the honor of the nation that the person or property shall be respected by the national armed forces. The violation of a safeguard is a grave violation of the law of war and, if committed by a person subject to the Uniform Code of Military Justice, is punishable under Article 102 thereof with death or such other punishment as a court-martial may direct."[8] Why is the punishment so serious? Because "the honor of the nation" has been pledged. That honor must always have at least nominal force because, as already emphasized, the purpose of the war requires that the enemy trusts the foe, accepts surrender, and remains surrendered.

Military Passports, Safe-conduct Passes, and Cartels

The general assumptions of this chapter also hold for other specific matters that arise as relationships between hostile powers. Persons who live in an occupied area can obtain a military passport that will give them the right to travel and carry goods within that area. For people living outside an occupied area, a safe-conduct pass can be used to permit travel (for example, for ambassadors and other diplomatic personnel). In addition, cartels— agreements—may be worked out for such purposes as exchanging POWs.

Regarding all of the relations mentioned in this chapter, the FM insists that "it is absolutely essential that the most scrupulous good faith shall be observed by both parties, and that no advantage not intended to be given by the adversary shall be taken."[9] Under a state of war, it is quite acceptable to kill the enemy, to wound the enemy, or to cause the enemy great harm, but a breach of honor is forbidden. The enemy's confidence in the other side's word of honor must not be lost because the aim of the war is to have that enemy accept and trust the terms of surrender. A breach of honor might jeopardize the goal of the war.

8

War Crimes, Remedies, and Retaliation (Dirty Warfare)

The concept of a war crime is at the center of military ethics. What is a war crime, who is responsible for it, and what reprisals are justified against it? The business of this chapter is to respond directly to these questions. In addition, due to the events of the past few decades, we must pay new attention to the term *terrorism*. How is terrorism related to war crimes? After considering the general idea of a war crime, we will define terrorism.

Defining a War Crime

The term war crime covers any violation of the laws of warfare. Such crimes may be committed by military or civilian persons or by citizens of neutral countries as well of those of belligerents.

A special group of possible war crimes are called "grave breaches" of the Conventions. These specify four categories of acts, acts against:

a. *all persons protected by the conventions:* willful killing, torture or inhuman treatment, including biological experiments, and willfully causing great suffering or serious injury to body or health;

b. *prisoners of war:* compelling a POW to serve in the forces of the hostile power and willfully depriving a POW of the rights of fair and regular trial required in the POW Convention;

c. *persons and property protected under the Civilian Convention:* unlawful deportation or transfer or unlawful confinement, compelling a person to serve in the forces of a hostile power, or willfully depriving him of the rights of fair and regular trial required in that convention, the taking of hostages and the extensive destruction and appropriation of property nor justified by military necessity and carried out unlawfully and wantonly; and

d. *property protected by the Civilian, the Wounded and the Maritime Conventions:* extensive destruction and appropriation of property not justified by military necessity and carried out unlawfully and wantonly (British Manual p. 175).

Shortly, we will return to two of the matters included in the above list of grave breaches: biological experiments and the taking of hostages. First, however, to clarify the idea of a war crime, consider the list given in the manuals as *examples* of possible war crimes, appearing essentially in both the British and American manuals. (After the earlier chapters of this book, these examples should look quite familiar.)

a. treacherous request for quarter;
b. maltreatment of dead bodies;
c. firing on undefended localities and nonmilitary objectives;
d. abuse of or firing on a flag of truce;
e. misuse of the Red Cross or equivalent emblem;
f. use of civilian clothing or of enemy uniform by troops engaged in a battle;
g. using expanding bullets or poisoned or otherwise forbidden arms or ammunition;
h. improper use of a privileged building for military purposes;
i. poisoning of wells, streams, and other sources of water supply;
j. pillage (purposeless destruction);
k. compelling prisoners of war to perform prohibited work;
l. killing without trial of spies, saboteurs, partisans, and others who have committed hostile acts;
m. using and, in particular, deporting civilians for forced labor;
n. violation of surrender terms.

The British Manual continues the list with items *o* to *t* that are further "examples" of war crimes. Obviously these are not in order of seriousness. It would seem that item *q,* killing hostages, is more serious than taking hostages (in item *c* of grave breaches).

o. bombardment of hospitals and other privileged buildings;
p. participation in hostilities by civilians;

q. killing of hostages;
r. using asphyxiating, poisonous or other gases, and all analogous liquids, materials or devices;
s. using bacteriological methods of warfare;
t. genocide

Biological Experiments

Even when a nation has agreed to refrain from *using* biological weapons, it may still take the position that *research may be conducted on such weapons*. Research may be for the sake of defense against its use by others or for developing weapons that may only be used in reprisal. (Later we discuss the morality of reprisal.)

Experiments on human subjects were run by Germany and by the Japanese during World War II and have been widely publicized since. Of course, those crimes have been prosecuted and convictions have been obtained, but it is worth looking at how such activities develop.

Military medicine is devoted to solving medical problems that arise in warfare; therefore, every army needs a medical corps to learn how to manage the results of such problems as the burning of skin and the need to make extensive skin grafts in therapy. In an ordinary skin graft, skin is taken from one place on the body and put where it is needed, or skin might be taken from another person and used, provided there are careful matches of the biological factors involved. German doctors used people in concentration camps, primarily Jews and gypsies, to learn about grafting techniques. These prisoners were used as if they were merely laboratory animals, cut up in any way that seemed to be of experimental interest, as if they had no "human rights."

Since World War II, well-publicized advances have been made in medicine, including almost common operations in which organs are taken from one person and placed in the body of another. Kidneys in particular, but also hearts and other organs, have been successfully transplanted. We can imagine the pressure to use "available" humans as guinea pigs, but to act as if protected persons are available for such experiments is obviously to commit a grave breach of the Conventions.

Biological warfare includes causing disease by dropping behind enemy lines some small, infected animal; insects; or viruses that will cause disease. To discover how to put a chemical in the air or deliver it to the enemy some other way is a part of such research. There are chemicals, gasses, and diseases that can cause the enemy to become sleepy, less efficient, or ill, or can kill the enemy. The problem of controlling the delivery of such gases, however, is obviously tricky. How can such systems be tested? There was a strange case in which the Department of Defense acknowledged putting a biological agent in the air of the New York City subways to discover its effect on people. When people found out what had been done to them without their being asked permission, there was great public criticism, though the government claimed that the test caused no harm and that it was necessary to protect the country.[1]

Biological warfare has a dirty, hitting-below-the-belt, dishonorable aura about it. Even plans for essentially harmless incapacitating weapons seem to affect people negatively. Perhaps such weapons just don't fit the John Wayne image of a soldier. That there is a well-known biblical example of the use of biological weapons is apparently of no relevance. In the story of the plagues that the Lord loosed against the Egyptians, these weapons were used by the Lord, not by humans in human warfare. The plagues included swarms of insects, an epidemic of boils, and Egyptian water being turned into blood.[2] Of course, let us hope that it is an understatement to say that military morality has advanced beyond the primitive level of the biblical era.

Based on sketchy reports that may be erroneous, the Japanese army had a germ warfare section during World War II that used prisoners for experimentation. The questions of interest are obvious. What kind of disease will a particular germ cause? How fast does it develop? How long does it last? Is it contagious? Essentially, how long will something have a disabling effect on people? At the end of the war, U.S. Army intelligence learned about this section and could have charged the commanding officers with war crimes because the Conventions do not allow the use of innocent people in experiments. Biological experiments are not an acceptable way of punishing people, even people who are found by trial to be guilty of some crime. Instead of being charged as war criminals, however, the Japanese military officers who were operating this germ warfare section apparently made an arrangement with U.S. intelligence officers. They gave the United States the results of their experiments, which was presumably valuable information on the properties of various kinds of germ warfare. Germ warfare is difficult to use; it must affect the enemy but not one's own forces. The infectiousness and other properties of the biological agent must be known before it is used. In exchange for this information, U.S. intelligence agreed not to prosecute the Japanese for war crimes. Newspaper stories about these events did not appear until a few years ago.

If the above report is accurate (here I am accepting newspaper accounts), what can be said about the morality of the American decision? (I discuss the American side here because there seems to be little doubt that the Japanese activity constituted war crimes.) Apparently, a decision was made to accept records of biological experiments in exchange for not charging the Japanese personnel with war crimes. It is tempting to contrast this case with plea bargaining in civilian law. In the ordinary case of plea bargaining, a defendant is allowed to plead guilty to a lesser charge. In this case, as far as I know, there was no "lesser charge"; there were *no* charges!

We do seem, however, to have a parallel with a question in civilian law: Is it acceptable to use information that has been obtained in illegal ways? (This is the exclusionary rule.) If it took war crimes to make certain information available, should we gratefully use that information, or should we disdain to accept it? The latter is the moral high road: Publicize the situation, charge the guilty, and destroy the results of the experiments after the trials. The argument on the other side, however, is obvious. The pain and suffering that the experiments caused the victims cannot be removed by deciding to destroy the results. Because a future enemy may have such information, why not keep the records for study by our own biological warfare units?

Both arguments are somewhat vague, but I think that the tautology holds that the high road is higher than the other road. For one thing, the pain caused to the victims and their families may be somewhat eased by knowledge that the guilty were at least charged with a crime. Not to do even that, while benefiting from the results, is to become a part of the war crime—not a shining page in American military history. But censoring those pages of history is hardly the way to moral improvement.

Volunteering for Biological Experiments

Suppose protected persons volunteer for biological experiments? Are the experiments then acceptable? In deliberating about this idea, we may find it worthwhile to consider a parallel question that caused a heated dispute a few years ago. In civilian prisons in the United States, some drug manufacturers were using prisoners to test new drugs. It was said that the prisoners volunteered, knowing the risks. Why would they volunteer? There are three possible reasons: to get extra money, to have a possible positive effect on a parole board decision, and to be of service to humankind. The second reason—the chance to impress the parole board—can hardly be ignored. Under such conditions, can we think that accepting a call for volunteers is really what it means to volunteer?

Can a prisoner ever be said to volunteer? A volunteer is someone who is not compelled to take a certain risk, who has not been unduly pressured. In the prisoner/drug test situation, some commentators hold that the prisoners' civil rights were being violated. Other commentators take quite the opposite view, saying that as long as the prisoners had a choice and had not been compelled to "volunteer," they had the right to choose to be used for testing if they wished. If they understood the risk and still wanted to make the extra money or make that kind of effort to impress the parole board, their own right to choose should not be taken away. From the standpoint of the outside population and the drug companies, new drugs do need to be tested before being sold to the general public. The matter of understanding the risks is far from clear: Were there no risks, there would be no need to test. If the risks were perfectly known, there would be no need to test. In addition, the prisoners might require considerable education in pharmacology to appreciate the explanation of the risks. We leave the question of experimenting on civilian prisoners in the United States with the remark that different states and prisons have had different responses to this problem.

In the case of protected persons and POWs, the prohibition against causing serious injury or suffering is quite clear. Suppose a POW volunteers for a biological experiment. Article 7 of the Geneva Prisoner of War Convention gives the relevant answer: "Prisoners of war may in no circumstances renounce in part or in entirety the rights secured to them by the present Convention." They are not allowed to volunteer to waive their protections and permit what would be a grave breach.

Why not allow POWs to volunteer for such experiments? The assumption apparently is that it is not in the long-term interest of the individual, whatever short-term advantage is offered by the commanding officer of a prison camp. Essentially, the prisoner is being used to act (essentially a variety of fight) against his or her own side. Why not do that? This question goes back to the notion of military honor. Soldiers are assumed to be willing to fight for the sake of their loyalties; they are not to be compelled to fight. Item *b* of the list of grave breaches specifies that POWs not be forced to "serve," or risk their bodies and lives, for the sake of their opponent. Soldiers are not to be either slaves or mercenaries.

Therefore, compelling POWs to serve in the forces of their opponent is a war crime and a grave violation. For the reasons listed above—the violations of human rights as well as help to the belligerent—it is also a war crime and a grave breach to use POWs or protected persons for biological experiments. Because the significance of human rights is central to the matter, we might remind ourselves of the different attitudes toward such "rights."

Human Rights

By the phrase *human rights,* we refer to the idea that, within limits, every human has and should be allowed to exercise certain abilities: the ability to speak, to act, to work, and to be free of certain kinds of coercion. Social systems have differed and still differ over just what is contained in the list of such rights. The language of rights and the significance of the concept have been a basic part of American thinking since the writing of the second paragraph of the Declaration of Independence: "We hold these Truths to be self-evident, that all Men are created equal, that they are endowed by their Creator with *certain unalienable Rights,* that among these are Life, Liberty, and the pursuit of Happiness" (emphasis mine). Note that these rights are held to be the property of "all Men," not just citizens. (If the object of this section were a full study of basic documents dealing with human rights, the French Declaration of the Rights of Man, the United Nations Declaration of Human Rights, and the status of women's rights would also have to be considered.)

The war conventions hold that among the purposes of the law of war is "safeguarding certain fundamental human rights of persons who fall into the hands of the enemy, particularly prisoners of war, the wounded and sick, and civilians."[3] Regardless of their social systems, all parties to the war conventions have agreed that using POWs or protected persons for biological experiments is a serious violation of human rights.

The four moral styles certainly differ on a matter as basic as human rights. Social utility may accept one list of human rights at one time and change it when the community's benefit would be enhanced by such change. Nothing is more important than the welfare of the community. Individualism might deny that the enemy has any absolute human rights, unless that position can harm the individual who is judging the matter. A religious style may hold that only God has absolute rights, that humans are always to sacrifice their interests to God's purposes. And a universal fairness style may insist that human rights can never be sacrificed for any cause different from the goals of the humans concerned.

The Conventions' position on this matter is closest to universal fairness. The Conventions, as we have seen, make protection of "certain fundamental human rights" into an absolute that is simply not to be negotiated. However, while this protection seems to be the letter and spirit of the law, the history of field operations tells a different story. The fact that there are violations does not show that the law is pointless; rather, it shows the importance and the need for the law.

Taking Hostages: "Surrender, or I'll Kill This Child!"

Why not seize a civilian and threaten to kill that person unless some military gain is allowed? Perhaps we could take a family member or friend of the enemy and force a whole unit to surrender. Clever or despicable? Looked at from the other side, suppose the enemy holds a pistol to the head of one of our children and says, "Surrender or I shoot!" What are the alternatives for a soldier on either side of the hostage question? The convention makes one of the alternatives definite; taking hostages is forbidden. The response to the terrorist who does take hostages is more complicated and must wait until we have a more complete view of war crimes.

The Geneva Civilian Convention

Among other serious war crimes cited in item *c* of the list of grave breaches is the taking of hostages. The Geneva Civilian Convention is short and clear on the matter: "Article 34. The taking of hostages is prohibited." Here, a number of urgent questions present themselves. Exactly what is a hostage? Can hostages be taken in reprisal for such action by the enemy? Why not take hostages as a means of inducing the enemy to give ground, cease some operation, perhaps surrender? How do the different moral styles react to the question of raking hostages?

In ordinary language, a hostage is a person given or held as security for the fulfillment of some terms. In military language, a hostage is a person who (a) has taken no active part in the hostilities, (b) is captured and held prisoner, and (c) whose freedom is offered in exchange for an action of some sort. In a somewhat parallel civilian situation, if a child is kidnapped and held for financial ransom, the child is a hostage.

As we have noted earlier, attitudes toward taking hostages have changed historically. Hostages were once given or exchanged "to ensure the observance of treaties, armistices and other agreements depending on good faith . . . and they were responsible with their lives for any perfidy."[4] For a time there was the practice of placing prominent local residents on the front of engines of railroad trains to ensure the safety of the trains. In another example, trainloads of protected persons were placed on railroad sidings next to ammunition trains.[5]

In the case of hostages offered as a sign of good faith, the pattern appears to have been analogous to leaving a deposit in a commercial transaction. To induce a storekeeper or real estate agent to hold some object, rather than offer it for sale, we might give a deposit—a "good faith deposit"—with the understanding that the deposit will be forfeited if we do not complete the sale by a certain date. Now, however, all of such usages of protected persons as hostages or deposits, whether voluntary or involuntary, are clearly forbidden.

The Four Moral Styles

Why is the taking of hostages forbidden? Recall that on the first page of the first chapter of FM 27-10, the three purposes of the law of war were specified and that "safeguarding certain fundamental human rights of persons" was one of them. In broad terms, the right involved here is *the right to be treated as a person, not a thing.* As the universal fairness position was developed by its modern founder,[6] persons and things are essentially different. The significant difference is that while things may be used as means or instruments for their owners' purposes, persons may not be used merely as such means or instruments. We do have a special word for the situation in which a person is used only as an instrument for another's purposes— slavery. Because universal fairness rules out slavery, it must also rule out using people as slaves for the sake of any master. When a hostage is taken and threatened with injury or death as if he or she were merely a forfeited deposit, he or she is being treated as a thing, not a person; therefore, the universal fairness style forbids taking hostages.

What of the other styles? How do they lead one to think about taking hostages? Social utility makes a significant distinction between the majority and various minorities. The moral question for this style turns on what would benefit the majority. The matter of hostages is to be decided by considering the consequences of the action: What would happen to the majority in the short term, and what would be the long-term results? There may well be situations in which placing a few hostages at risk would be of enormous benefit to great numbers. Years ago (for example, in the edition of the British Manual published just prior to the current one), the view was held that a commander might take hostages to ensure decent treatment of the wounded and sick left behind in hostile locations or that a commander might take hostages when prisoners had been taken by "irregular troops," with a great risk that those prisoners might be badly treated.[7]

In the long run, it may be that the pattern of taking hostages would cause more problems than gains. If such a pattern becomes established as acceptable, the majority might find themselves at risk. Social utility, therefore, must balance the short- and long-term possible results, but the decision would be based on the results for the majority, not on the human rights of the hostages.

If the commander's moral style is individualism, the decision whether to take hostages will turn on what will be best for that commander. He or she must balance the risk of being caught breaking the Hague Convention and committing a war crime against the risk of harm if hostages are not taken. As an individualist, the answer will depend on the commander's estimate of his or her security.

The religious position on morality takes as its key question service to God or to whatever is a substitute for God. This style believes that a *higher interest than human rights, the happiness of the majority, or individual power* exists. That higher interest is whatever is the desire of God. If God is taken to be the nation, then whatever is the desire of the nation is to be pursued. If God—or national security—is best served by one course or another, that course must be followed.

To be sure, the hostage problem is not merely the matter of taking as prisoners those who themselves have done no wrong, although that alone is a serious violation of the Geneva Civilian Convention. The point of taking hostages is to threaten to punish them for the acts, or the lack of certain acts, of the enemy. If the enemy does not respond as desired, is the threat to be carried out?

Historically, we find both answers. Recently, publicity has been given to situations in which terrorists have taken hostages and not killed them because they had somehow become friends; however, many examples attest that the outcome may be otherwise:

During the Second World War, Germany regularly carried out the mass shooting of hostages on such an unprecedented scale that the punishment of this atrocity was declared by the United Nations to constitute a major purpose of the war. As early as October 1941, the President of the U.S.A. (at that time neutral) denounced the German practice of killing hostages by way of reprisals. In Art. 6 of the Charter of the International Military Tribunal the killing of hostages appeared among the war crimes over which the Tribunal had jurisdiction. The Tribunal found that the German forces had resorted to the practice of keeping hostages in order to prevent or to punish any form of civil disorder and that, in an order issued in 1941, [General] Keitel "spoke in terms of fifty or a hundred lives from the occupied territories of the Soviet Union for one German life taken." Subsequently, various war crimes tribunals held the killing of hostages to be a war crime. There is no doubt as to the correctness of those decisions. Modern war—total and scientific—tends to blur the distinction between combatants and noncombatants. But that is not a sufficient reason for the deliberate killing of innocent persons. Such measures calculated to instill terror are violations both of legal rules and the fundamental principles of humanity.[8]

Why not punish hostages for the actions of other members of their group? We consider first the matter of reprisals and then return to the question of collective punishment.

Remedies and Reprisals

Suppose one side commits a war crime. What response by the other is acceptable? The official answer is found in the manuals under the heading of "Remedies and Reprisals." A *remedy* is a means of repairing the situation. *Reprisal* is close to, but not quite, a polite word for revenge. When something very harmful is done to one party, what can be done in response to maintain balance? If the enemy has committed a war crime, can such a crime be committed in retaliation? What can happen if they torture prisoners to get information? Suppose that the fact of the torture is accurately established by such things as photos and reports of escapees. Can the offended side torture their prisoners? Suppose the enemy has killed innocent women and children or used POWs for biological experiments. Can the same be done to the enemy? What, under the Conventions, can and cannot be done in answer to the enemy's war crimes?

Following FM 27-10, four sorts of remedies must be tried before resorting to reprisals.[9] These are:

1. Tell the world. Report to public opinion, the world's opinion. Explain that "our opponents are barbarians who use gas warfare, forbidden weapons, torture," or whatever the particular case is. To produce public criticism, publicize the violations. No nation wants to have the rest of the world think that it is dishonorable, that it doesn't behave and fight in a civilized fashion. Step one is publicity. People—and one hopes, nations—are ashamed of a bad reputation.
2. Protest and demand compensation. In the Persian Gulf in the spring of 1987, Iraq shot at a U.S. warship, and about thirty U.S. sailors were killed. Naturally, because we were not at war with Iraq, a demand for compensation to the families of those killed was made. (So far we have no reports of Iraq's complying.)

How is this sort of message communicated to the enemy during a war? It is sent through the so-called Protecting Powers—the neutral powers—or the ICRC or by a parlementaire sent by the commander in the zone.

Among the questions raised is the matter of the amount of compensation. What is the proper compensation for the death of someone who was tortured for information? For an unexpected death under such circumstances? Parallels with civilian compensation seem reasonable, although not quite the same. We could estimate the future earnings of the individual over his or her expected working life and compensate accordingly, but if the soldier were to live through the torture or through legitimate interrogation and escape or be returned to his or her own unit and continue to serve, he or she might be killed the following day in routine battle. These difficulties are not significant, as awkward as they may seem. We have formulas and precedents for civilian and military compensation: The usual problem is how to get the guilty parties to admit their liability and agree to compensation. Of course, the family whose innocent child has been killed will not be satisfied with a bank transfer of money or a bag full of paper marked "dollars" or "yen." While money does not replace a loved human, it does serve as a symbol of the mistake, the violation of civilized patterns of warfare.

3. Request neutral states to press the offending side to observe the law.
4. If the offenders can be identified and captured, punish them as war criminals. We consider matters of punishment of war criminals below.

If these four kinds of efforts are not successful, if the opponent continues to commit war crimes, reprisals may be taken. FM 27-10 makes the point, however, that even at this stage the enemy may be "more likely to be influenced by a steady adherence to the law of war on the part of their adversary."[10] The British Manual makes a similar point: "A certain caution should be exercised before deciding to institute reprisals, as in some cases counter-reprisals may follow, thus defeating the purpose of the original reprisals."[11] The commander must decide whether he or she is dealing with such cases, those cases in which— as the British put it—"a certain caution" is to be exercised. On what can the commander base that decision? Presumably the C. O. will consider what is known of the opposite commander and of the history of that unit of the enemy from any available intelligence reports. It could be counterproductive to take reprisals if the enemy command has stopped the practice and punished the offenders involved.

A reprisal is an act of retaliation by conduct that would otherwise be unlawful, and it must be for the purpose of enforcing future compliance, rather than flat revenge. Note, as explained above, other remedies must first be exhausted before resorting to reprisals.

Against whom may reprisals be conducted? Not POWs. Not protected civilians. Even if POWs have committed the crime or if the crime has been against your own forces after the POWs were taken, you cannot retaliate against them. You cannot be "as bad as they are."

Excessive Reprisals

The act that is used as a reprisal cannot be "excessive"—more serious than the crime against which it is directed. While the reprisal must not be more violent than the act to which it is a response, it need not be the same act. As noted above, if hostages, POWs, and protected persons cannot be the targets of reprisals, who can be? Essentially, enemy soldiers. What is "excessive" is a matter of judgment.

An acceptable target is specified at the end of item *c* (FM 27-10, p. 177), Reprisals can be visited upon enemy troops; however, if they have surrendered, they cannot be punished. If they have not surrendered and they are still fighting against you, you do not have the responsibility to treat them as POWs, and you can punish them.

The purpose of reprisals is discussed in FM 27-10 item *d*, page 177. The first point is significant: Reprisals are never permitted *merely for revenge*. Revenge is supposed to be a savage primitive idea: You hit me, so I'll hit you. The Roman *lex talionis*, or law of retaliation, has both a sense of equality—the apparent fairness of causing equal pain—and a sense of uncivilized instinct. The civilized reflex is to accept a legal or governmental procedure rather than to commit a personal act of revenge. Of course, when a third party, such as a governmental agency, makes the decisions, that party makes them in its own interest—and may want to consider rehabilitation rather than mere *lex talionis*.

As a last resort, reprisals can be used to induce the enemy to stop. There is still, however, a necessary limitation and procedure: Reprisals can never be employed by individual soldiers, except on orders of a commander. Both the American and British Manuals insist on this point: "never on the responsibility of the individual soldier."[12] The commander should give such orders only after careful inquiry into the offense and must be very sure of the facts because he or she will be responsible and may be tried for a war crime unless the basis is quite clear. The report of what happened must be true. After the commander has determined that the offense did indeed occur, the highest military authority available should be consulted. If the commander judges that the only way to stop the enemy from continuing a war crime, such as the use of illegal weapons, is to respond by another or the same illegal activity, then that commander may give such orders and take responsibility for the accuracy of the description of the situation. Other possible ways of stopping the enemy from continuing the illegal activity must first be tried and found to fail. Nevertheless, a commanding officer may take the responsibility for a reprisal when nothing else stops the enemy's illegal action.

Before leaving the subject of reprisals, we should mention that from at least one impressive viewpoint reprisals are no longer permitted under international law. The distinguished and well-respected historian Quincy Wright says that "the United Nations Charter abolished the traditional right of reprisals, as declared by the Security Council in April 1964, by requiring Members to settle their international disputes by peaceful means and to refrain from the use or threat of force in international relations except in defense against armed attack or under authority of the United Nations." He goes on to distinguish between "the obsolete doctrine of reprisal . . . [and] the right of self-defense against armed attack."[13] If this is the case, are reprisals no longer permitted, even under the limited conditions set forth above? I may be wrong, but I don't find Wright convincing.

Collective Penalties

Collective penalties are not allowed; in fact, they are flatly prohibited. As the Geneva Civilian Convention (GC) puts it: "No protected person may be punished for an offence he or she has not personally committed. Collective penalties and likewise all measures of intimidation or of terrorism are prohibited."[14] If it is known that one or more of a group has committed a crime, to punish the group indiscriminately is to give a collective penalty. This is not fair because it involves punishing individuals who are not personally guilty. In Anglo-American law, the mistake of punishing the innocent is taken to be more immoral than the mistake of not punishing the guilty.

Who is guilty of a war crime, those who commanded it or those who carried it out? Both, but not other soldiers wearing the same uniform or from the same country. We do seem to have a regular or natural reflex that suggests that if we cannot find the guilty person, we may then seize and punish someone who is from the same group or community as the actual criminal. If your brother, fellow citizen, or member of your unit commits a crime and we can't reach him, we will punish you. *If there is such a thing as a case of personal innocence in the situation,* collective guilt is simply not fair to the individual who is personally innocent. In defense of the bombing of civilian areas such as Dresden, Hiroshima, and London, it has been held that war is a relationship between all the citizens of the nations involved. If that view—a variety of the "total war" position—were adopted in the Conventions, then the notion of collective guilt would have to be modified. However, it is clearly forbidden at this point to punish a group for the crimes of some member of that group. The question of group knowledge and acquiescence is troublesome and far from clear in all cases, particularly in cases in which knowledge of a crime is covered up.

Collective Guilt

If the whole military unit knew and made no objection to the commission of a war crime, are they also guilty? Because crimes are to be reported and prevented if the observers are able without unusual risk to themselves, individuals who make no objection to or no report of a crime are also responsible for it. In such a case, they are personally involved in the act of covering up or of not reporting their knowledge. Withholding information, however, is ordinarily not dealt with as severely as the original criminal act.

Can there be a group criminal enough that mere membership in it can be grounds for punishment? After World War II, an International Military Tribunal was organized by the four major Allies—the United States, Great Britain, France, and the U.S.S.R.—to punish the "major war criminals." The Charter of the Tribunal

> provided for the trial of groups and organizations and gave the Tribunal the power to declare them criminal. It was laid down (in Art. 10) that where a group or organization was declared criminal by the Tribunal the national authorities of Signatory States should have the right to bring individuals to trial for membership in such groups or organizations.[15]

Three organizations were declared to be criminal and found guilty of crimes against humanity as well as ordinary war crimes.

The German General Staff and High Command were accused of being such an organization, a criminal group, but were acquitted on the grounds that the members did not constitute a "group" within the meaning of the Charter of the Tribunal. The Tribunal did, however, go on to state that the members had committed "outrageous war crimes and should be tried for these acts."[16]

The idea that membership in a group may be considered a crime is repugnant to the tradition of individual civil rights. "Mere" membership is said to be simply a right to choose one's associates. The opposite viewpoint holds that when an organization is known to be engaged in war crimes, to join it is to assist in those crimes. It should be quickly added that the war crimes trials after World War II depended on much more specific individual criminal activity than mere membership; however, the question of "guilt by association" has not disappeared. In twentieth-century American history, a great deal of attention was given to cases involving membership in the Communist Party and cases involving "criminal associates." (I would like to be able to say that guilt by association has been clearly rejected in American practice, but the matter is not that clear.)

Before leaving the question of criminal groups and membership in such groups, we should note the following comment in *The Nuremberg Judgment, 1946:* "Crimes against international law are committed by men, *not by abstract entities,* and only by punishing individuals who commit such crimes can the provisions of international law be enforced" (emphasis mine).[17] The distinction between actual persons and "abstract entities" forces us to choose between theories of reality—nominalist vs. realist.

The nominalist view holds that only individuals exist and that there are no abstract things such as classes, groups, or corporations; these are only names. The opposite position, the realist view, holds that in addition to individuals certain abstract entities really do exist. The realist might believe that a class, a club, a corporation, or a nation exists independently of those who happen to be its members at a certain time. U.S. law uses both positions in different circumstances. For tax and other purposes, corporations are considered to be persons. For voting and for eligibility for military induction, abstract entities have no status.

Corporations are not biological persons, but they do have impressive life spans and sometimes formidable power. Do they really exist, or are they merely names for the activities of individual persons? There is a long history of argument over the matter, but for the purposes of this study, we can take the nominalist hard line that restricts reality to individuals. We can also use various abstracts as pragmatically helpful without the need to "believe" in them as real. Although we never see the Commonwealth of Pennsylvania, it is useful to act as if there is such a thing. We can see the officers of the Commonwealth, the equipment owned by it, and the land within its borders, yet never see the state itself. Perhaps the state is a fiction, but it is a useful fiction, and that usefulness is enough for our purposes.

Punishment for War Crimes

Under the Conventions, each government has agreed to search for people who are alleged to have committed or ordered war crimes. Such persons are to be brought to court, *regardless of their nationality*. We will pass over the features of the various courts that may have jurisdiction; they range from a general court-martial under the UCMJ to a number of other military tribunals and to domestic as well as international courts. Note, however, that the obligation covers finding and punishing individuals, referring to the perpetrators who are either members of the enemy forces or of one's own. Paragraph 507 of FM 27-10 titled, "Universality of Jurisdiction," covers both persons who are charged as perpetrators and those who are victims.

A war crime is to be the business of the United States, regardless of the nationality—or lack of it—of the victim! According to paragraph 507 of FM 27-10, such an offense against just about anyone is within "the jurisdiction of the United States military tribunals," claiming an impressive range for U.S. jurisdiction. This wide range is not as chauvinistic as it may sound: Other nations make the same claim. Not merely a country's own nationals, but anyone who commits a war crime is liable to be tried and punished by any nation. As the British Manual puts it, "War crimes are crimes *ex jure gentium* (against the common law of mankind) and are thus triable by the courts of all States."[18]

The British text goes on to say that "persons accused of war crimes are properly charged not with an offence against the municipal law of the belligerent but with an offence or offences against the laws and customs of war."[19] The Hague Conference of 1899 required a "previous trial" before punishment; the British Manual mentions that a trial before punishment is "fundamental"; and the American Field Manual adds the significant detail that it must be "a fair trial on the facts and law."[20] Desirable as that is, the American specification of a fair trial on the facts and the law can be hard to produce in the emotional atmosphere of a trial room attended by dozens of relatives of victims.[21]

My Lai

Do nations try their own soldiers as war criminals? Do they convict and punish their own personnel? Yes, sometimes. The case of Lt. Calley is an example of a trial that came about because an American reporter publicized certain facts, and an American court-martial convicted an American lieutenant for killing Vietnamese civilians—old men, women, and children. It must be added that an American president intervened to mitigate the sentence.

The facts of the My Lai war crime are probably familiar to most readers of this book. In November 1969, the world learned the facts from Seymour Hersh, a reporter who was awarded a Pulitzer Prize for uncovering the story. Only the naive would ask why the story had to come from the press, not from the Pentagon, and, as usual, the naive would have asked an important question. Shortly, we will consider the special importance of the press and publicity in these matters.

On 16 March 1968, a large number of helpless civilians (more than five hundred)[22] who lived in the My Lai No. 4 hamlet of Son My village in Vietnam were slaughtered by an American army unit. Lieutenant William Calley, Jr., the immediate officer in charge, was tried and convicted. Shooting women and children at point-blank range can hardly be considered anything but a most serious war crime. That some women and children use weapons to attack does not make other women and children legitimate targets. The report about the My Lai massacre drew a lot of attention, of course, and led to books, articles, and public debate. One side took it to be an obvious war crime and expected that the command structure over Lieutenant Calley would also be found guilty. The other side "understood" how such things happen in a war like the Vietnamese War and protested the court-martial of Calley and the decision that found him guilty.

The order to attack and kill civilians in the village of My Lai was the basis for court-martial and conviction of Lieutenant Calley. Here we have a clear case of a nation that charged, tried, and convicted one of its own officers for a war crime. That President Richard M. Nixon used his power to affect the sentence does not take away from the military response to the war crime—more accurately, perhaps, the military response to the publicity about the war crime. President Nixon's response can be interpreted several ways, some less critical of him than others. It was noted that the charge of responsibility for the crime stopped at the lieutenant and the company commander; it might well be held that superior officers also shared responsibility. The case of General Yamashita struck some commentators as relevant, and we quickly review it here.

The General Yamashita Case

The general in charge of the 14th Army Group of the Imperial Japanese Army in the Philippines (in World War II) was convicted and hanged because troops under his command committed war crimes. The charge against him was that he "failed to discharge his duty as commander to control the operations of the members of his command, permitting them to commit brutal atrocities . . . and he . . . thereby violated the laws of war."

General Yamashita had no knowledge of the behavior of his troops because his communication lines had been cut. He was not derelict in training them nor had he led them to believe that they were carrying out his orders or wishes. He was found guilty and executed *because be should have known what his troops were doing!* He appealed his conviction to the U.S. Supreme Court but was turned down on the grounds that "commanders . . . are to some extent responsible for their subordinates."[23] To what extent? To the extent that General Yamashita was hanged even though he neither ordered nor knew what his subordinates were doing. The Court, the majority, held that he should have known what he could not have known because the

Americans had cut off his means of communication—an unfair decision to civilian ears but perhaps not in the military viewpoint. *The point is that command responsibility cannot be evaded*; almost nothing can count as an acceptable excuse.[24]

The Yamashita case was serious and unique on many grounds: the charges were for enormous atrocities; the court-martial seemed to violate due process in bringing additional charges on the day the trial began without giving time for the legal defense to be prepared; the appeal to the U.S. Supreme Court was novel; and the question of command responsibility when a commander is cut off from his troops was vague. We will discuss just the first and fourth of these points.

The bill of particulars against General Yamashita alleged "a series of acts, one hundred and twenty-three in number, committed by members of the forces under petitioner's command . . . as a result of which more than 25,000 men, women and children, all unarmed non-combatant civilians, were brutally mistreated and killed, without cause or trial."[25] Apparently these facts were not in dispute, but the matter of responsibility was.

The majority on the Supreme Court noted that General Yamashita was the military governor of the Philippines as well as commander of the Japanese forces. They concluded "that the allegations of the charge, tested by any reasonable standard adequately allege a violation of the law of war and that the commission had authority to try and decide the issue which it raised."[26] This left the decision of the court-martial standing, and General Yamashita was executed.

The Yamashita precedent suggests that not merely Lieutenant Calley but his company commander, Captain Ernest Medina, and the structure up to and including General William Westmoreland had command responsibility for My Lai. Should General Westmoreland and the American theater commander be held responsible for everything done by any small patrol under their command? Paragraph 501 of FM 27-10, titled "Responsibility for Acts of Subordinates," gives a reasonable answer to the question:

> Thus, for instance, when troops commit massacres and atrocities against the civilian population . . . the responsibility may rest not only with the actual perpetrators but also with the commander. Such responsibility arises directly when the acts in question have been committed in pursuance of an order of the commander concerned. The commander is also responsible if he has actual knowledge *or should have knowledge*, through reports received by him or through other means, that troops are about to commit or have committed a war crime and he fails to take the necessary and reasonable steps to insure compliance with the laws of war or to punish violators thereof (emphasis mine).[27]

The question of command responsibility depends in large part on the commanding officer's knowledge. The critical paragraph above, however, holds that he *should have knowledge* through reports, and so forth, of behavior involving war crimes. A commanding officer need not know many things; for example, the order in which the first sergeant put on his shoes this morning does not matter. Behavior involving war crimes does matter: A commanding officer should know, is expected to know, about war crimes being committed by his troops. Like General Yamashita, even if the commanding officer did not know, he should have known and, on that account, is liable for court-martial and death, if found guilty.

The Officer/Enlisted Personnel Distinction

The matter of command responsibility is one of the reasons for the distinction between officers and enlisted personnel, and this is perhaps the only reason that can stand up under examination. If officers do not accept the responsibilities of command, such benefits as higher pay, different uniforms, quarters, mess halls, and clubs become pointless privileges. (We return to this subject in Chapter 12.)

Command Responsibility

Where does this leave the command structure in the My Lai case? Commanding officers are responsible in the literal, not the honorific, sense of the word. They are liable to be called by a court-martial to answer questions about (1) the training about war crimes given to the personnel involved in the My Lai massacre,[28] (2) the orders given at various levels, (3) the reports made, (4) the cover-up, if any, and (5) their own involvement and knowledge: Where were they at the time? What were they doing? How close were they to My Lai? What did they know of the unit's actions? When did they know of the actions? How did they respond to the formal and informal reports? On the face of it, honorable senior officers would not allow a lieutenant, a captain, and the enlisted men to be the only ones held responsible. (If there are good reasons for the apparent irresponsibility of higher command, I don't know them.)

The Minority in the General Yamashita Case

So far we have considered the majority decision by the U.S. Supreme Court in this case and ignored the minority position. Both Justices Wiley B. Rutledge and Frank Murphy pointed out that the Fifth Amendment guarantee of due process of law applies to "any person"; therefore, it covers, as Rutledge put it, "all men, whether citizens, aliens, alien enemies or enemy belligerents. . . . This long-held attachment marks the great divide between our enemies and ourselves. Theirs was a philosophy of universal force. Ours is one of universal law, albeit imperfectly made flesh of our system."[29] Both justices found that due process of law had not been given to General Yamashita.

One part of Justice Murphy's dissent puts the matter in sharp terms and is frequently quoted by critics of the decision:

> These charges amount to this: "We, the victorious American forces, have done every thing possible to destroy and disorganize your lines of communication, your effective control of your personnel, your ability to wage war. In those respects we have succeeded. We have defeated and crushed your forces. And now we charge and condemn you for having been inefficient in maintaining control of your troops during the period when we were so effectively besieging and eliminating your forces and blocking your ability to maintain effective control. Many atrocities were committed by your disorganized troops. Because these atrocities were so widespread we will not bother to charge or prove that you committed, ordered or condoned any of them. We will assume that they must have resulted from your inefficiency and negligence as a commander. In short, we charge you with the crime of inefficiency in controlling your troops. We will judge the discharge of your duties by the disorganization which we ourselves created in large part. Our standards of judgment are whatever we wish to make them."[30]

Justice Murphy makes it look as if the strict interpretation of command responsibility is being applied to a defeated enemy. A rule or a law that does not apply to all persons similarly situated does not pass the universal fairness test. The justice goes on to say:

> The only conclusion I can draw is that the charge made against the petitioner is clearly without precedent in international law or in the annals of recorded military history. This is not to say that enemy commanders may escape punishment for clear and unlawful failures to prevent atrocities. But that punishment should be based upon charges fairly drawn in light of established rules of international justice and recognized concepts of law.[31]

Justice Murphy's conclusion was that "In no recorded instance, however, has the mere inability to control troops under fire or attack by superior forces been made the basis of a charge of violating the laws of war."[32]

One wonders what senior officers think about the General Yamashita decision and his execution. If the decision was sound, then it enforces a very strict construction of command responsibility. From that viewpoint, we must pursue and court-martial higher command in the My Lai case. On the other side, if the Yamashita decision was wrong—as the minority on the Supreme

Court held—if the actual lack of knowledge of the commanding officer should be an acceptable excuse, then the U.S. government has made a serious error in the decision. In that case, the United States should apologize to the Japanese government and to the family of the general.

The two situations differ in several ways. General Yamashita's enemy cut his communications; therefore, a reasonable case can be made for the United States making amends by taking both alternatives mentioned above. Using a strict interpretation of the notion of command responsibility, the United States should hold higher commanders responsible for the My Lai massacre as well as apologize to the Japanese government and the family of General Yamashita. Politicians may call this simplistic; however, it would merely be simple consistency in applying universal fairness.

Sentences, If Convicted of a War Crime

The Conventions require that the accused persons "shall benefit by safeguards of proper trial and defence." The U.S. Field Manual specifies "a fair trial on the facts and law."[33] In a number of countries, the civil or military laws specify certain protections such as, for the British, the requirement that the protecting power be notified of the charges and evidence before the trial and that sentences of death not be carried out until a specified time after the prisoner is notified of the sentence. This stipulation is to give the prisoner time to appeal. The British code provides a ten-day period before carrying out the sentence.[34]

We have already seen that war crimes can bring the death penalty. We should take notice of the statement in FM 27-10 immediately after the sentence on the possibility of the death penalty: "Corporal punishment is excluded."[35] It seems odd that the death penalty is allowed, but corporal punishment is not. Flogging would appear to be a milder punishment than death. Of course it is, but apparently, death is considered more dignified for both the victim and executioner. This idea parallels domestic law: Some states have the death penalty but have given up such "cruel punishments" as whipping.

While the death penalty is available for war crimes, more lenient penalties have also been used. The British Royal Warrant of 1945, applying to civilians as well as the military, provides:

A person found guilty by a Military Court of a war crime may be sentenced to and shall be liable to suffer any one or more of the following punishments, namely:
(i) Death (either by hanging or shooting);
(ii) Imprisonment for life or for any less term;
(iii) Confiscation [of property];
(iv) A fine[36]

"Don't Blame Me; I Was Ordered to . . ."

Is it a reasonable excuse to claim that superior orders forced someone to commit a war crime? The textbook answer is "No"; it is not an excuse![37]

Why not? Certainly soldiers have accepted the duty to obey their superior officers. True, *but they have the duty to obey only lawful orders.* The essential question is not: Was the act ordered? Rather, it is: Was the order lawful? There is no duty to obey an unlawful order.

How do military personnel know whether an order is lawful? Their training is supposed to give them the basic principles. What is and is not lawful is spelled out in the Conventions. All parties to the Conventions specifically agreed to teach them to their military forces. So, the individual cannot deny moral responsibility for an illegal act; however, there are mitigating circumstances.

Suppose the individual simply did not know that the act that was ordered was unlawful. Imagine a case in which he or she could not, for some reason, have known. Obviously, then, he or she does have an excuse, a defense against the charge of committing a war crime.

It should be noted that even when claiming that one was merely following orders is no excuse, the fact that the individual was following orders may be considered a mitigating factor in deciding on the punishment. The court can say that a person is guilty of a crime, but that person will not be punished to the full possible extent because he or she was given orders. The defense that the person was following orders, while not a factor in determining guilt, may be a factor in determining the degree of punishment. The decision about whether an act was a crime is quite different from the decision on punishment for that act.

In defense of a person charged with a war crime, a number of ordinary reflexes are to be considered: (1) All lawful orders are to be obeyed by everyone; (2) conditions may not permit a slow and careful analysis of legal niceties; (3) there are borderline questions that simply are not spelled out clearly, anywhere; and (4) an act of reprisal is acceptable—even if, when considered alone, it would be a crime. Along with these possible defenses, we must not forget that the individual member of the armed forces is responsible for his or her actions and has a limit to his or her duty. The limit is the limit of national and international law. Again, there is no duty to obey unlawful orders.

The focus on legal and illegal acts suggests that attention to the matter may breed an army of guardhouse lawyers. That would hardly be desirable, but it is also quite unlikely. Proper basic training can teach the Hague and Geneva Conventions and give all personnel a reasonable notion of the nature of a war crime. This knowledge protects them personally and protects their nation from the danger of criminal acts. It should give them more confidence about the scope and limits of legitimate action. There is a risk, of course: Can knowledge of war crimes be so threatening that it will cause nightmares and paralyze action? That risk can be met by intelligent presentation. Consider a civilian parallel: Knowledge of the risks of driving a motor vehicle does not seem to stop that activity. A government that avoids the risk of giving their personnel knowledge of the Conventions has chosen an illegal and shortsighted style.

With proper basic training, including explanations of the Hague and Geneva Conventions, all personnel will know what war crimes are. If a superior officer orders that a village of civilians be burned, his or her subordinates will know that that order is illegal. Of course, the order can include a supplementary comment justifying or explaining that it is an act of reprisal. Without a clear acceptance of responsibility for a reprisal, there is no duty to carry out the illegal order. Of course, personnel who are low in the order of command usually do not refuse the orders of those high in the command order. But they are supposed to do so in the restricted cases when crimes are ordered; otherwise, they can be punished for committing war crimes. Does it ever happen that troops refuse orders under such circumstances? Yes, it does, and not only in fiction: In the My Lai case, some members of Lieutenant Calley's patrol refused to kill civilians.

The variety of war crimes that have been reported is enormous, and this chapter is certainly not a history of the subject. For example, there is the strange class of actions—crimes—by an army against its own civilian population. Whether these are war crimes may be a moot point. Consider testimony in a recent case, heard in Tokyo and Naha District Courts, dealing with the Battle of Okinawa during World War II:

> Professor Masahide Ota of the University of Ryukus, an authority on the Battle of Okinawa, was the first questioned at the Naha District Court Tuesday.
>
> In his testimony, Professor Ota said that one-third of the Okinawa population were victimized in the war—at least 298 of them killed by the Japanese Army. . . . Ota said one of the characteristics of the Battle of Okinawa was that the Japanese armed forces forced many local residents to commit murder and suicide. [Ota] surveyed murder records described in histories of cities, towns and villages in Okinawa and in materials kept in the Defense Agency. According to his survey, 49 murder cases were confirmed as to when, where and why they occurred. Their total victims were 114. In addition there were 184 killing cases, the eyewitness accounts for which were believable. . . . More than half of them were killed *on suspicion* [emphasis mine] of spying for the U.S. Army.
>
> In addition, . . . four mass suicides with 483 victims, confirmed by eyewitnesses, were carried out under the order of the Imperial

Japanese Army. Ota said that more than two-thirds of the cases involving the killing of residents by the Imperial Japanese Army occurred after June 23, 1945, when the fighting on Okinawa was virtually ended.

He suspects that the Imperial Japanese Army murdered the citizens to prevent them from surrendering to the U.S. Army.[38]

It should also be noted that the Japanese Education Ministry differs with the reports above and asserts that most of the victims on Okinawa, apart from those killed by the U.S. Armed Forces, committed suicide. Suicide or murder? These differing views have led to major disputes over the way current Japanese school textbooks, which require the approval of the Japanese Education Ministry, report the matter.[39]

What would make the order to kill one's own civilians a war crime? It is the same war convention that makes directly killing enemy civilians a war crime: Civilians are not honorable targets. Most of the protections given to civilians also apply to the relations between a government and its own nationals; however, there is a significant difference. Even if enemy civilians cannot be forced to contribute to the surrender of their own nation, civilians might be considered to be persons who can be required to contribute to the success of their own side. If they could have been drafted for military service, why not require them to sacrifice for the same end, even if they are civilians? They are not required to make that sacrifice because they have not made the agreement that is part of the swearing-in ceremony; they have not promised or agreed to sacrifice anything or to follow the orders of the commanding officer. To force them to follow orders that they have not willingly accepted is to treat them as things rather than as persons, as slaves rather than dignified humans.

Just what should a commander do when military or political superiors order criminal acts? The British Manual gives a short answer: "The commander concerned may have no alternative but to resign his command"[40]—no "moral" alternative, that is.

Is Military Necessity an Excuse for a War Crime?

The answer here is perfectly clear: Military necessity is *not* an acceptable excuse for a war crime: "Military necessity has been generally rejected as a defense for acts forbidden by the customary and conventional laws of war . . ."[41] The laws of war were framed while considering the matter of military necessity. Even if a particular action is the only and necessary way to reach a certain military goal, no military goal justifies criminal acts—at least, according to the book. We have yet to examine the "dirty-hands" theory of command (see Chapter 9).

Terrorism and the Concept of War Crimes

In broad terms, we can classify terrorism as the position that advocates fighting outside the laws of warfare, fighting without the restrictions of the professional military code. A recent definition calls it "the deliberate and systematic murder, maiming, and menacing of the innocent to inspire fear for political ends."[42] The special feature is not the matter of political ends; legitimate warfare can hardly be understood without political ends. As Clausewitz put it, "War cannot be divorced from political life; and whenever this occurs in our thinking about war, the many links that connect the two elements are destroyed and we are left with something pointless and devoid of sense."[43]

Obviously, the problem is not that there are political purposes but that the terrorist acts beyond the limits of the laws of war. This behavior leaves established communities with the problem of choosing the means with which to oppose the terrorist. Before dealing with this, we must consider briefly the question of what motivates terrorists.

First, there is the obvious point that all "terrorist" groups are not identical. The "Red Brigades" in Italy in the late 1970s seemed to be composed of students and factory workers. In the same country and during the same period, the "Armed Proletarian Nuclei" (referred to in the European Press as the NAP) seemed to have come out of a rather different source—the prisons—and to be made up of former prisoners. Various Middle Eastern groups have distinctly political, and some others distinctly religious, goals. The war in Iraq begun in 2003 gives us several organizations that fit this description. To this list, we might add such groups as those in Northern Ireland (now under a different and more peaceful framework, one hopes), South and Central America, Pakistan, and Japan. These are far from having the same goals.

When can a group be called "terrorist," and when is a group legitimately "revolutionary"? This question is often a difficult one because each side is apt to call the other "terrorist." It is hard to avoid classifying one's allies as angels and one's enemies as demons. We have to answer that a group is not "terrorist" because of its goals or its decision to use warfare to win its goals. The goals of changing the form of government, the dominant religion or lack of it, or the dominant pattern of property ownership are certainly not marks of terrorism. To use warfare to win these goals is still within civilized patterns; the Declaration of Independence argues for the right to those goals and that means. Terrorism, however, makes the decision to carry on acts of war and of violence without accepting the limits of warfare. That is the reason for contempt, for hatred, of terrorism. To take hostages, to kill hostages and prisoners without legitimate trial, and to attack noncombatants is to violate the laws of warfare. That is the point.

A Moral Defense for Terrorism?

Now to the questions above: Why do groups (or individuals) decide on terrorism? Why the obvious unfairness of attacking civilians (for example, by setting a bomb in a bus station)? For the different groups, there may well be different answers. For those who may be called religious fanatics, who believe that their God is on their side giving them orders, mere matters of international law such as the war conventions are trivial. The essentially political groups have sometimes argued that their violence is necessary to produce a changed and improved world, or they have argued that their violence is less than "the invisible violence that surrounds us daily." This last remark is from a book on the origins of Italian terrorism of the 1970s, *Never Again Without a Rifle*,[44] in which Alessandro Silj traces the various roots of terrorist groups. The title apparently refers to the need to avoid surrendering because of police brutality. Silj concentrates on groups that formed to bring about social and political reforms but that became terrorist because, in their own thinking, nothing else could be done to reach their goals. Such groups hold that the established system is essentially violent in its treatment of the poor and of those who want basic changes in the system. In other words, the terrorists adopt the moral viewpoint of social utility.

An effort to construct a rationale for terrorism might follow this line: The established government uses terror to maintain itself; therefore, terror is permitted as reprisal. Certainly, the use of reprisal is recognized under the Conventions, and we have devoted considerable space above to that use. Under this defense, however, there are limits to reprisals. For example, reprisals are forbidden against protected civilians and against hostages.

Suppose the terrorist answers that the rule against taking hostages, as well as the entire war convention, was invented by the established governments to limit the ability of rebels to fight against those governments. We must agree that the Conventions do favor a powerful established government over a small, weak, and unsupported group. Legal systems usually do. That point follows a famous remark that Anatole France wrote in his novel *Le Lys Rouge (The Red Lily)*: The majestic equality of the law is shown by the fact that both rich and poor are forbidden to sleep under the bridges of Paris, to beg in the streets, and to steal bread. We must agree that laws that apply equally to everyone may still favor certain groups and harm others. By itself, that is not an argument against any particular law because all laws apply differentially. According to some legal theorists (such as Bentham), the exact point of law is to create inequalities but to create them in desirable directions.[45]

The terrorist, therefore, would have to argue the matter of reprisals against hostages on its own merits and could not get support from a blanket criticism of the entire system of laws of warfare. Is there a moral argument that can be used to defend taking, threatening, and killing hostages? Universal fairness does not allow it, but the other three positions could be formulated to do so. Individualism and some, not all, of the religious positions can manage to defend sacrificing people against their will. By assuming that it is required for the welfare of a majority, social utility can also countenance such sacrifice. None of these defenses is satisfactory, however, because each falls outside the parameters of universal fairness. As we held in Chapter 2, the other three styles can count as moral only when they do not violate the limits set by universal fairness.

Conclusion: Terrorism sacrifices people against their will, chooses targets that violate military honor, and has no moral defense.

The concept of a war crime is the main idea of military ethics and calls for general knowledge of a number of subjects: what a war crime is, how it is publicized, how it is punished, how soldiers are taught, and how the general civilian population gains an understanding of such a crime. If publicity matters, and it does, knowledge must be widespread. Military excess can be restrained only if there is embarrassment because everybody knows what is involved. "Everybody," in this case, means both the military and civilians. This need for knowledge leads to the importance of teaching the Conventions at the high-school level, a point that Chapter 12 presses. First, we turn to the dirty-hands theory of command.

9

The Dirty-Hands Theory
of Command

If we take our subject seriously, the theory of leadership known as "dirty hands" must be considered. Without this theory, a discussion of military morality would seem unreal. Briefly, the theory holds that in order to govern an institution, one must sometimes do things that are immoral. To act properly as a mayor of a city, a chief of a police department, a head of large corporation, or a commander of an engaged military unit, one must have morally dirty hands. Further, this theory insists, we do not want leaders who are so concerned with their own personal morality that they will not do "what is necessary" to solve the problem or win the battle. A commander who is not willing to get his or her hands dirty is not going to be successful. We have an inept leader if we have a person so morally fastidious that he or she will not break the law when that is the only way to success.

The phrase *dirty hands* may have been taken from Jean Paul Sartre's play of that name *(Les Mains Sales)*, but the idea is much older. One classic source is Niccolô Machiavelli's *The Prince*, published after his death in 1532:

> Experience shows that princes in our times who have done great things *have cared little for honesty.* . . . It is not necessary for a prince to have the good qualities mentioned above, but it is necessary to seem to have them. I would say this: to have them and use them *all the time is dangerous,* but seeming to

have them is useful. He should seem to be pious, faithful, humane, honest, religious, and to be so. But he should have his mind so prepared that when occasion requires, he is able to change to the opposite. . . . *It is often necessary to act contrary to faith, charity, humanity, and religion in order to maintain the state.* . . . If possible, he ought not, as I have said before, turn away from what is good, *but he should be able to do evil if necessary* (emphasis mine).[1]

In Machiavelli's view, it is "dangerous" to have as prince and commander an individual who has more respect for honesty, morality, and military honor than he has for the future of the state. Is Machiavelli right? Can an effective commander be a "goody-goody"—always going by the book, always obeying the laws of war? Some authors think that the problem is not solvable, that there is no answer to it.

Illustrations of dirty-hands situations are found both in and out of military history. Whenever we are tempted to use an immoral means to reach a desirable goal, we have the problem. The serious version faces us when the goal absolutely *must* be gained, and the *only* way to reach that goal is morally unacceptable. Carl Klockars calls it a "Dirty-Harry case."

Dirty Harry

Dirty Harry is the term Carl B. Klockars uses in his study of the above problem in police work.[2] He takes that name from the title of a 1971 Warner Brothers film in which a police inspector tortures a psychopathic killer in order to force the killer to tell where he has confined a young child. The child had been buried with enough oxygen to keep her alive for a few hours. The psychopath is the only source of information on the location of the child, and apparently torture is the single way to make him talk. Dirty Harry is the police inspector who applies the torture. The effectiveness of the means is irrelevant to the moral issue. In this particular film, although the killer reveals the child's whereabouts, the child is already dead when help arrives and the killer is set free because Inspector Harry's way of getting the information is not admissible in court. Even if Harry's use of torture did save the life of the child or if it had resulted in the conviction of the psychopath, we would still have the moral question.

The Dirty Harry case is one example of this moral issue as it applies to police work. Unfortunately, dirty-hands questions are not unique to international warfare either. While these cases are quite clear in military and police work, they can occur in more diffuse forms in trying to reach almost any goal. Of course, the obvious military parallel to the Dirty Harry case is the matter of torturing newly captured prisoners to get information. To make the parallel complete, the situation should be one in which the information *absolutely must* be obtained and which *only* torture of the prisoner can produce. (Chapter 10 considers torture in more detail.)

In his well-known and widely discussed book, *Just and Unjust Wars*,[3] Michael Walzer introduces the dirty-hands problem by saying, "I have left the hardest question for last,"[4] and then: "The available answers are all likely to make us uneasy." In "The Dirty Harry Problem," Klockars calls the problem "insoluble."[5] According to these commentators, a robust cheerfulness or confidence in one's judgment is hardly enough: These problems may be unsolvable. One wonders just what is so impossible here?

Simply put, a dirty-hands problem is a case in which only immoral or forbidden *means* can reach a necessary *goal*. This calls for separate attention to means and to ends or goals. Consider the range of styles in which we might respond.

Four Styles

Universal Fairness

From the assumptions of this view, no one can be used merely and totally as a means to the goals of others. So, torture of prisoners is wrong, and no goal can be so important as to justify an immoral means. Take the extreme case: Either torture a particular prisoner or the war will certainly be lost! According to universal fairness, that war should be lost. (There is more to be considered here, but it will wait until we have discussed the other three styles.)

Social Utility

The social utility attitude would consider the matter in terms of its overall result. It would insist that the means are questionable but only immoral *when looked at in isolation from the major goals of the activity*. The majority of persons concerned will benefit greatly from torture of the prisoner, as they must win the war. The torture, therefore, is justified.

Individualism

Suppose the commanding officer considers whether it is to his or her personal advantage to take the risk of being caught and court-martialed for torture of the POW. The advantage to him might be a successful mission—a successful conclusion to the war—and the great satisfaction of having personally contributed to that national goal. If the torture can be done quickly and covered up, the personal advantages may be appealing. The risks include the chance that, even with the torture, the war might be lost and that he or she will be tried by the enemy for the violation. From this standpoint, the individual may use any means if it produces a personal advantage.

Religious Styles

While there is more than one religious style, these often have in common the view that the commands or goals of God or the gods are sacred. Sacred goals must be fought for, and these goals are so absolutely important and desirable that there are no restrictions on the means to be used. In a religious war, if torture of a POW is necessary to achieve God's purposes, so be it. As mentioned earlier, this is a narrow view of religion: The variety of ideas of God and varieties of religion are certainly not well represented by this comment, taking the "commands or goals of God" as the only interpretation for any religion.

After this quick review of apparent alternatives, where are we? There are three positions that may countenance dirty hands, and one, universal fairness, that categorically rejects such means. We now turn to two prominent authors who find themselves defending, with certain qualifications, the use of dirty hands: English philosopher Bernard Williams and American political scientist Michael Walzer.

The So-called Moral Value of Guilt

In one study of dirty hands, Bernard Williams puts heavy reliance on the notion that there are different "sorts of persons."[6] He directs his comments on dirty hands to the activities of politicians, but his conclusions bear on the general problem: "There are actions which remain morally disagreeable even when politically justified." If they are politically "justified," Williams wants to have them done, but he is not willing to make rules about them or to trust just anyone to carry out these justified but immoral (he prefers the term *disagreeable*) acts. He wants us to put in positions of power "only those who are reluctant or disinclined to do the morally disagreeable when it is really necessary." If we pick this sort of person, we may expect or hope that he or she will not also have dirty hands "when it is not necessary." It is easy to grasp at least a part of Williams's point. Habits are notoriously hard to break, and the habit of getting dirty hands can obviously be a problem. What solution does he offer? Williams has the notion that there are different "sorts" of persons and that some are "reluctant" to behave immorally. These persons, when they do behave immorally, suffer a "genuine disquiet" (p. 63).

Williams's reliance on the "sort" of person who suffers "genuine disquiet" is quite close to a conclusion that Michael Walzer reaches.[7] Walzer discusses the case of Arthur Harris, the commander of the British Bomber Command in World War II who directed the forces that carried out the British terror bombing of German cities. Walzer takes it that Churchill was as guilty of dirty hands as was Harris. However, while Churchill never gave that description of the bombing of German civilians, never called himself and Harris guilty of dirty hands, he did do (actually, did not do) something that Walzer finds significant. After the war, the British Fighter Command (Tactical Air Force) received great public honors, including a plaque in Westminster Abbey with the names of those who died defending Britain. No such honors, however, were paid to Bomber Command (Strategic Air Force), although it had suffered greater losses, and their commander, Arthur Harris, received no public honors either. Why? Walzer thinks that it is because Churchill and the British public were guilty of dirty hands in the bombing of civilians and that they recognized their guilt. Walzer holds that this British *guilt* is a significant moral matter.

Just what is the value of that British guilt? Walzer says that when "collective survival" is at stake, the leaders must be utilitarian and must choose the social utility pattern. Afterward, however, they should feel guilty: "And they can only prove their honor by accepting responsibility for those decisions and by living out the agony."[8] Strange honor. Walzer's people who live out the agony and Williams's people who suffer genuine disquiet are much the same. Are there such people? If so, what special moral value would they have for us in this problem?

Consider these two cases:

1. Someone stabs you in the back, and as you fall to your death, you realize that *the killer feels guilty.*
2. Someone stabs you in the back, and as you fall to your death, you realize that *the killer does not feel guilty.*

Is there a serious difference between the two? Is the killer in case 1 a more moral or better person because he or she feels guilt? Is he or she less likely to do it again? Does the existence of guilt have any value for the victim, the killer, or the world? We turn to each of these questions below. Walzer tells us that without guilt there is less agony and less honor. (Personally, I hold guilt to be a specious notion and find both Williams and Walzer taken in by an almost empty idea.)

Whether a person who feels guilt is less likely to repeat the behavior is unclear and certainly unproved. People get used to their feelings, discover that they can live with their guilt, and may even come to enjoy it in a way. It would take a lot of evidence to make a case for the view that guilt protects us from repeating an act, and it is probably impossible to get such evidence. One use of the term *guilt* can be noted in the following parole situation.

Suppose a prisoner in a civilian prison is called before a parole board. The board has the power to reduce the sentence and perhaps to grant an immediate release on parole. The prisoner is asked, "Are you sorry about the crime that you committed?" If he or she shows no remorse, repentance, or guilt, the board will not be inclined toward leniency. So, the prisoner expresses "profound guilt" by insisting that because of constant feelings of guilt and of sympathy for the victim and the victim's family, he or she has not had a solid night's sleep for all the years in prison. How can the parole board decide whether the prisoner does feel guilty or merely says so? Equally, can the prisoner, him- or herself, know which is the fact?

Guilt is a well-known term that has been used for centuries, but it still may be an empty word with no real content.[9] Presumably, we learn to express guilt and to recognize the appropriate situations in which to express it, but this social learning may take place without any such thing as an actual feeling of guilt.

Regret over mistakes is a more general category. Certainly we make mistakes that we are sorry about, but where guilt means regretting a moral error, the truth is far from obvious. We may regret being caught, a different matter from regret for moral decay. Some people say that they can distinguish between regret over being caught and guilt over a personal moral indiscretion, but it is hard to find their arguments convincing. Neither Walzer nor Williams has given us a usable basis for dealing with the problem of dirty hands.

If we turn from the question of the morality of the individual to the morality of the community, we may find a helpful viewpoint. Start with a general statement of the problem from Walzer: "A nation fighting a just war, when it is desperate and survival itself is at risk, must use unscrupulous or morally ignorant soldiers; and as soon as their usefulness is past, it must disown them."[10]

This parallels the conclusion that Klockars reached in his analysis of the Dirty Harry problem. Klockars insists that the police must sometimes break the law in apprehending those who break the law. His advice is that we allow police to break the law themselves and gain the benefits of their dirty hands, but then he urges "the punishment of police who resort to dirty means to achieve some unquestionably good and morally compelling end."[11]

Both Walzer and Klockars hold that we must acquiesce, and even approve and sometimes order, our agents' use of dirty hands. After reaching our goals by such means, we must then punish or disown those who have carried out our requirements! Why this reversal? Why punish those who essentially carry out our orders? Because that punishment shows both us and the world that we know we are guilty!

We return to one of the questions above: Is there any useful difference between an immoral action that is and one that is not followed or accompanied by so-called guilt, as in the case of the stabbing? With respect to an individual, as suggested by the parole board example, we can never trust a statement of guilt. Without needing any confidence in the intention, we can, however, be aware of behavior.

In the case of a social group such as a nation, an expression of guilt accompanied by appropriate actions may have significant consequences. Appropriate actions might be compensation to victims and punishment of those who ordered and carried out the dirty deed. Such a group expression of guilt constitutes a parallel to the religious idea of becoming a new person, of making a radical change in the ultimate moral basis of one's motives. Can a nation become a new nation? Can a nation behave badly and then become morally new? Japan and the two Germanys after World War II are perhaps examples of efforts to do this. The Germans have exhibited supporting behavior by making substantial financial compensation to Jewish victims. While the idea is not completely imaginary, history is not cluttered with examples of national moral rejuvenation. Still, if expressions of guilt are predictions of desirable behavior, we need not be completely suspicious of the existence of guilt.

Collective Morality

The question of collective morality is somewhat novel. It refers to the morality of the nation itself and not to the morality of its individual citizens. The nation here is thought of as a collective entity, not a distributive one with its members being considered one at a time. It is this entity that Jean-Jacques Rousseau called "this public person" and "a moral and collective body."[12] If, as the nominalists put it, there is no such entity as the nation itself, then it can hardly have moral properties. However, even a nominalist view of reality can allow that there is an entity such as a nation, provided that it is given a definition in terms of actual individuals. Such a definition might be that a nation is a thing composed of all the citizens living at certain times and under certain legal systems and, perhaps, all the territory within certain bounds. Just as all the furniture in a room can be thought of as one thing, although made up of separate pieces, a nation can be considered one thing, although made up of separate individuals. In this sense, a nation can name something that certainly does exist, and one may consider that nation's behavior and make judgments about that behavior.

If a nation changes its legal system, changes its main political officials, and makes serious restitution for damages, we might call it an essentially new nation. If an expression of guilt for dirty hands led to those changes or to some movement toward those changes, the expression of guilt would have pragmatic meaning. If nothing happens as a result of the expression of guilt, that guilt must count as empty.

A Kantian Solution to the Problem of Dirty Hands

Even if we do not find a perfect solution, we can get some assistance with our problem in the work of Immanuel Kant. While writing on a different but related matter (the question of the possibility of humanity reaching a state of permanent peace), Kant analyzes the relations between politics and morality.[13] This question is close to the dirty-hands issue because *politics* refers to the machinery used to reach desirable goals and *morality*, for Kant, refers to the duty to follow rules that can be universalized. This view of morality is the universal fairness position that we take to be the basis of the war conventions.

Kant contrasts *a political moralist* to a *moral politician*. The first, the political moralist, shapes morality to fit political ends. The second, the moral politician, makes his or her political activities fit within moral limits. In our case, we must contrast a *military moralist,* who would restrict morality to military bounds, to a *moral militarist,* who would restrict military activity to moral limits. The former subordinates principles to ends, the latter ends to principles. Kant respects only the one who keeps principles intact, taking moral principles to be absolute—that is, the moral militarist. The title of this book follows from Kant's distinction.

What advice would Kant have for those who must weigh the alternatives in the dirty-hands problem? He offers two rules. These are derived from the idea that, as Kant puts it, "Every claim of right must have [the] capacity for publicity."[14] If it can't be made public, it can't be right. Let us dwell a moment on this before we apply it to dirty hands.

The Hague requirement implies that there be a declaration of war before the first act of war. A public declaration of war, publicly worn uniforms, and careful attention to the requirements of military honor are all connected with this assumption about the test of publicity. However, the details of a planned attack or other action need not be made public in advance; that's not required by Kant's principle. A declaration of war is a public announcement of the sort of action that will be taken, not a promise to publish all plans in advance, but all actions, including military actions, must have, as quoted above, the *capacity for publicity*. Kant puts the heart of the matter in two principles—one negative and one affirmative.

The Principles of Publicity

> *"All actions that affect the rights of other men are wrong if their maxim [rule] is not consistent with publicity."*
>
> —IMMANUEL KANT, "PERPETUAL PEACE"

The maxim or rule must be immoral if it "cannot be *openly divulged* without at the same time defeating my own intention, i.e., must be kept *secret* for it to succeed, or if I cannot *publicly acknowledge* it without thereby inevitably arousing everyone's opposition."[15] Note that it is the rule or maxim of the action, not the action itself, that must be able to stand publicity. The line between assassinations and legitimate military actions is drawn on this principle. Assassination rules must be kept secret in order to succeed; military rules need not be.

As an example, Kant discusses the case of a people who are oppressed by a tyrant. Can they use rebellion to overthrow him? A powerful ruler can openly say that he will punish by death the leader of any rebellion; a small group of rebels without wide support would have to keep their maxim secret. Conclusion: Under such circumstances, a rebellion is not justified.

In a second example, Kant takes the case of a nation that has made a certain promise to another nation but later finds that its own "well-being is at stake" unless it is released from that promise. To break its promise would be to follow a rule or maxim like this: If an agreement is difficult or disagreeable, this nation will simply break it. Ah, Kant insists, if this maxim were known, other nations would not take seriously the word or promises of such a nation. Conclusion: Such a maxim would be self-defeating because it would be destroyed by publicity. This result shows that a maxim is wrong.

Kant gives other examples of the negative principle, but these should do for the moment. He then points out that the negative principle alone is not enough for a decision. When a proposed action fails the test of this principle, it is wrong; however, all proposals that pass the test may not be acceptable. Kant mentions that a ruler who has "decisively supreme power, has no need to keep his maxims secret." Therefore, Kant offers *the affirmative principle*: "All maxims [rules] that *require* publicity (in order not to fail of their end) agree with both politics and morality."[16]

To require publicity in order to work is something different from merely being able to stand publicity. If a maxim (rule, law) requires publicity to be effective, then the public is not going to be suspicious of the question about which rule is being used. The political goal—of having the public satisfied with the conditions under which it lives—is more likely to be attained when the public is aware of the rules of the system than when these rules are kept secret.

Can these two principles solve the dirty-hands problem? Start with the Dirty Harry question. Can Inspector Harry Callahan's maxim pass both the negative and affirmative tests? He would state his maxim as: "When the life of one member of the community is at stake, I will take away the rights of the suspected criminal." The community would hardly accept such a maxim because of the enormous danger to themselves in a rule that allowed the loss of their right to be free of torture. Under Harry's maxim, a citizen's being "suspected" but not convicted of a crime would be enough to allow the police to use torture. Conclusion: The publicity principles deny Harry his right to torture to get the information. When you go by the book, it must be an open book—open to the public.

The formal proof that Dirty Harry was dirty is not really surprising. That's how he got his name. The question of this chapter still remains: If we know that an action is wrong, that it is obviously immoral taken by itself, may we still use it to reach an absolutely desirable goal? Harry is quite aware of the restrictions against police brutality and against the use of torture by the police; however, he chooses the risk of this violation over the risk of the loss of the child's life. The child also has a right—the right to police protection when threatened by a psychotic killer.

This balance of risks, this way of preferring one risk to the other, is Harry's style. We can easily understand the other way of balancing those risks, another style, but we cannot find one style always more desirable than the other. We can, however, make a different judgment. We can raise the question of the general results of one style or the other over time, and we may find that in the long run there are general advantages to a mixture of styles. To the question "Was Harry right?", we must say that he was not. The conflict of rights between the child and the suspect leaves us with no way of preserving all rights. However, suppose that the question is presented to us as "Would we be delighted to have found that his choice saved the life of the child?" Our answer must be "Yes, indeed." If we give contradictory answers to the same question, we are incoherent. If we give different answers to different questions, the matter is far from the same. We can say "No" to the first and "Yes" to the second.

If we ask one question, we must criticize Harry. If we ask another, we are enthusiastic over Harry's objective. Which question *should* we ask? Which way should we balance the risks of error? That question is equivalent to asking if there is one perfect style. To that, we can respond as follows: Any style that is morally acceptable must lie within the boundaries of the two principles of publicity. If the maxims of the moral actor can satisfy both the negative and affirmative tests for publicity, those maxims are acceptable. If Harry or his department could make his maxim public and if the maxim needs publicity in order to work, it would be moral. If one granted the argument that, after such publicity, psychopathic killing would not occur, Harry and his department could go public and be heroes. With a case that strong, Harry would not be dirty.

Application to the Terror Bombing of Germany

With this in mind, let us return to the dirty-hands question involved in the terror bombing of Germany. Suppose that Commander Harris and Prime Minister Churchill had made their maxim public. Would the British public have accepted, even in World War II, this rule: "To win this war, to crush the morale of the Nazis and thereby speed their defeat, we will bomb civilian populations in German cities"? Even if the British had, there is the matter of world opinion. To publicize this maxim would have been to accept the idea that civilians are legitimate targets. No government seems quite ready to take responsibility or blame for such an enormous change in military morality.

We have not yet considered the affirmative principle in connection with the terror bombing of German cities. Did the Harris/Churchill rule *require* publicity in order to be effective? If the objective of terror bombing had been to make clear to the victims just who is responsible for the terror, then the bombing would have worked only if it had been known to its targets. Accepting this argument, both negative and positive principles of publicity might have permitted the bombing, had the British been willing to face the consequences of allowing publicity for their rule. However, the high moral position of the nations at war against Nazism was inconsistent with terror bombing of innocent civilians. Conclusion: The bombing was not justified.

Again we have a choice of pertinent, significant questions. Is the essential question: "Is it right to bomb the German civilians?" Or, does the moral issue turn on the question: "Is this bombing of civilians going to end the war more quickly than any other method?" We can give different answers to the two questions. To the matter of bombing innocent civilians, we must say "No"; however, to the question of our desire for an early end of the war, we may say "Yes." The answer to the second question is bought at the cost of the first.

Does our desire to end a war justify committing war crimes, having dirty hands? No. A major purpose of the war conventions is to deny exactly that; however, without justifying the crimes, even while clearly condemning them, we can still point to the actual consequences of those crimes. We can note, with honesty, just what the crimes have led to without agreeing that the crimes were desirable or praiseworthy. (That the bombing of German cities crushed morale is far from obvious. The opposite effect may have occurred.)

The Reign of Terror

Kant himself followed the pattern above in his views of the French Revolution. He did not justify the Reign of Terror, which included the barbaric use of the guillotine on about twenty-five hundred people, but he did note the feeling of pleasure, close to enthusiasm, that he and others had from the news of the overthrow of the monarchy and the moves to republican government.[17] Did he feel guilty about the Terror? We must answer the two questions involved separately. He condemned it and those whose acts it was; he regretted it, but this regret did not mean that he could not celebrate the gains brought about by the French Revolution and even its period of Terror. This was no cover-up of the crimes. He wrote that the Revolution "may be so *filled with misery and atrocities* that no right-thinking man would ever decide to make the same experiment again at such a price, even if he could hope to carry it out successfully at the second attempt" (emphasis mine). He calls an atrocity an atrocity; the French revolutionaries had dirty hands. His next sentence considers a separate question: "But I maintain that this revolution has aroused in the hearts and desires of all spectators who are not themselves caught up in it a *sympathy* which borders almost on enthusiasm."[18]

The Fallacy of Many Questions

It is commonplace in logic to mention the fallacy of many questions. Consider the classic example, "Have you stopped beating your wife?" This question presupposes a prior question, "Have you started beating your wife?", and an affirmative answer to that. The fallacy consists in treating two or more questions as if they were but a single issue to which one answer would be adequate. Some of the questions raised about dirty hands are cases of the fallacy of many questions. Examples might be the question, "How do you justify the terror bombing of Germany?", and the question, "Don't you justify ending the war as quickly as possible?" Before answering either one of these, we would want to separate the questions involved and distinguish between our view of the means and our view of the results.

Can a commander (consciously?) choose to use dirty hands to accomplish his or her mission? As argued above, the two publicity principles are the required test. Hands are not dirty, however, if the maxim of their action passes the publicity tests. What if the maxim fails the tests; what if publicity is not acceptable or required?

Awareness of the sturdy fallacy of many questions can help separate the pieces of the problem, but that awareness does not tell us how to deal with those individual pieces. Must we countenance dirty hands? Must we justify them in some cases? Despite the various threads of the issue considered above, the answer should be "No."

What, then, is the attitude toward those who have done the work, who have dirty hands? They must be punished for the crimes, of course. It is not enough to think that they will suffer "guilt" and that such suffering is adequate punishment. It is merely a romantic myth to assume that those with dirty hands are "living out the agony," as Walzer put it. Such a maxim would run like this: "Hire people to commit war crimes and then disown them and hope that they feel guilty and live in agony afterward." We could not publicize such a maxim because it would justify almost every war crime. If we were strong enough to get away with it, we would not need it; with less strength, we would be afraid of becoming the maxim's victims. Formally, that maxim fails both publicity principles: We would be afraid to have it known, and it does not require publicity to reach its goal.

Does this leave us with the hypocrisy of Walzer's sad conclusion "that a nation fighting a just war, when it is desperate and survival itself is at risk, must use unscrupulous or morally ignorant soldiers; and as soon as their usefulness is past, it must disown them"?[19] Merely to punish those who have done our dirty work, at our command, is certainly not adequate. We must consider two variations of the problem.

In one set of cases, the war crimes are not absolutely necessary to winning the war. Then, if we hold that crime should not pay, we must insist that war crimes should not pay; therefore, those who are responsible for war crimes are to be punished and the victims compensated (where compensation is possible). This principle must also apply to those who employ and direct the physical perpetrators of the crimes. The politicians and the citizens who are responsible for and benefit from the crimes must not be allowed to pretend innocence. They can be punished and can pay compensation.

In another set of cases, let us assume that war crimes are *absolutely necessary* to winning a war. Can we ever suppose that war crimes and only war crimes can do it? It must be extremely hard to establish such a necessity, and, even with *necessity*, even if the war cannot be won without the crime, that may not be *sufficient*. Wars are notoriously hard to predict; they take surprising turns. To know that one or more war crimes are *both necessary and sufficient* to win a war would take a greater ability to predict the future than anyone can claim. However, even if we had such unavailable knowledge, we have concluded that unless both publicity principles are satisfied, dirty hands still cannot be justified. There are hands so dirty that we should not use them to win a war. There are wars that should not be fought and wars that should not be won. The moral hope, of course, is to fight only those that should be won.

There are three possible conclusions to a war: It may be won, it may be lost, and it may end in a stalemate of one sort or another. The United States has not won all of its wars, but it has not lost any to an invading force. A stalemate in Korea or a withdrawal in Vietnam is far from a loss to an invader. The style of response to the dirty-hands choice may well differ in the three different kinds of threat. Reluctance to use dirty hands to win or to reach a stalemate might not be reluctance in face of a risk of loss or perhaps of surrender to an invader. Despite the anticipation of a different attitude in a different situation, despite the moral panic to be expected from the threat of losing a war, *dirty hands* is simply a new name for an old pattern. The old name was *war crimes,* and an honorable military cannot choose them under either name.

In the next chapter we must consider how to apply these views of dirty hands to the questions involved in torture.

10
Torture

Tony Lagouranis, who spent a year in Iraq as a U.S. Army military interrogator in Abu Ghraib and other prisons, says that he "noticed something very disturbing. People are absolutely fascinated by torture. As soon as someone learns that I was an interrogator, I can see him formulate the next question. . . . 'Did you torture anyone?' It comes from people all across the political spectrum, from people both disgusted by torture and from people who actually want the troops to do it." [1] I'll leave to the psychologists the question of why people are so fascinated by torture. This chapter will deal with moral and legal aspects of the military use of torture.

The extremes of torture are (1) the civil liberties view that no violation of basic human rights can ever be justified; and (2) the pragmatic view that measures are to be judged by their effectiveness. Significant voices in this debate are those who try to find a middle course, such as Michael Ignatieff [2] and the author (S. Miller) of the article on torture in the *Stanford Encyclopedia of Philosophy*.

In the last decade, particularly since the military action against Iraq, there has been a significant increase in the number of books and articles on torture, as events such as the scandal at the Abu Ghraib prison force the United States and the world to rethink their views on the subject.

The Evolution of Torture

The use of torture is hardly new to the twentieth century. The Bible calls the reader to "Remember those in prison as if you were there with them; and those who are being maltreated [tortured?], for you like them are still in the world."[3] Torture was common in ancient Greece and Rome and became less frequent after the rise of the Roman Empire. Between the twelfth and fifteenth centuries the Roman Catholic Church used torture on accused heretics. Where we use the word *interrogation,* the Church used *inquisition:*

> By the mid-thirteenth century the Papal Inquisition applied to heretics the Roman law on treason, for it was assumed that the accused could be guilty of the highest treason of all, namely, treason to God and the faith. Hence a heretic was presumed to be guilty, was deprived of adequate legal defense, could not know and challenge his accusers, had no public trial, and was tortured if he refused to confess. Although the Papal Inquisition was never established in England, in the Tudor Age men accused of treason to the king suffered a similar kind of treatment. No wonder that in reaction to this, in the Tudor Age, the maxim arose which later became part of our Fifth Amendment: no man shall be compelled "to accuse himself" or "to be a witness against himself."[4]

Apparently it was the revulsion against torture that led the framers of the Constitution to write the part of the Fifth Amendment that makes it unconstitutional to compel self-accusation. The amendment is not restricted to citizens alone: It insists that "no man" is to be compelled, or forced, to be a witness against himself (in a criminal case). That appears to cover both POWs and protected persons. To continue with some of the history,

> Nonetheless it was Roman law, not the English common law, which first laid down the principle that normally the man accused of a tort or a crime should be presumed innocent. Implied as it is in the Magna Carta, the presumption of innocence was first literally stated, it seems, by Jean Lemoine, a canonist and cardinal in the time of Pope Boniface VIII [1294–1305]. Making use of Stoic-Roman-Christian ideas of legalists and canonists, he declared that every man accused of a crime had the full right to a public trial and to full legal defense by lawyers, and documents, and witnesses. For every man, he declared, "is presumed innocent until proved guilty" (*qui libet praesumitur innocens, nisi probetur nocens, . . .)*"[5]

The principle of "innocent until proved guilty at a trial," and the Fifth Amendment's objection to compelling self-incrimination from "any person," seems to apply to prisoners and protected persons and to forbid torture. The question of self-incrimination is crucial, because one major goal of torture is often to compel persons to testify against themselves. (Apparently we must choose between keeping a significant part of the Fifth Amendment or nullifying the amendment and accepting torture as legal.)

Torture was legally abolished by most European countries by 1800, but then

> Torture reappeared in the 20th Century, in unexpectedly high proportions . . . widespread in states that used law as a means of imposing ideology, as in fascist Italy, Nazi Germany and the Soviet Union under Stalin. In the latter half of the century its use spread widely in Africa, Asia, and Latin America and became an extra-legal means by which governments and wealthy elites suppressed political opposition and waged terrorist campaigns against civilians (often impoverished peasants) seeking reform."[6]

At an early point in this matter, the United States played a significant part in opposing torture, in the "Lieber Code." As mentioned earlier, this was the Civil War product of Frances Lieber that became the Army's *General Orders 100*. Commissioned by Abraham Lincoln, the Code prohibited torture. This was the first time a government had published a code for its military operations. It was quickly copied, almost exactly, by the major European nations. Since then, there have been the 1929 Geneva Convention on treatment of Prisoners of War, the 1949 Geneva Conventions, and the 1948 UN Universal Declaration of Human Rights (among others), all following the United States' lead in prohibiting torture.

The *Geneva Convention Relative to the Treatment of Prisoners of War, 1949,* includes a section [article 17] on the questioning of prisoners. It contains the following clear requirement:

> No physical or mental torture, nor any other form of coercion, may be inflicted on prisoners of war to secure from them information of any kind whatever. Prisoners of war who refuse to answer may not be threatened, insulted, or exposed to unpleasant or disadvantageous treatment of any kind.[7]

A Definition of Torture

The idea of torture and maltreatment raises a number of serious questions. First, is there a clear and widely accepted definition of torture? Recently, definitions of *torture* have become a political matter for the United States. For our purposes, we will start with a reasonable description that Donald A. Wells offers in his *Encyclopedia of War and Ethics:* "The infliction of excruciating physical pain or unbearable psychological torment for such reasons as punishment, extracting confessions and information, or intimidating and instilling terror in others."[3]

What are and what are not cases of "excruciating physical pain" and of "unbearable psychological torment"? Since the start of the military action in Iraq, these issues have been disputed between the U.S. military and the political administration of the U.S. government. For a time the political administration was willing to allow actions that an ordinary reading of the Geneva Conventions forbids. This has brought criticism, including that from Major General Antonio M. Taguba, the officer who led the U.S. Army's investigation into the scandal that ensued from revelations that U.S. soldiers were torturing detainees in Iraq's Abu Ghraib prison: "the fact is that we violated the laws of land warfare in Abu Ghraib. We violated the tenets of the Geneva Convention [on torture]. We violated our own principles and we violated the core of our military values."[4] General Taguba criticized both the civilian leadership of the Defense Department, and those officers who knew better but went along with the civilians.

The Geneva Convention makes clear that torture is not to be used on either prisoners of war or protected persons. The term *protected persons* is defined by the U.S. Army's FM 27-10, dated July 1956, as "all persons [in the hands of a belligerent] who have engaged in hostile or belligerent conduct but who are not entitled to treatment as prisoners of war." (The U.S. Army's "Interpretation" of the Geneva Convention, article 4, found on p. 98 of the same FM.) Several sections of the Geneva Convention emphasize the prohibition against torture used on either prisoners of war or protected persons. (For information on protected persons, see the Geneva Convetion's article 32, FM 27-10, page 107, and for the Geneva Convention on prisoners of war, see article 17, FM 27-10, page 37.) The Geneva Conventions category of "protected persons" seems to be a reasonable status for belligerents who are captured but do not qualify as POWs.

Arguments For and Against the Use of Torture

There are obviously arguments on both sides of the question of the use of torture. First, we will look at the argument for using torture, followed by arguments against its use.

Those who approve of the use of torture hold that there are situations in which the rapid gain of information can make a great difference to a war effort, or an effort to save lives. To learn the plans of the enemy before those plans are carried out is obviously a most valuable piece of information. In addition, there are those who do not advocate torture as a regular tool but instead, one that is brought out only when absolutely necessary. The "ticking bomb" situation, a frequently used argument, is considered later in this chapter.

As compelling as it might be to justify the use of torture for gaining information, there are a number of arguments against torture. One argument against using torture in warfare is that it violates the trust of the opposing side. This trust comes into play during a surrender, which is the object of a war. To win, the enemy must surrender and stay surrendered, and to really surrender there must be some trust on each side. If one side behaves so brutally that its members engender hate rather than trust, the war will not end. If the war does not end, the goal of winning the war is lost. There have been cases in which wars have gone on for generations (Northern Ireland and Palestine/Israel, among others). So, to win a war, it is a military advantage to follow the restrictions of the Geneva Conventions, which means no torture of prisoners.

Yet another argument against torture is that the U.S. justice system rules inadmissible confessions obtained by torture. This becomes an issue when those persons in U.S. custody confess to a crime and will be tried in U.S. courts. As some distinguished commentators, such as General Wesley Clark, have pointed out, "Since 9/11 the Bush administration has sought to categorize members of Al Qaeda as 'unlawful combatants,' rather than treat them as criminals"[5] or as prisoners of war. An "unlawful combatant," however, is a criminal, and the criminal justice system is the obvious place to deal with criminals. This means that should a prisoner confess to any wrongdoing during a session that involves torture, it is possible that a U.S. court will throw out that confession.

A very important argument against torture involves the trustworthiness of information obtained. One who is tortured may make up any story to stop the torture. In addition, torture can make an innocent man or woman confess to murder, whether or not he or she committed the crime. There are documented cases of police interrogation that have produced confessions to crimes that the subjects did not commit. Convictions are sometimes undependable (an understatement). Such was the case for four men on death row in Illinois who were later exonerated by Governor George Ryan.

While the risk of low, or no, accuracy is always there, those who believe that torture should be used in certain cases are impressed with the risk of great loss in not getting advance information. That issue is explored later in this chapter.

For a firsthand response about using torture to obtain information, let us return to the account of Tony Lagouranis, a U.S. Army interrogator at Abu Ghraib and other places in Iraq who wrote about his experiences after his discharge. Lagouranis's book describes his path from opposing torture to doing a small amount of it—called "torture-lite"—to doing more and more of it, and finally to hating himself and the army for doing it. So-called "torture-lite" methods included putting prisoners in stress positions (prisoners have died from long and painful stress positions), depriving them of sleep, leaving lights on continuously, playing extremely loud rock music for days, subjecting them to various diet patterns, and placing prisoners in stress positions outside in any kind of weather, although the nights in the desert could drop to 40 degrees. Lagouranis and his fellow soldiers also used dogs to intimidate prisoners. A prisoner's cell might have no windows and a prisoner might have no human contact for months. Going to and from the interrogation room would involve a head-and-face covering so that the prisoner never saw the sky.

Interrogators were to follow the Interrogation Rules of Engagement (IROE), but these rules changed depending on which camp one was in and on the dates of the interrogation activity. While the Rules specified that the prisoners were to have at least four hours of sleep a night, the chief interrogator at one camp decided that the four hours could be broken up into five pieces (48 minutes at a time). An interrogation might also include showing prisoners parts of relatives' bodies and clothing from relatives as a form of additional intimidation.

A recent study of CIA interrogation methods (mentioned in the Lagouranis book) found that psychological techniques such as covering a prisoner's head and face, putting prisoners in stress positions, and limiting food and sleep—"torture-lite" or no-touch torture—were more successful in obtaining information, on the whole, than physical methods. However, Tony Lagouranis quotes a retired FBI agent, Joe Navarro, who was an expert in interrogation, on four main reasons why torture is, overall, *ineffective*:

1. A torture victim will say anything to get the torture to stop.
2. The stress that pain creates confuses the subject and he simply can't remember details well enough to produce good intelligence.
3. The torture subject may die or go into shock, and give no information. [One commentator mentioned that torture in a police department can easily be covered up, but a dead body is a problem.]
4. The torture victim, if he tells the interrogator anything at all, is likely to give one piece of information, or very little information, whereas a cooperative source will talk and continue talking.[6]

Navarro adds that he believes that torture strengthens the resolve of the detainee, making it more difficult to obtain the sought-after information, despite using extreme methods. He cites Senator John McCain of Arizona, who, after having his shoulder torn from its socket by interrogators in Vietnam, said he was more determined than ever to keep his silence. A few years ago, as Senator McCain was arguing about his anti-torture amendment on the Senate floor, he told an opponent tersely, "It's not about who they are," meaning the terrorists. "It's about who we are."

Lagouranis also points out the difference between a confession and a piece of intelligence that might be useful to the military. A confession is backward-looking, and not the forward-looking kind of information that a commander wants in the field or that an investigator needs in order to thwart a terrorist attack. A confession of past activities is not a forward-looking piece of intelligence of use to the military.

Lagouranis notes that it is not the present pain/torture that the victim fears, but the escalation of it. To torture, then, one must always threaten something more severe. He quotes a CIA manual, saying, "the threat of coercion usually weakens resistance or destroys it more effectively than coercion itself." Chess players may know the story of Emanual Lasker, a great world chess champion, who was to play a man who couldn't stand cigar smoke. Lasker agreed not to smoke. After a few moves, Lasker laid a cigar on the table, along with some matches, but he never lit it. His opponent was so upset by the threat that he crumbled. Threats can be more powerful than actions; however, to threaten without being able to carry out the threat is useless, according to the same CIA manual (p. 245 in Lagouranis), that Lagouranis quoted.

Arguments Favoring the Use of Torture Only in Certain Situations

Some people who do not advocate torture on a regular basis do favor using it in particular situations. These proponents are (1) those that hold that there needs to be a legal pattern for protecting people who use torture under certain circumstances, and (2) those who hold that in emergencies there can be a "one-off" use of torture.

A Justification for Torture in a "Ticking Bomb" Scenario?

First, there are those who want a legal pattern under which torture can take place. Alan Dershowitz, a prominent lawyer, has argued that legalized torture is defensible after getting a warrant, a torture warrant, from a judge.[7] The "ticking bomb" scenario is often used as part of this argument. Suppose that the police know that a nuclear weapon has been set somewhere in a large city, and that they have caught someone who, they say, knows where the bomb is and how to stop it from exploding. If torture is the only way of getting the information and saving the city and thousands of people, why not torture? Constitutional guarantees do not mean that society has to allow itself to be destroyed, as Richard A. Posner emphasized in his book's title, *The Constitution is Not a Suicide Pact.*

In the "ticking bomb" situation, why not torture? Well, this matter has several assumptions: Do the police *know* that such a bomb has been set? How do they know it? And do the police *know* that their prisoner could either disable the bomb or give them accurate information if he were tortured? In the real world, not the world of imaginative examples, it is most unlikely that the police would really know both of these required matters. To institutionalize torture for so unlikely a case would invite the great evils of regular torture. Dershowitz proposed that only tightly controlled and restricted forms of torture would be legally admissible. But the history, the records, show (from Israel and other places)[8] that things move from torture-lite, to torture-medium, to torture without restriction. The "torture warrant" would not work in the time frame of the ticking time-bomb scenario. To work, the torturer must threaten even greater torture and be prepared to do it, as I've mentioned.

A Justification for One-Off Acts of Torture in Emergencies

The phrase *one-off* is used in England and Australia to mean an act that follows no pattern or law but is merely a unique event. As outlined in Chapter 9, in *Dirty Harry*, Inspector Harry Callahan used torture to find the whereabouts of a kidnapped child who had only hours to live. Torture was against department regulations, but Harry decided to use it to achieve what he thought was a defensible goal. This looks to be an effort at a one-off, one-time-only, use of torture. The "one-off" use of torture set no pattern; it followed no rule or regulation that could be used again.

Another, similar, example has been reported by John Blackler, a former police officer in New South Wales, Australia. On a very hot day, a mother stopped for petrol, leaving her three-year-old son asleep on the back seat of her vehicle. She went in to the station office to pay the bill, leaving her keys in the ignition. While she was in the service station, a man drove off in her car. Police wound back the service station's surveillance film, noted the man's appearance, and told the woman that the thief would just leave the car when he noticed the baby in the back seat. The police, waiting at the railroad station, caught the man, but the car was nowhere to be seen. Since the car thief had things from the car in his pockets, they thought that they had the right person. He denied the theft, saying (forgetting grammatical niceties), "It wasn't me." But the thief refused to say where he had left the car. The police knew that in another twenty minutes, in the heat of that day, the child would be dead or brain damaged. Appeals to decency, to reason, or to self-interest were of no avail. Explaining the difference between a minor charge and a murder charge got nowhere. Then, the police went for a serious beating, and that worked. The report (in the *Stanford Encyclopedia of Philosophy*) says, "kneeling on hands and knees in his own urine, in pain he had never known, and realizing that the beating would go on until he told the police where he had abandoned the child, he finally told them." The child, when found, was dehydrated, too weak to cry, but after ice packs and dehydration procedures, it was clear that the child would not experience any long-term brain damage. The child was saved.

In this case, torture seemed justified. The police had reasonable belief that (1) torture would probably save an innocent life, (2) the car thief was not innocent, and (3) there was no other way to save the child's life. This appears to be a "one-off" case of justified torture. No legal pattern was set, no authority approved it. I don't know if the police were complimented or criticized.

Still another example of an effort at a "one-off" act is the terror bombing of German cities at a certain stage of World War II. There was a point when England was fighting alone, and it was certainly possible, perhaps likely, that the Nazis would win. Chapter 9 includes a quote from Michael Walzer, making the point. "that a nation, fighting a just war, when it is desperate and survival itself is at risk, must use unscrupulous or morally ignorant soldiers, and as soon as their usefulness is past, it must disown them."[9] Why is it necessary to discredit them, when they carried out those "required" orders? It is necessary to discredit them to make clear that this was a "one-off" case and not a basis for repetition.

One last example is the 1995 case in which the Philippine police stopped a plan to bomb eleven U.S. airlines after gaining information tortured out of a Pakistani suspect. But this is a red-herring example, because the police did not know there was such a plot, they just routinely tortured this fellow and were surprised that he told the story of the plot. They were also surprised that he survived, since they had physically tortured him for weeks. (This example also is taken from the *Stanford Encyclopedia* article on Torture).

Does a so-called "one-off" case stay just one-off? One hopes so, but the risk of repetition is always there. In the case of the early bombing of German cities, that bombing went on well after the British gained strong allies (including the United States) and the risk of losing to the Nazis became unlikely. There seems to be no easy formulation of torture or terror bombing that carries no risk of error.

Political Categories Do Not Predict Attitudes Toward Torture

Traditional political categories don't easily apply to positions on torture.[15] Allan Dershowitz would permit torture, if regulated by judicial warrant. Liberal senator Charles Schumer has criticized the idea that "torture should never, ever, be used." William Safire, a self-described conservative, labels torture "barbarism."

Of course, the United States, a nation which prides itself on being a democracy, is not the only government to use torture in recent times. In 1999, the Israeli "Supreme Court backpedaled from an earlier permission to engage in 'torture-lite,' in emergencies, because the interrogators were torturing two-thirds of their Palestine captives."[10] In the Argentinian Dirty War, which lasted from 1976–1983, "One scholar reports that at first many of the officers carrying out torture [dropping people from aircraft into the ocean, etc.] had qualms about what they were doing, until their priests reassured them that they were fighting God's fight. By the end of the Dirty War, the qualms were gone, and hardened young officers were placing bets on who could kidnap the prettiest girl to rape and torture. Escalation is the rule, not the aberration."[11]

Conclusions

Consider again the arguments on both sides of the question of the use of torture. Those who approve of Dirty Harry's action, and certain other examples of torture, hold that there are situations in which the rapid gain of information can make a great difference to a war or police effort. To learn the plans of the enemy before they are carried out, for example, is a most valuable piece of information. On the other side is the matter of loss of trust that can make it more difficult or impossible to gain a surrender to end the war.

Having examined all sides of the question of using torture, what can we conclude about the morality of using it at all? Looking back to Chapter 2, we find a discussion of the four moral styles. How do these apply to questions about torture? While there are different moral styles, morality demands that, "All variations must follow rules that could be universalized to apply to everyone." The rule/assumption in torture is that it is acceptable if it provides useful information. Can this rule be universalized? Would we agree that we are proper objects of torture if during that torture we would provide useful information to someone? Hardly. Kant has another objection to that torture rule: It uses individuals as means to a goal not their own. It makes them slaves. Therefore, torture is not moral.

Finally, historian Michael Ignatieff makes a cogent argument against the use of torture. According to Ignatieff, "Torture might break apart a network of terrorist cells, but it would also engender hatred and resentment among the survivors of the torture. Extreme measures, like torture, preventive detention, and arbitrary arrest, typically win the battle but lose the larger war."[12] In addition, Ignatieff writes that a democracy should not need torture in order to sustain itself. In his view, it is "the very nature of a democracy that it not only does but should fight with one hand tied behind its back. It is also in the nature of a democracy that it prevail against its enemies precisely because it does."[13]

11

Nuclear Devices and Low-intensity Conflicts

Nuclear Weapons

Are nuclear weapons acceptable or forbidden as a means of waging war? Two responses will be offered to this question. The first is based on a reading of the Conventions and the second comes from an analysis by an eminent contemporary philosopher, Richard Wasserstrom.

Are Nuclear Weapons Covered by the Existing Conventions?

When we consult the existing manuals on the question, we find a strange situation. They include only extremely brief references to the most powerful weapons of all and only oblique comments on their usability. In its July 1956 edition, FM 27-10 has a single sentence in the paragraph on atomic weapons that states that these weapons "cannot as such be regarded as violative of international law in the absence of any customary rule of international law or international convention restricting their employment."[1] The British Manual, in its two-sentence paragraph on nuclear weapons, states that there is no rule dealing specifically with such weapons and so their use is governed by the general principles of international law.[2] The authors of FM 27-10 (the Judge Advocate-General department) agree with the British and others that new and unmentioned weapons are to be governed by the existing customary rules.

Which existing rules might apply? Looking at FM 27-10, we find in paragraph 34, "It is especially forbidden . . . to cause unnecessary suffering." Because "unnecessary" means beyond the requirements to gain the military objective, the extended suffering produced by the radiation from nuclear weapons places these weapons in the forbidden class. In the changes made to FM 27-10, dated 15 July 1976, we find paragraph 41 expanded to include the statement that "those who plan or decide upon an attack, therefore, must take all reasonable steps to ensure . . . that these objectives may be attacked without probable losses in lives and damage to property *disproportionate to the military advantages anticipated*" (emphasis mine).[3] This change essentially repeats and emphasizes the point of paragraph 34. Are there military advantages that require the killing, devastation, and long-term medical consequences of nuclear weapons? Within the framework of acceptability to the war conventions, we cannot imagine any such advantages.

The United States has renounced use of any riot-control agents and chemical herbicides in war unless there is presidential approval in advance.[4] FM 27-10 distinguishes between "incapacitating agents" that produce symptoms that persist for hours or even days after exposure and agents that produce "merely transient effects that disappear within minutes after exposure." The Geneva Protocol of 1925, ratified by the United States in 1975, is considered by the United States to prohibit the "incapacitating agents" that cause symptoms that last for hours.[5] If weapons producing symptoms that last for hours are forbidden (as first-strike weapons but not in retaliation), one would expect that the symptoms produced by nuclear weapons would also be a basis for forbidding those weapons.

The 1925 Protocol prohibits the use of "Poisonous, or Other Gases." The "radiation poisoning" of nuclear weapons must come under this category. Radiation poisoning is certainly a variety of poisoning. Radiation "fallout" and the concept of a "nuclear cloud" certainly come under the concept of a "gas." The common dictionary definition of a gas is "any toxic mistlike substance dispersed in air, used in warfare to poison an enemy."[6] This definition alone bans the device.

The British Manual considers that "the diffusion of poisonous and asphyxiating gases from cylinders or otherwise than by projectiles—a practice instituted by German forces during the First World War—whether or not within the prohibition of the use of 'poison or poisoned weapons' . . . was illegal in so far as it exposed combatants to unnecessary suffering, conduct prohibited by [Hague Rules 23(a)]." If those asphyxiating gases are illegal, any asphyxiation caused by the nuclear bomb would also be illegal.

The paragraphs above include quite a list of items in the military code that make the case against acceptability of nuclear weapons. The case seems clear even without mentioning the inability of users to discriminate between military and civilian targets, except in the possible case of very small "tactical warheads." Are nuclear weapons acceptable? A fair reading of the military code requires an answer of "No." The existing Code does cover such weapons: Nuclear weapons violate the Code by causing unnecessary suffering, by being poisonous, by being disproportionate to the military mission, and by being indiscriminate. Any one of these features would require honorable soldiers to explain that such weapons are forbidden.

Would a Nuclear War Be a War?

While considering the matter of nuclear weapons, it is instructive to review what we mean by the concept of war,[7] Definitions of war are easily found, but it is especially to the point here to consider what is assumed by almost all definitions, often without being explicitly stated.

1. A war is an activity that takes place over a significant period of time. It requires some time to raise an army or supplement one that already exists. Even a draft law in place takes time to operate. Basic training and specialized training cannot be completed in an instant. It takes time even to declare to all relevant parties that a war is taking place or that it will take place. A war is expected to involve some strategy and tactics, and these also take time to develop. The citizenry will need to have reasons for the war explained or argued for. If there is a minority opposed to the war, that group, at least in democratic countries, will need time to think and decide on its response, be it loyal opposition, passive resistance, or whatever.
2. A war traditionally takes place within boundaries. Some territory is, and at least some is not, a target of any of the belligerents. Some country is expected to be neutral and to serve as a protecting power and as a means of communication between the belligerents.
3. On the whole, the laws of war are expected to be obeyed, with some infractions. Some persons are to be considered noncombatants; some institutions, such as hospitals, churches, and schools, are to be considered safe from attack.
4. In the usual historical example, a war is fought by men and women. These people—soldiers—expose themselves to danger, and some may behave heroically.
5. A war is expected to end with a formal surrender, a written agreement, or articles of surrender.

The scenarios that we are offered for a nuclear "exchange" contain none of these historical features. Let us assume that in a matter of a few minutes two countries devastate each other. Could that be called a war by the criteria listed above?

166 / Chapter 11

In a nuclear exchange, there is no time for the process in item 1. There is no time to raise and train an army and no time for strategy or tactics, and none is needed because both countries are devastated almost immediately. There is no time for the civilian population to consider its changing interests as the war develops because there is no development.

The requirements of item 2 are missing completely. Nuclear fallout apparently covers the globe or, at least, the hemisphere in which the explosions take place; therefore, the ordinary boundaries of nonbelligerents are not immune to clouds of radiation fallout. The danger does not stop at borders. Again, there is no time for the ordinary activities of the protecting powers and neutrals.

The patterns in item 3 will not be observed. Noncombatants, as well as combatants, are victims. Hospitals, churches, and schools are destroyed along with the old notion of legitimate target.

As far as item 4 is concerned, the war is fought by machinery, not by brave men or brave women. Command decisions may also be made by machinery—computers. Soldiers may be in no more danger than civilians. With complete devastation, no soldier may be in more danger than another, so there is no basis for heroism.

As for item 5, if no command structure or government is left, no entity exists to offer or accept a surrender.

Conclusions

A nuclear exchange would not be a war; it would be "omnicide." Because the term *suicide* is a bit too restrictive here, the term *omnicide* has come into use for this kind of situation. Familiar definitions of war would also not apply. According to the British Manual, "War is for the purpose of overcoming armed resistance,"[8] but if there is no original entity left, then no one has overcome anyone's resistance. According to the familiar theory of Karl von Clausewitz, "war is . . . an act of [political] policy,"[9] but political policies aim at increasing the power of their constituents, not destroying them. The term *destroy* comes from a paper by former Secretary of Defense Robert S. McNamara: "The West's existing plans for initiating the use of nuclear weapons, if implemented, are far more likely to *destroy* Western Europe, North America, and Japan than to de*fend* them" (emphasis mine).[10]

All nuclear weapons are not of equal power. Does the conclusion above apply to small tactical warheads that are delivered by artillery shells to acceptable military targets? No one knows, but what we have as a basis for judgment weighs heavily against their use.[11] There seems to be no hard or dependable theory by which to predict that use of such "small" warheads would or would not lead to the use of more powerful nuclear weapons. Even if the immediate target was quite acceptable, the problems of extended fallout, noncombatant effects, and long-term results of the weapon would remain. The obvious tactical choice may be, "Use 'em or lose 'em."

Instead of accepting that alternative—either using battlefield nuclear weapons or having them captured by an enemy—we can prepare a third possibility. Essential components must be destroyable. If the small nuclear weapons cannot be made unusable before capture, then such weapons are obviously not fit for the battlefield. An artillery unit with such weapons would be in almost the same position as a terrorist with a bomb: "Don't touch me or else I blow up everything!" This is hardly an example of military honor. Even if these weapons could be dependably destroyed on the battlefield, the other violations would remain.

Although the case for or against battlefield nuclear weapons is not as absolutely clear as the case against the larger devices, it is very similar. We must, therefore, conclude that nuclear weapons are not acceptable weapons of war because, as argued above, they are essentially forbidden by the international conventions and their use would produce not a war but omnicide.

FM 100-1 (August 1981) includes a statement of unique relevance here: "In conflicts with major powers, the United States may be faced with situations where the achievement of an advantageous position for conflict termination *may require a political decision to use nuclear weapons*" (emphasis mine).[12] Because of the special features of nuclear weapons, the quotation implies that this is not a military decision alone. A most serious moral question arises here: *Should the military accept a political decision about military morality?* Toward the end of this chapter, we return to this conflict between political morality and a moral military. The conclusion there will be that military honor cannot be abdicated, that the military must not resign their conscience to politicians.

The Tactical Choice to Defeat Japan

It is frequently mentioned that in World War II President Harry Truman had to choose between invading the Japanese homeland or using the atomic weapons. The estimates of the cost of an invasion included an enormous loss of lives, both ours and the those of the Japanese. So it is usually concluded that President Truman did what cost fewer lives: He used the atomic weapons.

The third option is almost never mentioned: a blockade of Japan— actually, a blockade and aerial bombing. It was considered at the highest levels, although it is barely mentioned and was not discussed in the public media.

In a review of a book on naval blockades, Professor Bruce Ellemen of the Naval War College's Department of Maritime History, wrote that "in World War II the U.S. blockade against Japan was so tight that it may have been the most effective naval blockade in history" (Professor Bruce Elleman of the Department of Maritime History, Naval War College, in *Naval War College Review*, Vol. 60, Number 4, Autumn 2007, p. 147). If the blockade was that effective, why not continue it instead of dropping the atomic weapons? A blockade was considered, in combination with conventional bombs, as the material below shows.

My historical quotes come from an unclassified CIA publication, *The Final Months of the War with Japan: Signals Intelligence, U.S. Invasion Planning, and the A-Bomb Decision* by Douglas J. MacEachin (Central Intelligence Agency, Center for the Study of Intelligence, CSI 98-10001, December 1998). The author, Mr. MacEachin, was a member of the CIA from 1965 to his retirement in 1997, was Deputy Director for intelligence at the CIA from March 1993 to June 1995, as well as holding other major positions there.

In the Mac Eachin publication cited above, the first paragraph of this CIA work reads, "A number of key Navy and Army Air Force officers led by Fleet Admiral Ernest King, Chief of Naval Operations, and General H. H. "Hap" Arnold, Chief of the Army Air Force, argued that a combination of sea blockage and aerial bombardment could produce a Japanese surrender without the need for a ground invasion." Why did this view not become the basic plan? The CIA report goes on to indicate the opposing view: "Army Chief of Staff George C. Marshall and his Army planners, however, believed that Japan's surrender on the terms being demanded by the Allies [unconditional surrender], could be assured only by invasion of its home territory." Mr. MacEachin then adds that the debate "appears to have reflected organizational competition"; on one side the Navy and Air Force, on the other the Army.

In early July 1944, The Joint Chiefs of Staff approved a report by its planning group "that said unconditional surrender was to be achieved by undermining Japan's ability and will to resist through sea and air blockade, intensive air bombardments, and destruction of Japanese air and naval strength . . . and ultimately by invading and seizing objectives in the Japanese industrial heartland." The report continues, "The U.S. military leadership did not treat the situation as an either/or choice of invasion versus blockade and bombardment, but as a melding of the two concepts" (p. 1).

One published version of a Truman letter says that General Marshall told the president that an invasion might cost as many as a million casualties. The CIA report says that there has been "considerable debate" about the basis for such a figure, and that it may be "a product of an *ex post facto* campaign to but forth a rationale for having used the atomic bomb" (p. 27).

The need for an *unconditional surrender* was said to be based on the idea that we had forced Germany to accept that, and so the Japanese should be required to do no less. Even that was not totally agreed to by all top military personnel. Admiral Leahy "had supported the blockade-and-bomb strategy in earlier debates, and he was the only participant in the 18 June

1945 White House meeting recorded as saying that he did not think unconditional surrender was worth a high cost in American casualties" (p. 34).

"Whether the Allies' demands [unconditional surrender] could be achieved without capturing any part of the Japanese homeland was really what the debate between invasion and bomb-and-blockade was all about" (p. 37). (Refer back to Chapter 7 for a discussion of the morality of unconditional surrender.)

The prospect of the Soviet entry into the war's Pacific Theater has also been noted as a reason to go for an early defeat of Japan. However, the absence of public knowledge and discussion of the blockade alternative leads to a distortion of history. It is time to rectify that.

Low-intensity Conflicts, Covert Actions, and Psychological Warfare

We can think of a nuclear exchange as one end of a range of intensity, with small conflicts as the other end of the range. The small or low-intensity conflicts may or may not be proceeded by a declaration of war, and just what group is participating in and supporting the conflict may not be clear or public. Various names have been attached to these situations, usually *special operations, low-intensity conflicts,* or *covert operations.* In describing opponents, the terms are apt to be *guerrillas, subversives,* or *terrorists.* The term *insurgency* has become a bit more neutral; we might at this point respectably support or oppose a group described that way. (Where psychological warfare does not involve military force, it would not be included; see "Special Warfare," below.) The question for us is this: Does the professional military ethic need to be modified in the face of these somewhat new lowintensity conflict (LIC) situations and the several kinds of activity grouped under "special warfare"?

A New Morality for the New Style of Fighting?

A large volume of literature has been devoted to this matter in the last decade, and some of it bears on the question of morality.[13] The February 1987 issue of *Military Review* included a collection of articles that focused on LICs. In the introductory piece, Major Thomas J. Kuster, Jr., shocks us with the contemporary relevance of President John F. Kennedy's June 1962 graduation address at the U.S. Military Academy at West Point. Is a LIC a new form of warfare? Kennedy said that it is:

No nuclear weapons have been fired. No massive nuclear retaliation has been considered appropriate. This is another type of war, new in its intensity, ancient in its origin—war by guerrillas, subversives,

insurgents, assassins, war by ambush instead of by combat; by infiltration, instead of aggression, seeking victory by eroding and exhausting the enemy instead of engaging him. It is a form of warfare
uniquely adapted to what has been strangely called "wars of libera-
tion," to undermine the efforts of new and poor countries to maintain
the freedom that they have finally achieved. It preys on economic un-
rest and ethnic conflicts. It requires in those situations where we must
counter it, and these are the kinds of challenges that will be before us
in the next decade if freedom is to be saved, a whole new kind of
strategy, a wholly different kind of force, and therefore a *new and
wholly different kind of military training* (emphasis mine).[14]

Does this "new and wholly different kind of military training" require a
wholly new kind of military morality? That question must be sorted out
with special care. The terms that President Kennedy used include both acceptable and unacceptable actions under the Hague Rules and the Geneva
Conventions:

1. In his sentence describing this new warfare, the president's first
   three terms (*guerrillas, subversives, insurgents*) are political pejo-
   ratives and raise no matters of military morality. For example,
   they might have been applied to General Washington and his
   troops at Valley Forge. It can help our moral balance to recall that
   Washington's Army, the members of the Army that won our independence, could easily have been called guerrillas, subversives, and
   insurgents.
2. Assassins certainly violate the military code. The Hague Rules
   and FM 27-10 are quite clear about assassination.
3. The distinction between "war by ambush instead of by combat"
   is a bit strange here. An ambush is a legitimate tactic, *if* carried
   out by soldiers in uniform following the Hague Rules. The president, however, had a perfectly clear point if *ambush* is a general
   reference to acts of war without a declaration of war or to acts of
   war by persons who are not attached to any obvious military unit.
4. The reference to "war by infiltration instead of aggression" requires a definition of *infiltrate*. The common dictionary meanings
   are "to move into an organization surreptitiously, usually as its
   employee, for covert espionage" and "to move into an enemy
   area furtively on special military assignment." Where the reference is to espionage, the ordinary military response would seem
   to be adequate. Where the infiltration is done for the sake of sabotage or for attacks on civilian and other illegal targets, such acts
   are war crimes, and the president's tone of moral contempt is certainly well placed. The judgment about what is immoral infiltra-

tion and what is a morally acceptable action depends on intentions and actions. On the face of it, the conventional military ethic—(the Hague Rules and Geneva Conventions)—gives us the categories for classifying and understanding the varieties of infiltration (in uniform, out of uniform, with weapons, without weapons, and so forth).

5. The strategy of "seeking victory by eroding and exhausting the enemy instead of engaging him" is no violation of military honor. Why not exhaust the enemy instead of engaging in combat? The ancient tactic of the siege is a time-honored, perfectly acceptable example. Because *siege* carries the idea of surround and attack, a better example would be merely surrounding, cutting off all supplies, and waiting for surrender.

In view of the above, it would seem that President Kennedy's proper concern with the new threats from "guerrillas" and so forth did not call for new and different military responses. However, ten years before that address by the president, something new was underway.

Special Warfare

In 1952, the U.S. Army established a Psychological Warfare Center for developing capabilities for both psychological warfare and "special warfare." Some definitions are needed here. In 1962, ten years after the center was organized, Secretary of the Army Elvis J. Stahr defined the basic category:

Special warfare is . . . a term used by the Army to embrace all military and paramilitary measures and activities related to unconventional warfare, counter insurgency, and psychological warfare.[15]

The term *paramilitary* means auxiliary to or supplementary to a regular military force. For the other special terms, we find straightforward definitions in a historical study by Colonel Alfred H. Paddock, Jr.:

Unconventional warfare primarily encompassed guerrilla operations and subversion to be carried out within enemy or enemy-controlled territory by indigenous personnel, supported and directed by U.S. forces.

Counterinsurgency, on the other hand, included all actions, military and political, taken by the forces of the United States alone or in conjunction with a legal government to prevent or eliminate subversive insurgency.

Psychological warfare encompassed those activities planned and conducted to influence the opinions, emotions, attitudes, and behavior of the enemy, the indigenous population, and neutral or friendly foreign groups to help support U.S. objectives.16

Paddock adds that, according to Secretary Stahr, these three elements of special warfare included the capability to fight, "*as* guerrillas as well as *against* guerrillas." We should note, as Paddock does, that the concept of special warfare has undergone various changes in its less than thirty years' history since Secretary Stahr's comments. Our interest here, however, is not its history but its morality.

Several questions immediately occur. Are "indigenous personnel" used because we want them to commit war crimes on our behalf (as well as on their own)? Why do we "support and direct" them if they are not proper military units? Are the political actions mentioned under "counterinsurgency" actions to be taken by U.S. military units? What are the limits on these political/military acts? Here is one extreme example: May a U.S. soldier (in or out of uniform) run for political office in a foreign country in order to achieve U.S. military goals? While operating as "guerrillas," may U.S. soldiers commit war crimes? After some attention to covert operations, the subject of psychological warfare also remains to be considered.

Covert Operations

The term *covert operation* names an action that is planned to be secret—to be covered—so that it looks like something else. To remain unknown, personnel may need to be out of uniform. They may need to assume a completely nonmilitary identity, such as the "cover" of a businessperson, newsperson, teacher, nurse, doctor, diplomat, or other civilian position. This much is familiar in the history of spying, and we have considered some aspects of it in the chapter on espionage. The goal of the deception in these cases, however, is more than intelligence; it is military action. That makes a difference.

Covert operations, on their face, are illegal under the international conventions that define military honor. The synonyms for *covert* are *hidden* and *secret*. *Covert* and *honor* are far apart; we give up one when we choose the other. The honor of the soldier depends in part on his or her willingness to display loyalties publicly. Honorable soldiers are not ashamed to show the flag, to show the world exactly for whom they fight. When the uniform is publicly and proudly worn, it tells the world for whom the soldier fights. According to the well-known FM 100-1, "Soldiers have no time or use for untruths or double meanings. Especially under battle conditions, truthfulness and sincerity among soldiers have no substitutes.[17] In the face of special warfare, this statement now has something of an out-of-date tone.

The penalty for spying may range up to death. As mentioned in the chapter on espionage, spying is so widely practiced that it is expected and, therefore, not considered a war crime. Covert action that goes beyond collecting intelligence and produces overt acts of war, however, is a flat violation of military honor. The penalty for a military operation that violates the laws of war may also be death, plus the charge of a war crime. That covert actions are not honorable should be obvious from the preceding chapters and be reinforced by the principles of publicity that were emphasized in Chapter 9 on the dirty-hands theory of command.[18]

Psychological Warfare

A short, clear definition of psychological warfare was given by the Psychological Warfare Division attached to General Dwight D. Eisenhower's Headquarters (SHAEF) during World War II. This kind of warfare was to be "the dissemination of propaganda designed to undermine the enemy's will to resist, demoralize his forces and sustain the morale of our supporters."[19] Tactical or combat aspects include using public address systems, radios, mobile printing presses, and leaflet bombs. These activities had certain successes: It was reported that "both Germans and Italians [prisoners] stated that the content of the leaflets had greatly influenced their decision [to surrender]. They all insisted they were mostly impressed with the veracity of our leaflets."[20]

Where veracity is an effective weapon, there can hardly be any moral objection to its use; however, suppose that a lie can also induce enemy soldiers to surrender. Isn't such a lie—disinformation, as we are sometimes asked to name it—more humane than a bullet? This is a well-known question in ethical theory, and major figures in the history of philosophy have developed positions on it.[21] For our purposes here we might simply recall that in Chapter 4 we discussed the effect of the Hague Rules on treachery toward the enemy, along with legitimate and illegitimate strategy. It was emphasized there that such questions must be considered in light of the purpose of war, which is to have the enemy surrender and stay surrendered. Treachery harms that purpose; therefore, psychological warfare has the same parameters as other military operations and the same problem of finding a line between an acceptable strategy to mislead the enemy and a loss of "good faith." Just as there are limits to the way in which the Conventions permit questioning a POW, there are limits to psychological warfare.

Broadcasting directed at enemy personnel has become an expected variety of psychological warfare. "Axis Sally," "Tokyo Rose," "Lord Haw Haw," and "Hanoi Hannah" are some of the well-known radio personalities and programs intended to weaken enemy morale in World War II and the Vietnam War. Our question is the morality, not the effectiveness, of the effort. These particular commentators were presented as "civilian" broadcasters who regularly just happened to have impressively detailed information about military movements, even those involving very small units. (I was once in a group of eight men who arrived on Corsica from Italy, and Axis Sally reported it that evening in her very attractive voice.) The newest music and detailed comments about troop movements and bombings that were sometimes announced in advance were used as audience lures for propaganda. Then came passages explaining that the war was being lost, that further fighting was pointless, and that back home the girlfriends were probably just about to be unfaithful with safe and rich civilians who had avoided service.

We can hardly have a moral objection to this disk-jockey-propaganda kind of broadcast; however, people have objected to what was called "instigation of treason." This call is one beyond the expected inducement to surrender; it is a call to renounce sworn loyalty to one's government. To urge enemy soldiers to be disloyal to their commander or government entails a certain risk. The goal of the war may well be to have that government or that commander surrender. To instigate treason against that government may make it more difficult in some cases and less difficult in others to obtain that surrender. The main objection, however, is the moral maxim involved: If the call to the enemy soldiers is not merely to surrender but also to renounce their loyalty to their commander, then it may be understood as a call to break one's word whenever it seems advantageous to do so. The party that advocates such a maxim can hardly be trusted to keep its own word, to be bound by its own surrender agreements.

Of course, without falling into the moral problem of advocating opportunism, it is quite possible to argue that the enemy government is itself immoral and should not be defended. This matter is more complicated than a simple call to surrender or to renounce allegiance. A sophisticated psychological warfare unit, working on a clear factual basis, might be able to succeed in convincing its targets that their government was criminal—a *Vetbrecherstaat*, in Karl Jaspers's term.[22] Because there have certainly been criminal governments, our respect for an individual's loyalty must still permit moral distinctions between different objects of that loyalty. Brief slogans, however, may never be adequate as vehicles for convincing political analysis, and the matter can hardly be effectively transmitted in a short leaflet. Therefore, the basic material for such "strategic" political weapons as selling democracy is apparently in civilian hands, embassies, information centers (for example, the American Centers in many countries), and shortwave radio programs (such as Voice of America and Radio Moscow).

The concept of covert activity is also involved in psychological warfare. According to Paddock, during World War II, when the U.S. agencies were organized for psychological warfare, there were great differences in attitudes toward "open," "white," or "overt" as opposed to "closed," "black," or "covert" propaganda.[23] In the first kind of propaganda, you make public the authorship and purposes of the material; in the second, these are all concealed. The principles of publicity that emerged in the chapter on dirty hands can be decisive here: Only the material that can stand publicity is acceptable.

Where does this leave the morality of psychological warfare? When it is an effort to use the truth to gain a military goal, this type of warfare is to be accepted and applauded. When lying or "disinformation" is used, it cannot be accepted as an honorable weapon. (Of course, this is quite apart from legitimate tactics to conceal information from an enemy or to mystify or fool an enemy.)

Something of a stigma remains attached to the idea of defeating the enemy by tricky words rather than deeds. As one author writing about the period between the world wars put it: "Many military men wanted to have nothing at all to do with psychological warfare; it was not "real soldiering."[24]

Conclusions

Low-intensity conflicts involve combinations of factors. Honesty requires that we try to separate these different pieces and condemn *all but only* those that really violate the professional military ethic.

Does the conventional military ethic need to be ignored or violated in order to understand and deal with low-intensity conflicts? No, not on the basis of the evidence so far. For example, nothing in the *Military Review's* excellent issue on the subject (published in February 1987) requires that we give up the moral high ground found in a strict interpretation of the Hague Rules.

In a conflict between political and military interpretations of the bounds of a military action, we must carefully state the issues. Historians have noted "a theme that recurs at critical points throughout the history of special warfare—important governmental *civilians* intervene to prod hesitant and cautious uniformed Army leaders into taking action on concepts of an 'unconventional' nature" (emphasis mine).[25] This pattern is not surprising because there is a tradition of military honor, but there is nothing very clear on the matter of political honor.

As dangerous as these many low-intensity conflicts are and may continue to be for the democratic world, it may be even more dangerous to abandon the military tradition in the effort to combat them. When a local population cannot distinguish between the morality of our side and that of our opponents, we have lost! Of course, we must never drop our guard, but military honor *is* one of our guards. By not taking part in assassinations, actions out of uniform, violations of international law, or training others for such actions, we maintain both our own self-respect and the moral leadership that may well be significant in determining the outcomes of low-intensity conflicts.

Politicians ordinarily have little sense of military honor and the restrictions that it puts on acceptable missions. Of course, Paddock's history of special warfare regularly mentions that civilians have taken the lead in pushing "special" ways of fighting: Despite some civilian political pressure, "the Army continued through WWII to view unconventional warfare with a certain distaste."[26] More than just expressing "distaste," General Douglas MacArthur is said to have "steadfastly refused to permit OSS [the Office of Strategic Services] to operate in the South Pacific throughout the war, even when [General] William J. Donovan offered a plan to support guerrilla operations in the Philippines."[27] MacArthur's view must be balanced by others (for example, General Joseph Stilwell, who ended up praising the Special Forces they had first criticized).

The Fight against Al Qaeda, the Taliban, and Terror

What status is to be given to those who fight for AlQuada, and other non-governmental organizations? People who fight without the restrictions of the war conventions (Hague and Geneva), without concern for the soldierly requirements of at least a part of a uniform and of orders showing that they fight for an authority more than themselves, do not qualify for POW status. What are they defined as, then, when they engage in hostile activities? There is no internationally recognized category such as "illegal combatants." They are to be considered protected persons. The Geneva Convention on the protection of civilian persons, as interpreted by our FM 27-10 takes them to be included in "all persons who have engaged in hostile or belligerent conduct but who are not entitled to treatment as prisoners of war" (FM 27-10. para. 247, p. 98).

They, protected persons, must be "treated with humanity" (FM 27-10, p. 99), and not be made to suffer "murder, torture, corporal punishment, mutilation, and medical or scientific experiments . . . or any other measure of brutality whether applied by civilian or military agents" (FM 27-10, p. 107). Also, they may not be transferred to a country that is not a party to the Convention (FM 27-10, p. 111). What is called "rendition" is clearly ruled out by our own FM.

Is a fight against such persons a low-intensity conflict? Yes, unless the action calls for large-scale military units. There is no textbook answer to the question, "How many military aircraft are considered a large-scale operation?" In any event, the provisions of the war conventions are certainly applicable, significant, and necessary.

The military must have the moral courage to say "No" to politicians when they ask for violations of the international conventions that define military honor. Instead of quoting Clausewitz approvingly on the connection between politics and war, we might better think about General Eisenhower's response to Churchill's poison gas proposal mentioned earlier.

The problem of explaining military morality to the public cannot be ignored. The matter of the relations between the military and the civilian branches of the U.S. government is quite clear: The Constitution makes the military subservient to the commander-in-chief, the political leader. However, there is another facet to the matter. Illegal orders must not be carried out, but suppose the commander-in-chief gives an illegal order. While there seems to be no principle that can be trusted to resolve this matter in every situation, we must insist that a conflict of that sort be recognized, called to the attention of the commander-in-chief, and not decided without careful discussion of all the factors. Military morality is a military and a moral factor.

How should honorable soldiers respond when asked to violate the Hague and Geneva Conventions—to fight without a declaration of war, to commit war crimes while wearing or not wearing the uniform, to fight covertly—hiding their true allegiance. Responsible officers must have the guts, the moral courage, to respond as General Eisenhower did, to use the moral sense of an honest soldier.

12
Conclusions

The War Conventions as a Moral Code

Chapter 2 considered the range of moral styles. The rest of this book may be thought of as a discussion of various aspects of the war conventions. Now we have this question: What is the moral status of the style that follows the conventions and the moral status of the styles that do not? Specific and narrower questions about morality appeared in each chapter, but we are still left with the matter of the status of the conventions as a whole.

To judge moral status calls for us to locate three factors: (1) the moral *actor*, (2) the *beneficiary* of the acts, and (3) the nature of the *sacrifice* that the acts contain.

The Moral Actors

For the war conventions, the moral actor is sometimes the individual soldier, sometimes the individual politician, and sometimes that abstract thing called the nation. Even this outline is too spare a catalog of moral actors; it does not mention groups of soldiers (such as squads, companies, the Joint Chiefs, court-martial boards), and groups of politicians (congressional committees and review boards). These are the obvious moral actors who are to be restricted and judged by the Geneva and Hague Conventions; however, a most significant group has not yet been listed—the general public.

The public, citizens or not, are not merely the beneficiaries of the soldiers' and politicians' efforts; they are also moral actors. They finance the war, desire it more or less, and also sacrifice for it (even without considering the personal risks of area bombing). The Geneva Conventions include a section on publicizing their texts "as widely as possible, . . . and, in particular, to include the *study* thereof in their programmes of military and, if possible, *civil instruction,* so that the principles thereof may become *known* to all their armed forces *and to the entire population*" (FM 27-10, p. 11; emphasis mine).

In addition to this formal effort by the parties to the Geneva Conventions, there is also the clear statement in FM 27-10 that: "The customary law of war is part of the law of the United States, and . . . is binding upon the United States, *citizens of the United States, and other persons serving this country*" (FM 27-10, p. 7; emphasis mine). Why this effort to have the "entire population" know the principles of the conventions? One obvious reason is the fact that knowledge of what war crimes are becomes a restraint on their commission by the military. We pay attention to this below.

A second reason is to constrain the population from committing, asking for, or countenancing war crimes. Civilian populations have killed POWs without trial, engaged in marauding, and supplied poison gas for use in extermination chambers.[1] The war conventions restrict not only the military but the entire population to civilized conduct; therefore, the members of the general public are responsible for their own personal conduct as well as for the behavior of their employees.

For a principle to be morally acceptable on the basis of universal fairness, it must apply to everybody. The war conventions meet that test: They apply to all parties on all sides, whether in the military forces or not. They apply to the political leadership, the military leadership, and all the way up or down to include "the entire population" on all sides.

The Beneficiaries

Who are the beneficiaries of the war conventions? The titles of the Geneva Conventions (12 August 1949) specify the beneficiaries: "For the Amelioration of the Condition of the Wounded and Sick in Armed Forces in the Field," for the "Wounded, Sick and Shipwrecked Members of Armed Forces at Sea," "Relative to the Treatment of Prisoners of War," and "Relative to the Protection of Civilian Persons in Time of War." Because everyone is by definition either in the armed forces or not, these conventions apply to everyone. Combatant or not, one's status in war may easily change from one category to the other. The principle of universal fairness would seem to be comfortably satisfied by the universal range of benefit.

The conventions apply not only to all sides in international wars; they also carry minimum provisions: "In the case of armed conflict not of an international character" (FM 27-10, p. 9). Civil wars and lesser cases of "armed conflict" are covered by the main humanitarian restrictions, although the institutional details are somewhat different.

The beneficiaries are both the military personnel and the civilians on both sides. The military gain such benefits as POW status and freedom from "unnecessary suffering." Civilians gain a host of protections, as previous chapters have indicated: freedom from direct attack, warning of attack, various rights to medical care, religious freedom, protection against destruction of cultural artifacts, and so forth. Neutrals as well as belligerents gain protections. The beneficiaries are not only those involved in contemporary wars but also future populations that may be expected to benefit from the precedents of these restrictions on warfare.

Of course, those who would gain by breaking the conventions are not beneficiaries, at least not in the short run. Where torturing a captive to gain information would provide an advantage to certain parties, those parties are not beneficiaries, so they may think,—at least, not immediate beneficiaries. Where such actions as bombing hospitals and taking hostages are of use, commanders who must obey the restrictions may think that only their enemy benefits. The argument against those commanders holds that they benefit from the same restrictions on the enemy and from the improved chances of bringing the enemy to surrender.

Where a small revolutionary group may gain enormous leverage by taking hostages, that group can feel that the conventions benefit only the established powers. We discuss this "terrorist attitude" further in the next section on law. Excepting the "terrorist viewpoint," the benefits of the conventions are universal. Universal fairness is well satisfied.

The Nature of the Sacrifices

A sacrifice is not a trade, not a case in which one exchanges a loss somewhere for a gain somewhere else. A sacrifice is a loss—at least, a loss in the same currency, a loss in material terms—though there may be a gain in something intangible. To trade good treatment of your POWs for equal treatment of mine is not to sacrifice. To trade a restriction on gas warfare on my part for a similar one on your part is merely to trade. These are perfectly sensible trades, but they do not register as sacrifices.

Suppose that a commander refrains from obliterating a troublesome civilian village out of fear that knowledge of it may get out and provoke damaging publicity. This behavior would then be determined by personal or group advantage and not by morality. Suppose, however, that the action is somehow quite safe from publicity and the commander refrains from it merely because it would violate the convention. A command decision on that basis would be a sacrifice for the sake of the principles of the convention. Are there any such command decisions, decisions made purely out of respect for the laws of war and not for any material gain or trade and not even to impress one's subordinates? If there are, then the conventions have moral value. Conversely, if the conventions have moral value, they must occasionally produce such decisions.

Sacrifices made out of respect for the conventions can be made on lower levels than command decisions. A patrol that is itself in danger of discovery, yet does not seek safety by killing its POWs, would be an example of sacrifice. Would such behavior be stupid, rational, or inspired? Is it realistic or practical to be moral in this sense of morality? Chapter 2 considered several aspects of this issue. Our conclusion was that sacrifice is not "practical" in short-run material terms (gains) but has a different function. It is the way that values are produced. Our values are those beneficiaries for whom we are prepared to sacrifice.

To note that our sacrifices create our values is not to argue that we must constantly be sacrificing, constantly creating new values. We hardly expect our commanders to value the enemy more highly than our own forces and to show this by their sacrifices. We do expect some consistency in values so that we can predict and depend on the patterns of selfish and of sacrificial behavior by both our own forces and the enemy's. In the question of the sacrifices involved in the war conventions, we must acknowledge the risks that the conventions carry. For example, certain military objectives may have to be sacrificed in order to value the demands to fight without chemical weapons. That is the point—the moral point.

On any fair interpretation of the meaning of a moral code, the war conventions certainly qualify as such. The agents, the beneficiaries, and the sacrifices all satisfy the requirements of the moral style that we call universal fairness.

The War Conventions as International Law

A certain amount of power is needed to exercise the rights given by the conventions, and those without power of their own must depend on protecting powers, neutrals, the International Red Cross, and world public opinion. War criminals must be caught before they can be brought to trial, and they must be brought to trial before being punished. To carry out these and other provisions takes certain minimum powers, of course. The rights due under the conventions are not always enjoyed, as we all know. Laws are broken, conventions are violated, and recourse takes power. With all this given, are the conventions really laws or just empty political slogans?

Two different conceptions of law must be sorted out in order to respond to this question. From one viewpoint, laws exist only if there is a ready mechanism to punish violations. This view also holds that laws are an expression of the power to enforce and that it is pointless, therefore, to ask if a law is just or not. The only serious question is this: Is the law enforced or not? An unenforced law is a contradiction, not really a law. (This view is often associated with Thomas Hobbes.) Looked at in this way, there are no international laws unless there is an international police force with courts and punishments to deal with violations. We have some of these elements in place: an international court at The Hague and a United Nations with some power.

Chapter 4 put forward a conception of law attributed to Roger Fisher. He holds that the law has essentially two functions: (1) to tell us what to be shocked at and (2) to tell us what to do about it. The second function involves calling for the force of punishment, which is certainly critical, but the first function is also basic to the idea of law. This feature specifies exactly what counts as improper behavior or a violation of community values. We must know what a crime is. The Convention clearly explains that the international community forbids certain acts and would be shocked at their occurrence; therefore, we learn that we are to be shocked at their occurrence.

To say only this would be to pretend that the laws of war are merely positivistic assertions and that any law is as well founded as any other. On the contrary, the laws of war, the Conventions, can be explained and defended on a natural-law basis, and I have tried to do that. A brief (and oversimplified) explanation of these two poles of legal theory may be of some help.[2] A "positivistic" conception of law relies on the written law alone to decide whether an act is legal or not. A "natural law" position tries to relate a specific written law to a body of inherent rights in order to decide on the acceptability of that written formulation. This study has tried to gain some of the advantages of both viewpoints: It has assumed the natural law notion of human rights and has stressed the positivist attention to the exact wording of the Conventions.

According to critics, one of the tendencies of natural law theories and, therefore, a tendency in this book is the occasional blurring of the distinction between questions of morality and questions of law.[3] I admit the charge but offer the defense that the interest here is in making both individuals and institutions obey the law. A combination of fear of consequences and respect for morality may increase the chances of producing lawful behavior. Fortunately, the law to be obeyed can also stand moral scrutiny.

The answer to our question about the status of the war conventions should be clear: The Conventions are understood as international law because they serve as all laws do to indicate undesirable behavior and specify responses, even though the punishment mechanisms are *not yet* completely developed. One says "not yet" on the basis of certain assumptions about the history of law and legal systems. These assumptions come from Kant's philosophy of history, and they picture human civilizations as moving through history from small groups to tribes, villages, cities, states, nations, and finally to an international legal system. With each enlargement of the legal system, the human community becomes more moral because the degree of universal fairness is increased. More and more people come under the same set of rules. (For a more sustained description of Kant's view of history, see Appendix 1. It may also be noted that the U.S. Library of Congress has a program underway to put the definitions of key legal terms of all countries on a single data base, an aid to internationalism.)

After agreement that the laws of war are a legal system, the questions remain: Do they constitute a fair legal system? Do they give unfair advantages to established groups, to wealthy nations, to developed over less-developed nations? We must not be too hasty in responding to this charge.

A fair law must hold for everyone. That turns out, in the history of law, to be too broad. We have to refine the definition to the extent that a fair law must hold equally for everyone in the same circumstances. Why this qualification? Because of what we may call "the Red Lily effect."

The Red Lily Effect

When discussing this issue, we need the phrase *in the same circumstances* for a number of reasons. Those reasons were made quite clear in a famous passage in Anatole France's novel, *The Red Lily*,[4] mentioned earlier, in which the majestic equality of the law in France is demonstrated by the fact that no one, rich or poor, is allowed to sleep under the bridges in Paris, to steal bread, or to beg in the streets. Anatole France made an important point: Laws may be applied equally to all, but they do not affect all equally. In different financial circumstances, people have different interests in such activities as stealing bread. A law that is trivial for the rich is not so for the poor. Likewise, a law forbidding a particular weapon is trivial for a poor nation that does not have such weapons but it is an operative restriction on a rich nation that does have those weapons. In the other direction, a law requiring a high standard of housing for POWs may be a restriction for a poor nation but not for a rich one.

The "Red Lily effect" cannot be overcome by any magic words or tricks. People or nations in different circumstances are not affected equally by laws, including the Hague and Geneva Conventions. Wealthy nations with highly trained and equipped military forces may find it easy to obey the Hague and Geneva Conventions. Poor nations or groups may simply not have the resources to fight within the bounds of the Conventions. For example, suppose that a nation cannot afford complete uniforms for all personnel. The Conventions require that members of "volunteer corps" be treated as POWs when captured provided (to mention only this point) that they "have a fixed distinctive sign recognizable at a distance" (FM 27-10, p. 25). That rule does not require a complete uniform made by the best tailors in the world; it does require, at least, some clear "sign," some bit of material. If a group cannot afford it, they don't qualify for POW status (except in special situations, such as when there is no time to meet the requirement). The intent of the Convention seems to be to minimize the Red Lily effect, but that effect has not been and cannot be absolutely eliminated.

Does the Red Lily effect mean that the war conventions are unfair because they cannot put all parties on an absolutely equal level? Some groups may think so and give this as their reason for turning to terrorism as a weapon to equalize matters; however, their argument is not compelling because of the fairly minimal requirements of the Conventions and their enormous moral value to all parties. Chemical and biological warfare can sometimes be expensive. The restrictions on those kinds of warfare would not seem a special burden to small groups. Assassinations and taking hostages are not extremely expensive activities, and small groups obviously use these methods. (The arguments against them have already been considered in earlier chapters and need not be repeated here. Their availability at low cost still does not make a case for their acceptability. We must, however, admit that wealthy nations or groups need not stoop to taking hostages, while poor ones might.)

The Red Lily effect applies to all laws, but the laws of warfare seem to have been framed with particular care to avoid gross inequalities; that is, unfair applications to groups with different economic resources. We must always pay attention to the argument that a particular law can be improved. No laws, including the war conventions, have dropped from heaven in perfect form. Some residue of the Red Lily effect cannot be denied. For example, lions do have an advantage over mice: It is a bit easier to imagine a lion eating a mouse than the converse. In the nature of things, the powerful have advantages over the weak; but this is no reason to deny the value of law, generally, or the laws of war, specifically. Rather, it is a reason to insist on their value in order to protect the weak.

Education: Military and Civilian

Military Education

Military education must include serious efforts to teach the Geneva and Hague Conventions. This requires that soldiers pass examinations before completing basic training and certainly before receiving a commission. Merely giving lectures and showing films does not mean that the soldiers understand the Conventions. As experienced college teachers know, alert expressions and busy note-taking are no substitutes for testing. Until teachers grade the first set of examinations, they do not really know whether the lectures have succeeded. Ideas of war and war crimes are new to most students and, like everything new, to be well understood they must be field-stripped, examined, and put back together. These ideas must be discussed and argued, and then individual candidates must be tested on these matters.

To send military personnel into the field without teaching and testing their knowledge of the Conventions can be a dangerous mistake. To put weapons in the hands of those who do not know the restrictions on their use is to invite war crimes. The establishment of an Army Ethics Unit at Fort Benjamin Harrison a number of years ago was a healthy sign of new concern. The creation of that unit is just one of the activities that indicate that many voices are in agreement on this matter.

We can easily imagine a variety of educational activities. Military attaches of foreign governments could be invited to observe the teaching and testing of the laws of warfare. U.S. military attaches could accept invitations to observe the same in foreign military academies and training programs. Military secrets are not at risk: Each of the 170 or so governments that signed the Conventions has agreed to teach them to their military forces. All sides benefit from effective teaching and testing.

It might also be of service to give a standard test on the Conventions to candidates for commissions and to prospective graduates of basic training in several countries. To encourage interest in this idea, Appendix 3 offers a sample multiple-choice test on the Conventions.

Civilian Education

As pointed out earlier, the Geneva Conventions include the requirement that the contracting parties teach the contents of the war conventions to both the military and the general population in each country. They are to try to teach civilians, but it does not appear as if this part of the agreement has been given any attention. No government seems concerned with the matter. Consider the results. An eighteen-year-old can find him- or herself in service and, just a few months after leaving high school, may be carrying lethal weapons into military action. It takes time to think about and understand such aspects of a war crime as civilian immunity, forbidden weapons, military honor, legal and illegal orders, rights of POWs, and the status of cemeteries, hospitals, and buildings used exclusively for religious activities. No quick magic in basic training can replace the need for discussion and thought over time.

An obvious response would be to introduce into the high school curriculum a unit on the war conventions. Coming one or two years before graduation, it might well fit into American history, civics, or social studies courses. Various pacifist objections need to be met, but these can be overcome on the strength of several significant aspects of the proposal. First, the Conventions are matters of U.S. law as well as international law, and keeping our citizens ignorant of those laws is hardly an acceptable mission for the school system. Second, protection for the population of the world is at stake, and neglecting that challenge is educationally indefensible. Third, students' own safety and ability to make moral judgments may depend on having time to study, discuss, and think about the Conventions. By starting to think about the subject a few years before the need for personal decisions arises, students will have time to develop more mature judgments. What objections can there be to the education of high school students in a basic subject that may involve their own lives and the security of their families and their nation? If they are too young to think, then they are too young to fight. A distaste for war is understandable and acceptable; a distaste for reality is not.

Beyond the points made above, a fundamental reason for making the general public aware of the principles of the war conventions remains this: the assumption that, like all other people, military personnel are always drawn toward two opposed bases for action—the selfish and the moral. An aware public, like a policeman on the scene, makes it more likely that the laws will be obeyed.

Military Honor: A Romantic Myth or a Serious Matter?

In his carefully prepared history of U.S. military strategy and policy, *The American Way of War,* Professor Russell F Weigley documents the "unlimited annihilative aims" that have often characterized his subject.[5] Weigley forces us to consider the implications of what he calls the "ingrained American habit of thinking of war in terms of annihilative victories."[6] He gives examples to explain how this "habit of thinking" developed: "Indian campaigns early encouraged the notion that the object of war is nothing less than the enemy's destruction as a military power. The Civil War also suggested that the complete overthrow of the enemy, the destruction of his military power is the object of war."[7] World War II continued that idea of strategy: "The strategy of annihilation became characteristically the American way in war."[8]

Weigley does give his readers examples of some current opposition to his main theme. He develops the story of those who now press for "flexible response" and limited war. He finds, however, that "what we do today is governed at least as much by the habits of mind we formed in the relatively remote past as by what we did and thought yesterday."[9]

How does the habit of thinking of war as being aimed at annihilation of the enemy fit with the demands of military honor? This is one of the questions that face anyone with serious interest in military honor. Military honor requires that the enemy be treated with certain kinds of respect: respect for enemy soldiers' rights as POWs, respect for the enemy's civilians, and respect for the enemy's religious and medical institutions.

The attitude of the colonists who fought the American Indians developed from desperation, leading them to classify themselves as "civilized" and their enemy as savages.

> When the English colonists in America fought the Indians, they often fought in what both sides recognized as a contest for survival. In King Philip's War of 1675–76, the Indians came fearfully close to obliterating the New England settlements. When the colonists rallied enough to save themselves, they saw to it that their victory was complete enough to extinguish the Indians as a military force

throughout the southern and eastern parts of New England. . . . Not every Indian war was so overtly a struggle for existence as King Philip's War. . . . But the logic of a contest for survival was always implicit in the Indian wars [as it never was in the eighteenth-century European wars].[10]

The colonists' victory over the Indians was not only complete enough to "extinguish" them as a military force; it just about extinguished them in that part of New England. The American habit or appetite for annihilation had been created and was later to be phrased as "unconditional surrender."

To demand unconditional surrender is to demand that the enemy claims no rights. To claim no rights is to abandon the claim to be human! Turning again to Weigley, we find him calling "unconditional surrender . . . a characteristically American war aim" and a "policy objective which accorded thoroughly with the preferred American military strategy of annihilation."[11]

The problem should now be clear. As phrased above, How does this American habit of thinking of war as aimed at annihilation or unconditional surrender fit with the practice of military honor? It does not. Honor respects the enemy; annihilation does not.

Only by changing the concept of the aims of war can the concept of military honor be fully expressed. This change may require a very painful re-thinking of American military history, and that may require more honesty than nations usually show.

Abandoning the notion of war as annihilation is not a new idea. Shortly after the end of World War II, Admiral Arthur W. Radford said, "In planning to wage a war . . . we must look to the peace to follow. . . . A war of annihilation might possibly bring a Pyrrhic military victory, but it would be politically and economically senseless."[12] To extend the Admiral's point (and ignore the inter-service rivalries that were involved in many such high flights of statesmanship), as we exchange the aim of annihilation for the aim of a satisfactory peace, we may expect to find that military honor becomes increasingly significant. In this sense, we mean military honor to indicate the willingness to obey the laws of warfare, even at the cost of defeat.

Is this a recipe for defeat? No, but it does mean that there are certain things that an honorable soldier will not do even if victory depends on the decision. What are those things, and are they absolutes in any situation? Of course, these things must be affected by the context. Only mathematics is, as it is often defined, "invarient under translation"; that is, only mathematics remains exactly the same regardless of the situation—the context. Mathematical laws have no moral style; human soldiers do. A variation in human styles will still be possible even when the demands of military honor become stronger. As Chapter 2 argued, a choice of weights between Type I and Type II risks of error is a moral choice. In choosing a certain preference between success of the military mission and military honor, we make a moral decision.

Of course, morality is not completely ascribed to the whim of the moment. As Chapter 2 says, the acceptable range of styles must fall within the limits of universal fairness. Outside those limits, a style of action is not moral.

Why care about military honor? To expand on Admiral Radford's point, remember that the goal of war is an acceptable peace, not annihilation. The effort to force the enemy to surrender requires that there be acceptance rather than hate for the dominant power. That is the utilitarian reason. As stated in Chapter 3, there is also the foundation in human dignity.

Is it really necessary to obey the laws of war in order to make peace with the enemy? It may be argued that despite the area bombing of World War II, Germany and Japan accepted the terms of surrender and show no signs of reneging. On the other hand, relations between China and Japan are still cool. The Japanese army is still thought of in terms of "the Rape of Nanking" and the germ warfare experimentation camp in Harbin, China. Why the difference? Here is at least one speculation, ignoring economic factors, to explain it.

The Allies violated noncombatant immunity by such actions as their "strategic" bombing, the fire-bombing of Dresden, and the bombing of Tokyo. However, the German atrocities in their concentration camps gave the strategic bombing something of the sense of reprisal. The Japanese attitude toward the Americans is complicated by many factors—among them, the rather good behavior of the occupation forces after the surrender. Informal reports by adults who lived through that period say that they were quite pleasantly surprised by the Americans because they expected the victors to behave like Japanese troops, but instead, they were most gentlemanly. (Such comments cannot be accepted without analysis, but they have come to me from casual acquaintances as well as neighbors in Tokyo. Even some of the victims of Hiroshima, the "Hiroshima Maidens," appear less critical of the United States than of Japan, presumably because of dissatisfaction with their own government's assistance to them and gratitude for the cosmetic surgery that they received in the United States.)

While there are a number of factors involved in former enemies' attitudes toward the United States, the Chinese have different memories of their enemy. December 1987 was the fiftieth anniversary of Japan's massacre of three hundred thousand Chinese in Nanking (Nanjing). The atrocities that took place there earned the event the name of "The Rape of Nanking." Reports say that during the first six weeks of the Japanese occupation, more than two hundred thousand people in the city, including civilian women and children, were killed mercilessly as suspected guerrillas by the Japanese Army. More than twenty thousand women were raped before being killed.[13] At the Harbin (North China) germ warfare experimentation camp, "prisoners were infected with cholera, syphilis and the plague, and the speed of their deaths studied. . . . Blood was drained from some captives and replaced with that of horses, others were left to freeze to death. . . . Their captors called them 'maruta,' logs of wood."[14] With behavior like this, it is not surprising that the Chinese are still bitter toward the Japanese.[15]

What accounts for the dishonorable behavior of the Japanese military? Again, a variety of factors would have to be weighed in a study of this matter, and what follows merely touches on a few elements. Of course, the well-known racism of the Japanese cannot be ignored. If they believed that their emperor is actually divine and they are the greatest race in the world, no enemy could be on their level and thereby deserve their respect. The Japanese Military Code had certain such relevant items as the *Gunjin Chokuyu*—the declaration that disobedience to a superior order is to be treated as treachery against the emperor. Even after the traitor's execution, his dishonorable act was reported to the community in which his family lived, and the family was ostracized. A soldier's fear that his family would suffer in this way must have been a significant part of the pressure to obey every order, inhumane or not. The *Senjin-kun,* a declaration by General Hideki Tojo, maintained that the "honorable" spirit of the soldier is to prefer death rather than dishonorable surrender. This attitude created a tendency to despise POWs who, according to one informant, "were thought to be lost to shame." Of course, the second declaration of the U.S. Code of Conduct for armed forces also specifies no surrender (see Chapter 3) but leaves the possibility of an honorable surrender.

Comments on the dishonorable behavior of certain Japanese units are somewhat accidental; examples of dishonorable behavior can be found on all sides in all wars. The atomic bomb that was *perhaps* aimed at what it hit in Nagasaki (the Urakami Roman Catholic Cathedral) does not give the United States an episode for pride.[16] The Japanese may well have thought that honor as a soldier required exactly such behavior at Nanking. We are not born knowing what is honorable or what is moral; we must learn it, and after learning it, we must practice it. Without practice, we do nothing well. That maxim, common in the sports world, must also be used in teaching military honor—hence, the stress earlier in this chapter on serious education concerning the military code. But education is not sufficient to guarantee honorable behavior. Indeed, nothing can guarantee it, but we can hope to increase the chances for honorable behavior by combining education, example, and law.

Education requires information about the Conventions. That is the easiest part, and we have considered some suggestions for it. *Example* requires the inspiration of those who have chosen the honorable course. We might look to the men who refused to take part in the My Lai massacre for one example. The matter of honor and the interpretation of its classical examples are sometimes quite ambiguous. Consider the famous story reported by Cicero in *De Officiis* (Book III, Chapter 26):

Marcus Atilius Regulus commanded the Roman Army in the First Punic War, until captured by the Carthaginians in 255 B.C. After a time in captivity he was dispatched to Rome to try to arrange the return of some high-ranking prisoners. To kindle his ardour, the Carthaginians extracted an oath that, if he failed, he would return to Carthage to be put to death by torture. On reaching Rome, however, he urged the Senate to refuse, since the prisoners were worth more to Carthage than he was to Rome. His advice carried the day. Then, unmoved by the pleas of friends and peers, he insisted on keeping his oath and sailed back to Carthage. There he was returned to prison and kept awake until he collapsed and died.[17]

We may well consider whether this is the history of a rational man. What would we think if an American general had been captured by the Viet Cong and sent to Washington on the same terms? Would we expect or even want him to keep his oath and return after sabotaging his mission? Should he, or must we call it irrational if he did return? (These questions about the contemporary evaluation of Regulus are raised by Martin Hollis in "Reasons of Honour.") Of course, we wonder today why Regulus accepted the mission if he intended to advise Rome against the exchange. He may have come to his conclusion after starting the trip or reaching Rome. But that's not the relevant question. The matter that has interested Cicero's readers for centuries is the question of the sense of honor, the rationality of it in that sort of case. Having accepted the mission, how should one behave?

Most interesting examples of honor are complicated, but even the extreme cases are pedagogically useful. They give us images of various alternatives, and without images and models, judgment is very problematical. Tennyson's poem, "The Charge of the Light Brigade," gives another example of military honor, one that presses both the thought that there is something beautiful in such examples of honor and the thought that the line between honor and stupidity is hard to draw. In fact, that line may not exist.

When is the sacrifice justified? To that, each moral agent must give a personal answer, based on a personal concept of desirable style. At one end of that range, there is the view of Hobbes quoted in Chapter 3, "That which gives to human actions the relish of justice, is a certain nobleness or gallantness of courage, rarely found, by which a man scorns to be beholden for the contentment of his life, to fraud, or breach of promise". In this "heroic" image, opportunism is never considered, while in an alternative model, opportunism is the first principle. Perhaps it would be empty romanticism to expect to find or produce easily the "certain nobleness" that Hobbes defines. The world, however, gets on without angels. If we can be satisfied with less-than-perfect "nobleness" or honor, we can expect that the need for a decent self-image does give us at least the possibility of improving the chances of honorable behavior when it counts—that is, *when opportunism would produce a war crime*. At the least, we ought to avoid spreading the acceptance of opportunism.

Law is a guide to both military honor and civilian honor. The law tells us what is expected and what is forbidden. For the military, the picture is compounded by the need to consider both domestic law and the laws of warfare. The emphasis in this study has been on the role that the Conventions can play in teaching all parties just what is and is not acceptable. Ideally, we requite "going by the book," tempered by a bit of humanity and judgment. Because judgment may not be teachable, officer selection must never be casual. We cannot escape the need for officer-candidate selection that includes personal interviews and serious life-experience evaluations, as well as whatever examinations we have and can develop, but these comments on officer selection must not be misunderstood. The dependable basis for obedience to law is fear of publicity and concern for the respect of one's comrades. These, rather than "strength of character," are the assumptions about human nature that the U.S. Constitution presupposes in its separation-of-powers construction.

Two great philosophers have given us opposing ideas on the matter of trusting "virtuous" leaders. Plato thought that with proper selection and education dependable "philosopher-kings" could be produced. Many centuries later, Kant replied: "That kings should be philosophers or philosophers kings is neither to be expected nor to be desired, for the possession of power inevitably corrupts reason's free judgment."[18] While there may be historical examples to be cited by followers of both Plato and Kant, I find Kant's view the more dependable to the modern "liberal." Following Kant, then, while we must try to present our officer candidates and all military personnel with the ideal of an honorable military, we had better not hope that we can trust them with unchecked power after touching them with a magic wand.

Plato gave us a famous test of personal honor—the idea of the ring of Gyges. According to his story, a shepherd in the service of the ruler of Lydia found an old ring and put it on his finger. He discovered that it had a somewhat dramatic property: If the collet of the ring were turned in one direction, the shepherd became invisible; if turned in the other direction, he reappeared again. What would one do with such a ring, such power? Plato's story tells us that the shepherd "seduced the king's wife and with her aid set upon the king and slew him and possessed his kingdom."[19] Naturally.

Can we teach military morality by immoral means, by lying about our military history? It is rather odd pedagogy to try to teach honesty by lying about General Washington and the cherry tree. Plato's "noble lie"[20] for the better governance of his city does not seem compelling to the modern democrat. Plato, to convince the citizens to sacrifice themselves for the benefit of his perfect city, invents the myth of the metals, but because Plato thought that a myth—not a lie, but a suggestive story—was needed to make the citizens sacrifice, must we accept that strategy for citizens of a democratic state? I hope not. I assume, without arguing it here, that the citizens of the

United States will defend their nation without being lied to. I assume that we citizens of a democracy *can stand the truth* (in the William James phrase) and that we are tough-minded enough to choose our own style of behavior in a crisis. Most important, no one else is trustworthy enough to make that decision for us. I take it that the same sort of argument applies to military education: The truth about our military history and the truth about the world situation are necessary but not sufficient to increase the chances of honorable military behavior. Nothing is sufficient, but a balance of education, example, and the fear of the law is the best that we can do. Of these, *the fear of the law is the most dependable,* which brings us to the subject of publicity about military activities.

The Need for Publicity

Two obvious demands come into conflict. One is the need for secrecy in operational planning, strategic planning, weapons development, and related matters. The other is the need for a democracy to know what its own forces are doing on its behalf. The problem is to balance the two possible risks of error. One risk is the error of telegraphing one's punches, thus helping the enemy prepare. The other risk is keeping the public ignorant of what they are supporting, of what is being done in their name. A dictatorship has a much simpler problem: The public can merely be fed official handouts on whatever the dictator thinks they should be told.

Can a democracy fight a war as a democracy? Nietzsche's warning always hangs over us: "He who fights with monsters should be careful lest he thereby become a monster."[21] The enemy is usually thought of as a monster, and sometimes the enemy is. Nietzsche does not convince us, however, that he has seriously dealt with the problem of fighting monsters. It may not be possible to fight them without becoming like them, becoming one of them, having dirty hands, as Chapter 9 put it. Just mentioning all the problems involved in war between a democracy and other forms of government would take us far from the scope of this book; we will pay some attention only to the question of limiting the reporting by the news media. Can the United States fight without giving up the First Amendment to the Constitution? This amendment holds that "Congress shall make no law . . . abridging the freedom of speech or of the press."

"Loose lips sink ships" is a perfectly reasonable slogan on the walls of embarkation ports. To limit freedom of speech about troop movements before they take place is an obvious requirement. In World War II the news media never violated that limitation, never reported movements *before* they were completed. That also held true in Korea and Vietnam. What, then, is the problem? A ferocious debate has developed since Vietnam over the question of the impact of news coverage, particularly television coverage, of that war. Now, in Iraq, we have the pattern of "embedding" the press with military units.

Was the efficiency and the chance of success of the U.S. military effort in Vietnam damaged by the intense television coverage? An example of the debate over this appeared in the February 1987 issue of *Military Review*.[22] One writer, Major Cass D. Howell (U.S. Marine Corps), held that the "unhappy conclusion [of the Vietnam War]" was brought about "by a failure of U.S. will and not by a failure of U.S. arms." Howell blames television reporting for producing a shift of national feeling from support to opposition to the war effort and holds television responsible for giving the American public the idea that the Vietnam War was different, more immoral, than previous American wars. He gives examples of immoral acts in other wars to demonstrate that American forces were equally immoral in earlier wars.[23] Major Howell supports his point with examples such as, "During the Battle of the Coral Sea in 1942, the survivors of sunken Japanese transports were strafed in their lifeboats until the sea ran red with their blood. Commander 'Mush' Morton routinely surfaced his submarine to machine gun Japanese civilians on their fishing boats. Other wars were no different."[24]

In these other wars, the home front did not see the blood in color on their TV sets every night. So, Major Howell states, "In our next war, the television cameras must stay home! Television reporters can accompany their print brethren to the battlefield, but they must not be allowed to take cameras with them. They can file written dispatches or depart the country to file a videotape report sans battlefield footage."

Howell concludes that "Television is too powerful . . . it has too much impact. It is clear that if we accept this erosion of public will power, our cause, *however just and necessary*, is doomed" (emphasis mine). The decision on the justice and necessity of our cause is certainly a matter of the highest moral seriousness. Howell seems to want that decision made once by the political leadership of the nation and then not reconsidered as we go . . . understandable, but undemocratic in the extreme.

A variety of objections must be faced: (1) the people may *want* to reconsider, (2) the political leadership may have made an erroneous decision, (3) the situation may have changed, and (4) the cost in material, human, and or moral terms may have been wrongly estimated. *The tradition that a soldier must obey the last order presupposes that the order may be changed.* The ultimate authority must be as well informed as possible. In a democracy that authority is the people, not the commander-in-chief. Hence the public must learn the results of their military activity and learn in time to do something significant if they wish. They are also responsible for their activity; television can inform them impressively, as Howell fears.

In the debate in *Military Review*, Howell's opponent, Colonel Wallace B. Eberhard (U.S. Army Reserve, Retired), argued that public opinion about the Vietnam War was changed by a complex of factors and not by television alone. He held that the viewpoint behind the "sunshine laws" at state and federal levels is the one that ought to prevail. The public has "the right of access to events" and that—Eberhard's standpoint—includes events on the battlefield. (He is now a professor of journalism.)

Of course, continually changing and reversing orders can make efficient command impossible, but the case that Howell deals with, the Vietnam War, was not a history of continually reversing orders. Rather it was a slow change of mind of mind that took years to solidify enough to produce new orders—hardly an example of the inability of a democracy to be efficient while being democratically informed of the occurrence of war crimes. The main point is that a war is not just the business of professional soldiers; it is also the business of the nation for whom they fight. That the military may make the greater sacrifices does not justify keeping the public ignorant. Actually, area bombing, even with conventional weapons, may put the public on an equal level of sacrifice.

The argument against battlefield publicity is not an effort to keep the enemy from knowing what happened. After an action, they do know. It is an effort to keep the home front from knowing, and that suggests that the command is ashamed of something it has done. If so, that is exactly why the public should be informed. It was the home front that Major Howell was afraid to inform. He feared their response to a television-edited version of the truth. (Needless to say, all versions are edited in some fashion.) Of course the public appetite is a mixture and not merely a high-minded interest in preventing war crimes; the public appetite is also the fascination with drama, with life-and-death events. *The fear of publicity is one of the controls on excess.* It can function this way in all governmental institutions, civilian as well as military, but the risks of error are so high in military activity that the need for publicity can hardly be overstated.

To repeat Kant's view, as stated in Chapter 9: "Every claim of right must have this capacity for publicity."[25] Kant gives a negative and a positive principle of publicity. The negative reads: "All actions that affect the rights of other men are wrong if their maxim [principle] is not consistent with publicity."

Recall the stress in earlier chapters on the soldiers' pride in openly announcing to the world their loyalty by wearing a uniform that told the story. This negative principle of publicity is obeyed by openly declaring war before attack, by openly (in uniform) carrying on military operations, and by accepting the news media anywhere (with the obvious restrictions, noted earlier, on publicity *before* actions and on such activities as troop movements and strength).

The positive principle adds another element to the political side of the story: "All maxims that require publicity (in order not to fail of their end) agree with both politics and morality."[26] A document of surrender is a joint political statement and needs publicity in order to work, as this second principle asserts. This idea also applies to matters, such as a truce, that require publicity in order to take place. At this point, Kant's principles are so obviously moral requirements that they need no further explanation or argument.

Enemy Morality

The question of confidence in the morality of possible enemy forces must occur to any reader who has come this far. A parallel question arose in ancient ethical thought. Can there be just one honest person in a community? Can such a person exist? The more productive line of thought proposes to raise the level of the community rather than deal with a world that has just one honest person or just one honorable nation.

In our case, we want all the nations of the world—at least the 170 or so who have signed the Geneva Conventions (and the Gas and later protocols)—to make serious efforts to obey them. That obedience requires, as stressed above, teaching the Conventions to both military and civilian personnel. To increase international confidence in the educational level of the military (as proposed above), all nations ought to conduct testing of their military forces on the war conventions using a standard test. Such a test might be administered by the International Committee of the Red Cross or a committee of the Security Council of the United Nations. An international committee of training officers with the power to give tests and publicize the results would be an impressive educational tool. Fear of embarrassment at poor performance would become a motive for taking the subject seriously. An honorable military establishment should have the courage to risk such public testing.[27]

Summary of Themes

Law: It is the nature of law to tell us what to be shocked at and what to do about it. Laws do not prevent crime; they tell us what we are to call a crime and what responses to make. These features of law also hold for the laws of war—the International Conventions.

The Purpose of War: The goal of a war is to win, and that means to have the enemy surrender and remain surrendered. For several reasons, a certain level of human rights must be observed, including the need to win the war, to have the enemy accept surrender.

Universal Fairness: The boundaries of a morally acceptable rule are fixed by the principle that only rules that could apply to all are fair.

Moral Pluralism: Within the bounds of universal fairness, more than one style, more than one way of balancing the two risks of error, can be moral.

Honor: Military honor has dual requirements: obeying the commanding officer *and* obeying the Geneva and Hague Conventions. When these two requirements conflict, the Conventions are the legal orders, even when obeying them hurts.

Total War: War becomes steadily more democratic; everyone is at risk. All, not just the military personnel, must be educated, must know the laws of warfare. Everyone—officers, enlisted personnel, and civilians—is involved and responsible for their moral decisions.

The Professional Military Ethic: Where military honor forbids or demands an action, that honor should be the deciding factor. The matter may be explained to others, but not ignored. *The military must not resign its conscience to the politicians, or to anyone else.* The commander-in-chief must be obeyed: When honor forbids that, a soldier must resign rather than commit a war crime.

Courage: Immanuel Kant, on whose work this study relies, will have the last word, despite the fact that he can hardly be understood fully by reading a fragment out of context.

> For what is that which is, even to the savage, an object of the greatest admiration? It is a man who shrinks from nothing, who fears nothing, and therefore does not yield to danger, but rather goes to face it vigorously with the most complete deliberation. Even in the most highly civilized state this peculiar veneration for the soldier remains, though only under the condition that he exhibit all the virtues of peace, gentleness, compassion, and even a becoming care for his own person; because even by these it is recognized that his mind is unsubdued by danger. Hence whatever disputes there may be about the superiority of the respect which is to be accorded them, in the comparison of a statesman and a general, the aesthetical judgment decides for the latter. War itself, *if it is carried on with order and with a sacred respect for the rights of citizens,* has something sublime in it, and makes the disposition of the people who carry it on thus only the more sublime, the more numerous are the dangers to which they are exposed and in respect of which they behave with courage (emphasis mine).[28]

Appendix 1
Are the Hague and Geneva Conventions Obsolete?

REALITY TODAY

The reader of these chapters must be far from satisfied. The argument, thus far, has assumed that the fundamentals of moral military operations remain what they were taken to be about sixty years ago, at some point just after World War II. The fundamentals of the Geneva and Hague Conventions and the traditions closely connected with them have been used as the text and spirit of the subject. The contemporary world, however, features military actions without formal declarations of war or distinctions between combatant and civilian and with frequent taking of hostages and frequent acts of terrorism. There has also been open derision toward the Geneva Conventions. Therefore, the question is inescapable: Is the viewpoint of this book completely out of date?

Every subject has a history, a pattern of change over time. We should not be shocked to consider the hypothesis that the basic criteria of morality in military action also change over time. Let us give this hypothesis a fair construction and examine it. Each of the charges, above, needs attention.

In the stylized game called *fencing*, the rules specify that combatants must warn "On guard" before the first attack—a reasonable rule for a game between courtly ladies and gentlemen or between two romanticized medieval knights. Hostilities in our age, however, are not restricted to gentlemen. When the goal is more than a game, when it is of enormous moment, we would be childish to act as if we were merely fencing. Responsible guardians must and do put their commission as guardians above their romantic fantasies of being gentlemanly fencers.

There has been a great shortage of declarations of war in the past thirty years, but there has been no shortage of hostile acts. Many tons of bombs have been dropped and harbors mined without declarations of war. Perhaps the term *war* is obsolete and with it the need for a formal declaration. Politicians who say they abhor *war* seem to find *defensive actions* much easier to explain. And, the best defense may turn out to be an attack. I do not find this argument compelling, but I will hold my response until the other parts of the story are in.

The line between combatant and civilian is certainly a fundamental of the "old" ethic. That ethic assumed that a society could employ professional guardians to do the work and suffer the risks of combat on its behalf. As soldiering became more and more technical, using specialized and complicated weapons, it certainly seemed to require a professional force. To increase that force in emergencies, a draft of untrained recruits might be necessary, but such recruits would need long basic and specialized training in order to be able to serve in a modern force. To become soldiers, they had to learn the profession of arms—no notion of farmers merely taking the Kentucky long rifle from the rack over the fireplace and fighting for their country. With the idea of a distinct profession of soldiers came the notion of a distinct ethic that held between them. These professionals treated each other differently from civilians and had a different respect for each other than for civilians. The line between the professional warriors and the noncombatants became clear, and it was a point of honor to respect that line.

What happened to the old world of the previous paragraph? The story can be told quickly. Of the many forces at work in the world, we need to consider only two: the well-known and celebrated advance of specialization and the equally well-known and (one hopes) celebrated advance of democracy. Specialization and high technology produce the *military* need for an ever-increasing use of *civilian* scientists, specialists, factories, advisors, people, and products of many kinds. Military professionals cannot manage without constant research and without constantly replacing their computers, software, and hardware of all kinds. They must have the resources of the entire economy at their disposal or risk obsolescence, which means loss of the power to defend their society.

This need to connect closely, if not to make indistinguishable, civilian and military institutions leads to an obvious result. As it becomes almost impossible to separate one from the other, it becomes impossible to attack one apart from the other. Area bombing, therefore, is defensible because it is now a total society that protects itself, attacks others, and is heavily if not completely involved in its military activity. Because the military could not exist without its civilian economic and political base, it is trivial to try to continue the old separation between combat and noncombat elements. When a nation is at war, all of that nation may contribute and all of it can properly be expected to bear the consequences of its decisions.

The concept of *taking hostages* once referred to capturing people who were not themselves involved in a conflict, or at least not directly involved. In the modern technological world, everyone is involved, and so there are no innocent hostages in the old sense. Everyone is a combatant because everyone either contributes to one side or to another. Dog tags are not the essential identification; a passport or tax receipt is. As the title of a World War II book put it, *Only the Stars Are Neutral*. Is age a protected-person category? No, children can grow up to be soldiers, and the aged can inspire the young.

In the past, an action was called *terrorist* and looked upon with horror when it seemed to violate the concept of ancient chivalry. Assassinations of leaders and attacks on civilians were examples of terrorism; however, now that some of the major nations have used assassinations (the United States, for example)[1] and major nations participate in attacking civilian populations (the area bombing during World War II), the term *terrorist* is just a name for one's opponent. Either overtly or covertly, the major nations of the world no longer abstain from being what used to be called *terrorist*.

FOUNDATIONS OF THE REALITY VIEW

The above view of the world is general enough to deserve consideration. Although I do not at all agree with this view, the following is an effort to establish its foundations.

Everything changes. "We cannot step into the same river twice," as Heraclitus noted. The history of ideas is a record of change, and that holds for the ideas of everything, including those of acceptable warfare.

We are in an age of large corporate entities, of collectives. Individuals are trivial in economic, social, and military terms. From the standpoint of nations, which are major collective entities, individuals are irrelevant. Individual morality is a romantic anachronism. Nations are collective beings, and they fight as collectives, not as fragments. Combatants are those who are trying to destroy you and who pose an immediate threat. The emphasis on "immediate" is arbitrary: An entire community is involved in trying to destroy you when you are at war with a nation. That some are paid to wear one uniform and some another sort of clothing is irrelevant in the effort to destroy you.

Nations have no soul and are certainly not hoping to go to Augustine's City of God or to any other heaven. They exist only in this material world, and their greatest hopes remain materialistic. They care about power and territory. They care about people only when people increase their power. They demand absolute loyalty from their citizen–subjects. Absolute loyalty can mean absolute sacrifice. And they occasionally require wars.

By definition, wars are hostilities among nations. No common power exists to keep them in awe, and they must depend on their own strength for their existence. So, right and wrong do not have a place in relations among nations. As Hobbes explained, right and wrong exist only when there is a single power—a king—to enforce a command. When there is a single king, that king's commands are law—no king, no law; no law, no right or wrong.

It is perfectly acceptable to use treachery, fraud, deceit, and terror between nations. Agreements among nations are like the Nazi–Soviet non-aggression pact of August 1939. In less than two years, by June 1941, Hitler and Stalin were at war with each other. No surprise: That is the way nations act for their own benefit.

CONSEQUENCES OF THIS VIEW OF REALITY

According to the position outlined above, nations and other corporate entities are the holders of power, and an honest view of the world must say so. There are no *natural rights,* either for individuals or for nations; there is only the ability of the powerful. The only thing *natural* is that power overcomes weakness, that there are winners and losers; therefore, in the evolution of more and more powerful collective entities struggling to exist, we may expect increasingly desperate wars.

The history of evolution shows the development of more and more powerful entities. We now find that, not individual humans, but national collective entities have inherited the Earth and that individual humans are best understood as means for national goals. Agreements to protect individual human rights are just chips in the game that nations play. Like any treaty between sovereign nations, these agreements are as dependable as the non-aggression pact between Hitler and Stalin; therefore, no international treaties and no written or unwritten laws of warfare are to be taken seriously.

AN ALTERNATIVE TO SO-CALLED REALITY

Now we will consider a view that holds that there are periods of excess in which wild violations of law occur, but these swings move around a center that is quite different from the assumptions above. This viewpoint is a partial, not a complete, "good guys" theory. From this viewpoint, the world is making progress toward a more moral situation. Despite fluctuations, universal fairness is increasing its scope through history, and a more moral military history is to be expected in a progressively more moral world.

What might mark this moral progress? We might see more compassion for the poor, more attention to victims of tragedy and Third World famine, and to discrimination against children, races, religions, women, and aliens. Here follows some of the structure for such an expectation of the future of morality.

National Honor vs. Individual Honor

Those using common sense often make the mistakes that logicians call the fallacies of composition and division. These fallacies consist of the following arguments: If the members of a group have certain properties, then the group must also have them; and, if a group has certain properties, its members must have them. Seductive as these patterns of argument can be, they are not valid. The reason for calling attention to them here is to emphasize the distinction between the morality of individuals and the morality of the community of which they are members.

If we measure the morality of a community by the degree to which universal fairness characterizes group patterns, we especially note such matters as the absence of slavery, religious freedom, and equal rights for women and minorities. However, it may be the case that the members of a community have developed and enforce such legal patterns for reasons independent of their own personal morality. The United States became a more moral society after the abolition of slavery; however, we need not think that the members of the nation *personally* became more moral after the Emancipation Proclamation. Those who did not own slaves did not sacrifice any slaves to the new situation. Those who did own slaves were compelled to sacrifice to free those slaves. The nation moved significantly closer to universal fairness, but individual citizens did not obviously display any higher degree of morality. There is no reason to think that the postwar citizens had become any more honest, honorable, gentle, or virtuous. This case is one of many in which progress in community morality does not mean progress in individual morality.

The history of civilization looks to be a history of increasing group or community morality; that is, the same set of laws hold equally for more and more members of the group—equal fairness, legally. In terms of U.S. constitutional law, we speak of the extension of application of the "equal protection clause" of the Fourteenth Amendment (and of due process); however, as suggested above, the level of community morality and the level of individual morality are different questions, and the facts force different answers. While the history of civilization shows increasing community morality (with starts and stops and backsliding), it does not show the same thing for individuals.

The pessimists like to claim that individuals are less moral than they used to be, and the optimists hold that individuals have made and continue to make progress in their morality. The third and most impressive view to me is Kant's idea that human individuals seem to be no better and no worse in their personal morality at the present than in earlier periods. Their society makes progress, but the personal honor and morality of the present generation seems to be neither advancing nor regressing. There may be a tendency in each generation to sentimentalize their ancestors, at least their most immediate ancestors. Cicero tells the story of Regulus to claim that the Romans of his own day had degenerated from that earlier high and general level of honor. But if we take morality to lie in subjective intention, we can answer such questions only about ourselves. If morality is to be judged by behavior, the matter is often unclear (that is, the moral weight of the matter, the nature of the beneficiary, and the sacrifice must be considered).

What is clear is that there is a difference between the question of whether a group obeys its laws and the question of the personal motivation of the members of the group. The individuals may be quite selfish, in their own eyes; yet, they may appear to behave generously because of fear of being caught, fear of the law, and fear of publicity.

Rules or Character
Given the distinction between the performance of a legal system and the motives of individuals, one group of philosophers takes morality to reside in rules and judges the morality of anything and anyone by obedience to an ideal set of rules. Another group of philosophers takes the problem of finding an ideal set of rules to be vacuous and, instead of looking to rules, looks to the character of individuals—to their virtues—as the locus of morality. The issue is between rule-based and virtue-based morality. If names or name- dropping can help, the contest is between Kant and Aristotle. This second view, looking to an Aristotelian theory of virtues, deserves more attention than we have given it so far (or will give it in the short comment below).

According to the Aristotelian, or virtue-centered view, "We need to attend to virtues in the first place in order to understand the function and authority of rules."[2] What are called *qualities of character* are the essential matter, and although rules or laws are a convenient way to manage complications, they are not themselves the source or bearers of morality. We must find and trust people with such virtues as courage, loyalty, and honesty and not trust laws that can never be counted on to solve new problems.[3] Laws are understood as formal abstractions, and there are no reasons for choosing one set over another.

Kant's Philosophy of History
Opposed to the virtue theory is Kant's view of human nature. For him, as we have said, individuals are combinations of a moral incentive and a selfish incentive. Healthy humans always have both of these and so can never be trusted to be perfectly moral. They always have some ambivalence, some interest in selfish motives as well as moral ones. Kant takes the rule of morality, the categorical imperative that we considered in Chapter 2, to be an order that a rational person gives to him- or herself. If one is rational, then internal reason insists—orders—that only rules that

can be universalized are to be followed. But we are not only rational; we are also selfish, and the selfish principle proposes that we serve ourselves and ignore the orders of reason. Are there people so virtuous that they can be trusted not to be selfish? No, says Kant.

While individuals always remain subject to both the moral and the selfish principles, humanity as a group can make moral progress. This progress happens through law. The history of increasingly moral legal systems is the real mark of moral progress of the community. The present dangers, like previous ones, can be expected to lead to stronger worldwide legal controls and powers. For Kant, humanity's moral history shows progress, even while individuals do not. The threat of war leads to the construction of law. The same force that pushed humanity into domestic legal systems will push the world into an international legal system. That is Kant's answer: The dangers of unrestricted warfare will produce the fear that will force us into a world government. That is the optimistic answer to the moral pessimism of the first viewpoint above; that is the answer to so-called realism.[4]

In thinking about military matters, we can adopt some of Aristotle's and some of Kant's views of human nature. The concept of honor is based on a set of assumptions connected with Aristotle's notion of virtue, The concept of laws of warfare and their protection of human rights is Kantian. For the purpose of judging individuals, we can look for degrees of honor. For the purpose of judging laws and rules of warfare, we can use the Kantian ideas of natural rights and the progress of the human species.

What is our response to the charge that the Hague and Geneva Conventions are obsolete? Based on the Kantian philosophy of history, they are not. The broad pattern of human history shows increasing respect for the individual and increasing arrangements to protect individual human rights. When challenged by apparently new threats—from terrorism, new technologies, LICs, and the growth of corporate entities such as nations—the pattern of legal restrictions on acceptable military conduct can be expected to continue. In historical terms, the greater the danger, the more sophisticated the legal response. The danger to individual human rights grows greater daily, but the techniques for legal protections also grow. Despite temporary ups and downs, the morality of universal fairness that underlies the Hague and Geneva Conventions can and will be extended. There is no need to lose our nerve, our moral nerve.

Appendix 2
Topics Not Considered
in the Text

It may be useful to mention certain issues with which this study has *not* tried to deal, matters that one might expect to find in a book called *A Moral Military*. They range from the obvious—the "just war"—to the not-so-obvious, the possible end of the distinction between officers and enlisted personnel.

THEORY OF THE "JUST WAR"

We have not yet considered the basic question of when a war is justified. Two possible errors must be balanced: the Type I error is *not fighting when one should;* the Type II error is *fighting when one should not.* (The relationship between these two errors is discussed in Chapter 2.) An absolute pacifist is worried only about the dangers of the Type II error, fighting too much; an absolute militarist would be worried only about the dangers of the Type I error, not fighting enough. Each "absolutist" prefers to ignore the existence of one of the risks of error. An ideal "just war" theory would explain how to avoid both errors, but we have no such theory. Lacking a perfect theory, we are still forced to make judgments, to adopt one or another style.

What conditions or threats are so immoral that killing is justified in order to change or oppose them? Of course, this is a matter of the utmost significance, and the long history of concern with the "just war" must not be neglected. Our question, however, of *how* to fight is different from the question of *when* to fight.[1] Having said this, it must be quickly noted that these questions are not independent. The decision on whether to fight should be affected by an assumption about the means to be used and the cost. If the only way to fight is unacceptable, or if the cost is unacceptable, those assumptions must bear decisively on the decision about whether to fight. On the other hand, if a war is not justified, then even scrupulously fighting within the bounds of the war conventions will not satisfy all moral issues. Obviously, the questions of *when to fight* and *how to fight* are different but not independent. While this study is limited to the question of how, it is far from having exhausted the significant moral issues.

HISTORY

Military history and its interpretation certainly are relevant to the matter of understanding moral military activity. Here and there we have turned to bits of military history to illuminate a point; however, a sustained analysis of history is a different project. Fortunately, there is no shortage of military histories. The genre of historical writing in the West goes back, at least, to the military histories of Herodotus and Thucydides, not to mention Homer and the Bible. Recent histories bear directly on our subject (for example, I have already referred to eminent historian Russell F. Weigley's *The American Way of War: A History of United States Military Strategy and Policy,* an extremely important expert study of the nature and implications of American strategy).[2] Weigley and other historians serve us well, and their work is my excuse for limiting the treatment of history in this study. The history of the laws of war has not been my concern here; rather, it is the assumptions and implications of the present situation that I have tried to consider carefully. We must note, however, that the understanding of these is incomplete without their history.

Military activity has had impressive consequences for many nonpolitical aspects of civilization; these are ignored here. As an example of the influence on art, consider a remark about one of Napoleon's campaigns:

> The full impact of Egypt [Egyptian Art] was not felt until after Napoleon's Egyptian campaign (1798–99). Although in terms of military history the venture was a disaster, archeologically and artistically it was a triumph. The account and engravings which Baron Denon published, *Voyage dans la Basse et la Haute Egypte* (1802), helped to spread "Egyptomania" throughout Europe. Together with Greek and Roman forms and details, chairs became adorned with sphinxes, clock mounts were decorated with hieroglyphics and doorways designed as if entrances to Egyptian temples.[3]

COMMON MORAL PROBLEMS

Moral problems easily arise in any large institution, military or civilian. Stealing from the company, favoring one's friends, and self-advancement or self-protection at the expense of others are breaches of common morality. These can also certainly have military consequences (for example, selling weapons to the enemy); however, these are matters met with in ordinary civilian as well as military institutions and are not essentially military. I have, therefore, ignored them. As I write this, my eye falls on a headline in the morning paper: "*Pravda* Claims Soviet Military Is Full of Corruption":

> The Soviet armed forces are so riddled with corruption, poor discipline and improper personnel practices that their combat readiness has greatly diminished in many cases, the Communist. Party newspaper *Pravda* reported Sunday.

In a two-month period this year, Soviet military officers were fined 2.5 million rubles ($4 million) for various abuses of military regulations, including theft and willful damage to army property, *Pravda* said, quoting figures from the Military Procurator's Office. . . .

The report said corruption is rampant, especially among officers. Thefts of military property are on the rise, and the improper use of soldiers for non-military projects such as civilian construction has badly hurt combat readiness of some units, the report added. It also implied that some senior officers have been using soldiers for personal projects like private home repairs.

It said that there were cases of enlisted men and non-commissioned officers renting apartments on the black market and living off base in blatant violation of regulations.[!]

"We are now ruthlessly getting rid of procurators and investigators who take bribes, of drunkards and workers in the procurator's office who close their eyes to the violation of military law," [Lieutenant General Boris] Popov said.[4]

While these examples of corruption are violations of rules and they may, if true, have military consequences, they are not matters of the conduct of war. So, despite their interest value, we have usually (but not always) ignored violations of individual and *institutional morality* that are not directly matters of warfare. The cases of the honor code at the military academies and the recruiting scandals are not purely military. They have civilian analogues; yet, they did help make certain points in Chapter 3.

MILITARY LABOR UNIONS

A somewhat novel question has arisen in the last few decades. The Dutch Army has allowed a civilian institutional pattern to be followed; they have allowed a *labor union* to form within the army. From informal conversations with some veterans of that army, it seems that the union was formed to press for what were called improved "labor conditions" for enlisted personnel. Labor conditions cover rates of pay, duty hours, leaves, insurance, and dependents' benefits. Immediately one wonders whether, when under stress in battlefield conditions, the enlisted personnel will look to their officers or their union leaders (shop stewards). The concern is apparently vacuous. The union is involved only in working conditions as set by contract and not at all in military action or activities. While the matter of a soldiers' union and potential strikes (mutinies) raise interesting questions, they seem so close to civilian patterns that it has not yet made its way into our category of concerns for a moral military. The parallel with police associations and the history of those associations, however, suggests that this development may have to be taken more seriously in the future.

COMPOSITION OF THE MILITARY FORCES

The composition of military forces *is* a matter for concern. Military forces run a special risk of sacrifice for the rest of the nation. Is that risk fairly assigned? This is certainly a moral question. The move from drafted to volunteer recruits makes for a different composition of personnel. The proportion of blacks in the U.S. Army is higher than the proportion in the general population; the nation appears to be asking this minority to take a disproportionately large risk of dying for the benefit of the majority. Similar questions are raised by the ratio of men to women in the military. The screening tests for recruits have, in the past, involved a variety of factors, including psychological matters, national loyalty, sexual preference, religious concerns, and pacifism.

An obvious question here is the matter of the age bracket for recruits, drafted or volunteers. The draft patterns historically have called on eighteen- to twenty-five-year-old men. In an increasingly technical military world, we might expect that the age bracket would start higher than eighteen and might well range up to fifty—or up to the retirement age for senior officers. The criticism that the young are asked to die for the old cannot be easily answered by mentioning the need for youth to carry a full field pack all day in a desert. The world of technology is not based on eighteen-year-olds.

Despite the importance of each of these questions, neither they nor their theory are directly matters of military operations, and so they have hardly been mentioned here.

DISTINCTION BETWEEN OFFICERS AND ENLISTED PERSONNEL

The distinction between officers and enlisted personnel is long established and well understood. However, it is not perfectly obvious that a democratic nation needs to continue with that pattern of "classes." An invitation was once issued—by General Patton, I believe—that read "Officers and their ladies, and enlisted men and their wives are invited to a reception given by the Commanding Officer." Apparently officers were understood to have the company of "ladies," while an enlisted man simply had a "wife." Is the two-class system—different uniforms, pay rates, housing, food, and clubs—needed in the armed forces of a democracy? Would people refuse to accept the responsibilities of an officer without higher pay? Would our officers desert if their dependents' allowances were reduced to enlisted personnel levels? The serious question, of course, is: Would leadership suffer without the two-class system or might unit cohesion gain? We can easily imagine experiments to test these hypotheses.

The two-class system parallels the distinction in the civilian business world between management and labor. Because it is so close to the civilian pattern, the system does not seem to be uniquely involved in our question of how to fight. So, despite the interest value, this subject also is passed over with no more than the comment above (and one in an earlier section). The historical forces moving the world toward increasing equality may also make the future military and police forces into one-class entities. So far, there is not much evidence of change.

Appendix 3
Test on the Laws of Land Warfare

PART I: EXAMINATION

Instructions for examination on FM 27-10, The Laws of Land Warfare *(containing selections from the Hague and Geneva Conventions, the Gas Warfare Protocol, and U.S. Army commentary)*

This test is an effort to discover how accurately you can remember (or guess) *just what the U.S. government has agreed to* with respect to the several Geneva and Hague Conventions on the conduct of war.

The U.S. Army promulgates the agreements on the conduct of war in Field Manual 27-10; therefore, the questions are often stated in language taken directly from, or in terms close to, the Field Manual.

Please answer each question, not in terms of your own views or preferences, but *in terms of what you think the agreements actually state and the Field Manual specifies.*

Write *T* for true or *F* for false to the left of the number of each question. Then, compare your responses with the answers given in Part 2.

1. Field Manual 27-10 is suggestive but is not intended to provide authoritative guidance.
2. Even in war, certain fundamental human rights ought to be safeguarded.
3. Belligerents must refrain from employing any kind or degree of violence that is not actually necessary for military purposes.
4. Hostilities must be conducted with regard for the principles of humanity and chivalry.

5. Military necessity is a proper defense for acts forbidden by the so-called customary and conventional laws of war.

6. The law of war is binding on all individuals, ordinary citizens as well as military personnel.

7. The law of war comes from two sources, written treaties and unwritten or customary law.

8. The customary or unwritten law of war is also a part of U.S. law.

9. The unwritten law of war must be strictly observed by U.S. military forces, unless specific exceptions have been directed as reprisals by a competent authority.

10. The Geneva and Hague Conventions must be given the same respect as the Constitution and laws of Congress.

11. Knowledge of the texts of the Hague and Geneva Conventions is intended for military personnel only, not civilians.

12. The Geneva Conventions refer only to international war and make no restrictions concerning civil wars.

13. No one, not even military authorities, may take responsibility for prisoners of war unless they have had instructions in the Geneva Convention on Prisoners of War.

14. Hostilities must not start without either a declaration of war or an ultimatum with a conditional declaration.

15. There must be a reasonable length of time between a declaration of war and the start of hostilities. At least one day.

16. Bombardment of undefended towns is prohibited.

17. Military personnel are not allowed to declare that no quarter (mercy) will be given.

18. If an enemy soldier has laid down his or her arms, that person may then be wounded but not killed.

19. It is prohibited to fire on paratroops, or others apparently bound on hostile missions, while they are descending by parachute.

20. Persons descending by parachute from disabled aircraft may not be fired upon if they are apparently unarmed.

21. Assassinations of enemy soldiers or officers are permitted.

22. It is permissible to put a price on an enemy's head or to offer a reward for an enemy, "dead or alive."

23. Citizens of the enemy country cannot be compelled to take part in the operations of war directed against their own country.

24. Once at war, there are no restrictions on how to injure the enemy.

25. Field Manual 27-10 specifically forbids the use of atomic or nuclear weapons.

26. Weapons that employ fire, such as flamethrowers and napalm, are forbidden.

27. The use of gas warfare against human beings is prohibited under any circumstances

28. The United States has renounced first use of poisonous gases or other chemical weapons but has reserved the right to retaliate with them against a state that has done so.

29. The United States has renounced the first use of bacteriological weapons but has reserved the right to use them against a state that has done so.

30. The attack or bombardment, by whatever means, of towns, villages, dwellings, or buildings that are undefended is prohibited.
31. An undefended town may be attacked if it contains military objectives (factories producing munitions and the like).
32. When there are civilians in an area to be bombed, the commanding officer must do all in his or her power to warn the authorities before starting.
33. To pretend to surrender is an example of an acceptable trick or ruse of war.
34. As a general rule, a soldier must not directly lie to the enemy but must observe absolute good faith.
35. A belligerent may do anything to mislead the enemy that a rational enemy ought to have expected.
36. To broadcast to the enemy that an armistice has been agreed upon, when it has not, is an acceptable trick.
37. To give your word of honor to the enemy and then break your word is forbidden.
38. It is legitimate to use spies and secret agents.
39. Planting false information is legitimate.
40. Psychological warfare and deceptive signals are legitimate.
41. It is legitimate to pretend to communicate with troops or reinforcements that do not exist.
42. It is legitimate to deceive the enemy by bogus orders purporting to have been issued by the enemy commander.
43. None of the following can be used during combat to mislead the enemy: a flag of truce, the national flag of the enemy, the military uniform of the enemy.
44. Individuals not in the armed forces of the enemy who commit hostile acts are not to be treated as POWs and may be tried and executed if their actions were sufficiently serious.
45. To save him- or herself and the unit, a commanding officer may kill POWs.
46. Prisoners of war who are paroled on their promise not to escape are bound on their personal honor to stick to their word and not escape, even if there is such an opportunity.
47. Civilian hospitals, used only for medical purposes, may not be attacked.
48. The taking of hostages is permitted on certain occasions, as, for example, by way of reprisal for previous acts.
49. Military commanders are responsible for war crimes committed by their troops if they have actual knowledge, or should have knowledge, of those acts and do not punish the violators.
50. Any person, military or civilian, may be found guilty of a war crime.
51. Misuse of the Red Cross emblem is a war crime.
52. Spies may be killed without trial if their guilt is obvious to the commander on the scene.
53. Maltreatment of dead bodies, while not encouraged, is not a war crime.
54. You cannot be punished for a war crime if you were ordered to carry out the act.
55. Members of the armed forces may properly disobey a commander if the commander orders an action that would be a war crime.

56. Prisoners of war who refuse to answer questions may be threatened or harmed if that is the only way to get military information from them.
57. Prisoners of war who are wounded or sick must be cared for and treated humanely.
58. If the enemy do not take proper care of your wounded and sick, you may take similar reprisals against their wounded and sick.
59. Property belongs to whoever captures it.
60. If civilians have committed crimes and the individuals can not be identified, then a general punishment of the group or community is justified.

PART II: ANSWERS AND COMMENTS ON THE EXAMINATION

The answers are given immediately after the number of the question, followed by the number of the paragraph that locates the answer in FM 27-10 and, in some cases, by explanatory comment.

1. F The first sentence in the FM (para. 1) states that its purpose is "to provide authoritative guidance to military personnel on the customary and treaty law," based on treaty agreements among most of the nations in the world, including the United States. Treaty arguments appear in bold type and are binding on courts and tribunals; the rest of the text is guidelines.
2. T (para. 2, b)
3. T (para. 3, a)
4. T (para. 3, a)
5. F (para. 3, a)
6. T (para. 3, b and para. 7, c)
7. T (para. 4, a and b)
8. T (para. 4, b) The unwritten or customary law of war is to be understood as having the same status as Anglo-American common law.
9. T (para. 7, c)
10. T (para. 7, b) Under the Constitution, Article VI, para. 2, "All treaties made or which shall be made under the authority of the United States, shall be the supreme law of the land . . . anything in the Constitution or the laws of any State to the contrary notwithstanding." The Constitution does not allow Prince Metternich's attitude, in his reported statement, "What is a treaty? A sheet of paper!"
11. F (para. 14, a, b, and c) The Geneva Conventions specify the importance of "civil instruction" and the intention to have their principles "known to the entire population."
12. F (para. 11, a and b)
13. T (para. 14, b) Actually, this paragraph also requires that anyone who takes responsibility for a POW have a copy of the text of the POW Convention. Presumably, the text need not be carried by anyone below the rank of company commander.
14. T (para. 20, a) The Convention calls for the declaration of war to be "reasoned."
15. F (para. 20, a) No particular length of time is required. The Hague Convention specifies a "previous and explicit warning" before hostilities start. The term previous means that at least some time must elapse.

16. T (para. 39.) This paragraph states that such an attack is prohibited. It should be added that this position may be no longer be applicable given the newer doctrine that every citizen of a country at war is an enemy of the citizens of the opposing side.

17. T (para. 28) This is one of the patterns that the Hague Convention states "is especially forbidden." To declare that no prisoners will be taken, no mercy shown, is a clear violation of para. 28.

18. F (para. 29) "It is especially forbidden . . . to kill or wound" an enemy who has surrendered.

19. F (para. 30) If they appear to be on a military mission, they are legitimate targets.

20. T (para, 30)

21. F (para. 31) To commit assassination, one must be treacherous and must pretend not to be a soldier. Both are forbidden.

22. F (para. 31)

23. T (para. 32)

24. F (para. 33, b) "The means employed are definitely restricted by international declarations and conventions and by the laws and usages of war." All is not fair in war.

25. F (para. 35), As paragraph 35 holds, there is no customary rule or international convention restricting precisely atomic weapons.

26. F (para. 36) This paragraph holds that they are acceptable but should not be used so as to cause unnecessary suffering to individuals.

27. F The new paragraph 38 [in Change No. 1] must be consulted for details. The United States has agreed not to use poison gas in a first strike but is free to retaliate with such a weapon in response.

28. T [para. 38, b (of Change No. 1 of 27-10)] This holds that the United States will not use poisonous gases in a first strike but reserves the right to use them in retaliation for their use.

29. F [para. 38, a (of Change No. I of 27-10)] In the case of bacteriological warfare, the United States accepts the prohibition against first use and also against use in retaliation. (See Change No. 1, page 3.)

30. T [para. 39, a (Change No. 1)] The definition of "undefended place" is in para. 39, b.

31. F [para. 40, c (Change No. I)] Undefended places are not permissible objects of attack, even when they are classified as military objectives.

32. T (para. 43, a, b, c) Dropping of paper notices is one example of such advance warnings.

33. F (para. 50) To pretend to surrender is not acceptable. It is true that some tricks are and some are not legitimate, but only obvious or questionable lies are permitted.(such as saying that they are surrounded by a large number when they are not, or planting false orders.

34. T (para. 49) The enemy may be mystified and misled by many means but not by deliberately lying; however, this answer must be taken in conjunction with the answer to the next question.

35. T (para. 49) For example, after many such incidents, an order to surrender on the grounds that a force is surrounded is a trick that an enemy ought to suspect.

36. F (para. 50)

37. T (para. 50) This paragraph includes the sentence, "It would be an improper practice to secure an advantage of the enemy by deliberate lying when there is a moral obligation to speak the truth." Some examples follow and then para. 50 explains that: "Treacherous or perfidious conduct in war is forbidden because it destroys the basis for a restoration of peace short of the complete annihilation of one belligerent by the other."
38. T (para. 51) This paragraph lists these as legitimate ruses.
39. T (para. 51) This is not the same as giving your word of honor.
40. T (para. 51)
41. T (para. 51)
42. T (para. 51)
43. T (pan. 52)
44. T (para. 80)
45. F (para. 85)
46. T (para. 185) U.S. soldiers are not authorized to give parole, except for very unusual cases, and these must be approved by the senior commander. However, if persons are given parole, they "are bound on their personal honor" not to break their word.
47. T (para. 257) However, this protection may be discontinued if hospitals are used for "combatant action," such as observation posts, liaison centers, ammunition storage, and so forth (para. 258).
48. F (para. 497, g) The taking of hostages is flatly forbidden. They may not be taken in reprisal.
49. T (para. 501)
50. T (para. 499)
51. T (para. 504, f)
52., F (para. 78, a) No punishment before a trial.
53. F (para. 504, c)
54. F (para. 509, a and b) Acting under orders is no defense for committing a war crime. Soldiers are "bound to obey only lawful orders."
55. T (para. 509, b)
56. F (para. 93) No torture or other form of coercion is allowed. POWs are to give name, rank, age, and serial number. If they refuse even this information, privileges may be restricted, but no torture or coercion is permitted.
57. T (para. 215, a)
58. F (para. 214) Reprisals against the wounded and sick are prohibited.
59. F (para. 406) This paragraph states, "Private property cannot be confiscated." Para. 397 forbids pillage.
60. F (para. 448) Individuals may be punished only for their own actions; no collective penalties are allowed.

Notes

1. INTRODUCTION

1. *The* Department of the Army, *Law of Land Warfare*, FM 27-10 (Washington, D.C.: U.S. Government Printing Office, July 1956), pp. 182–183. This will be subsequently referred to as FM 27-10, as the U.S. Field Manual, or, simply, as FM.

2. *Ibid.,* p. 183.

3. *Ibid.,*p. 182.

4. *Geneva Convention for the Amelioration of the Condition of the Wounded and Sick in Armed Forces in the Field,* 12 August 1949, art. 47.

5. A very knowledgeable reviewer of this proposal (a publisher's reviewer whose name is thus unknown to me) has made the point that parents who object to having material as strong as *Cinderella* read in school would hardly accept training their children to become warriors. Quite so, at first blush. However, some of their children do become warriors shortly or directly after high school. Whether these children ever see service, education about the basic laws affecting their country and the world ought not to be opposed. Ignorance is not safety. War, like sex, can be learned in the street, but responsible education has its advantages.

6. The Geneva Protocol of 1925, which prohibited "Asphyxiating, Poisonous, or Other Gases, and of Bacteriological Methods of Warfare," was signed by the United States fifty years later, in 1975.

7. For example, in his extremely valuable *The American Enlisted Man* (New York: Russell Sage Foundation, 1970), Charles C. Moskos, Jr., mentions, "it has often been noted that front-line soldiers bitterly contrast their plight with the physical amenities enjoyed by their fellow countrymen, both rear-echelon soldiers as well as civilians back home" (p. 153). Moskos goes on to give a more

complete comment on the ambivalence of complaining about and desiring civilians' comfort.

8. This remark is not adequate by itself. Sometimes civilians are more enthusiastic than the military about particular weapons and targets.

9. In *War, Morality and the Military Profession,* ed. Col. Malham M. Wakin (Boulder, Colo: Westview Press, 1979, p. 201), Wakin gives Alfred Vagts, *A History of Militarism* (New York: Free Press, 1959), as his source.

10. Major Daniel M. Smith, U.S. Army, "The Army: A Search for Values," *Military Review* 60, no. 3 (March 1980): 11.

11. This distinction is analogous to Kant's distinction between "a moral politician," one who behaves morally, and "a political moralist," one who "forges a morality to suit the statesman's advantage." He develops this point in *Perpetual Peace* (p. 372). See the Ted Humphrey translation, *Perpetual Peace and Other Essays* (Indianapolis: Hackett Publishing Co., 1983). All references to the work of Immanuel Kant will follow the standard pattern, that of the pagination of the Prussian Academy (also called the Berlin) edition in twenty-two volumes. This is used in almost all modern translations of Kant. *Kants gesammelte Schriften* (Berlin: Preussische Akademie der Wissenschafren, 1900–1942).

12. William James, *Psychology: Briefer Course* (New York: Collier Books, 1962), p. 44l.

13. Peter L. Stromberg, Malham M. Wakin, and Daniel Callahan, *The Teaching of Ethics in the Military* (Hastings-on-Hudson, N.Y.: The Hastings Center, 1982). A valuable review of problems, goals, and teaching techniques, with a bibliography of books and journals.

14. See note 1.

15. Immanuel Kant's ethical theory is found in his *Critique of Practical Reason,* trans. Lewis White Beck (New York: Liberal Arts Press, 1956) and *Fundamental Principles of the Metaphysics of Morality* (sometimes translated as *Grounding for the Metaphysics of Morals*), as well as in his works on the philosophy of history and of religion, some of which are listed in the Bibliography.

16. 1 agree only in part with comments made by Richard A. Gabriel (Major, U.S.A. Reserve) in his review of Col. Malham M. Wakin's anthology, *Hastings Center Report* 10 (August 1980): 23–24: "the military is a qualitatively different type of social institution. That is the central challenge of any book on military ethics: to evolve a specific code of ethics and to evolve pedagogies for teaching that code." To call the military "qualitatively" different must not mean that basic moral distinctions have no scope. Police departments have many of the same features as the military, plus, the whole range of civilian social institutions presupposes the military institution's success for its own activities. Yes, there are differences, but let us note that military and nonmilitary institutions each intimately need the other and cannot pretend ignorance of each other's moral patterns. I quite agree with the second part of Gabriel's comment and hope that this work can make some contribution toward that pedagogical goal.

17. Elizabeth Flower, "Ethics of Peace," in *Dictionary of the History of Ideas,* ed. Philip P. Wiener (New York: Charles Scribner's Sons, 1973), 3:444.

2. MORALITY: WHY SACRIFICE MYSELF?

1. We shall take Aristotle's square of opposition to be a way of exhausting the alternatives. The quantitative aspects of *A* with respect to *B* must be one of these

four: All *A* is *B*, some *A* is *B*, some *A* is not *B*, and no *A* is *B*. Many introductory logic books develop these matters much further. The logical relations of the square of opposition hold between the four moral positions to be presented.

2. FM 27-10, p. 23.

3. FM 27-10, p. 22.

4. Immanuel Kant, *Grounding for the Metaphysics of Morals,* trans. James W. Ellington (Indianapolis: Hackett Publishing Company, 1981), p. 429.

5. *Ibid.,* p. 430.

6. Immanuel Kant, *The Metaphysical Principles of Virtue,* trans. James Ellington (Indianapolis: Bobbs-Merrill Company, 1964), p. 425.

7. Kant, *Grounding for The Metaphysics of Morals,* p. 429.

8. Immanuel Kant, *The Metaphysical Elements of Justice,* trans. John Ladd (Indianapolis: Bobbs-Merrill, 1965), p. 307.

9. *Ibid.,* p. 347.

10. "Treacherous or perfidious conduct in war is forbidden because it destroys the basis for a restoration of peace short of the complete annihilation of one belligerent by the other." FM 27-10, p. 22.

11. While this is not the place to argue the question, my own expectation is that world citizenship—the development of a single world government—is the clear and necessary development of the political structure of the world. Various kinds of *de facto* world citizenship, such as working as an official of the United Nations, are already obvious. The growth of the European Common Market is another impressive move away from the sovereignty of individual nations. And, most seriously, the dangers of having nuclear weapons in the hands of a large number of independent nations make it imperative to move to world law to control and to police these and other major weapons. The logic and morality of military actions, however, are not dependent on my expectations for world political history.

12. J. S. Mill, *Principles of Political Economy* (London, 1848); reprinted in *Social Reformer,* ed. D. O. Wagner (New York: Macmillan, 1959), p. 400.

13. Thomas Hobbes, *Leviathan* (1651), chap. XIII.

14. *Ibid.,* chap. XV.

15. *Ibid.,* chap. XIII.

16. *Ibid.,* chap. XIV.

17. *Hobbes,* chap. XIV, *Hobbes Selections,* ed. F. J. E. Woodbridge (New York: Charles Scribner's Sons, 1958), p. 279.

18. *Ibid.*

19. According to military historian Russell F. Weigley, U.S. Army desertion rates are low during war and high during peace. This does not support individualism as an explanation (private correspondence).

20. To repeat, we shall limit our comments to Western religion.

21. The passage in which essentially this argument is found is Plato, *Euthyphro,* starting at 10 d. Our term *good* is Plato's *holy,* and our *desire* there is *love.*

22. *Holy Scriptures* (Philadelphia: Jewish Publication Society of America, 5697/1937).

23. Exodus 20 and Deuteronomy 5.

24. James Turner Johnson, *Just War Tradition and the Restraint of War: A Moral and Historical Inquiry* (Princeton, N.J.: Princeton University Press, 1981), p. xxvi.

25. I take the historical analysis of James Turner Johnson, *ibid.*, and others, to be compelling. The lawyers and the military, as well as the theologians, put together what we now call the "just war theory."

26. For example, see Santayana's *Reason in Religion,* the third volume of his five-volume work, *The Life of Reason* (New York: Charles Scribner's Sons, 1905–1906: reprinted Collier Books, 1962).

27. From Santayana's *Dominations and Powers,* reprinted in part in *The Philosophy of Santayana,* ed. Irwin Edman (New York: Charles Scribner's Sons, 1953), p. 672.

28. *Reason in Religion,* reprinted in Edman, *Philosophy of Santayana,* p. 147.

29. There are examples of persons whose religion seemed to give them the basis and the courage to criticize tyranny as well as examples of those with similar religious commitments who showed no such courage. One of the courageous ones was Bishop von Galen, the Catholic bishop of Münster, Germany, who was reported to have taken part "in the only serious civilian protest in the history of the Third Reich." He delivered a famous sermon criticizing the Nazi program of killing those called "unworthy of life." People were killed as "unworthy" for religious or political reasons as well as for being medically incurable. See Neal Ascherson, "The Death Doctors," *New York Review of Books,* 28 May 1987, p. 30.

30. FM 27-10, p. 3.

31. Edgar A. Singer, Jr., "On a Possible Science of Religion," *On the Contented Life* (New York: Henry Holt, 1936).

32. The philosophical theory of reality called *nominalism* holds that only individuals exist, that abstract entities such as classes and essences do not exist but are simply names. There are blue objects, but *blueness* itself does not exist except as a name. In the case of a government, there are certainly individual officials, property of the government, real estate and boundaries, papers describing the laws of the government, an individual who is the head of the government, citizens, tax collectors, and so forth, but there is no such entity as the government itself, apart from individuals of one sort or another. From the nominalist standpoint, we can use the terms "the government" or "the nation," but this is merely a shorthand or abbreviation for certain individual entities that actually exist. The nation, as an entity itself, does not exist. To believe in the nation, therefore, is to risk the chance that the nominalist is wrong.

As an antidote to the position of the ultrapatriot—that one ought to take the nation as a religious goal—see the sophisticated work of Paul Schrecker. He argues that it is dangerous to "grant the political province unchallenged hegemony over the entire field of civilization," in *Work and History, An Essay on the Structure of Civilization* (Princeton: Princeton University Press, 1948), p. 27.

33. Kant, *Grounding for the Metaphysics of Morals,* p. 421.

34. These are also presented in more detail in FM 22-100, *Military Leadership,* October 1983, chap. 4, esp. pp. 86–88. The four values phrased in the 1981 version of FM 100-1 apparently derive from an article by General Edward C. Meyer, then Chief of Staff, U.S. Army, "Professional Ethics is Key to a Well-led, Trained Army," *Army,* October 1980, pp. 11–15. The same issue of *Army* also carried an article by General Donn A. Starry, then Commanding General, Training and Doctrine Command (TRADOC). In his "Values, Not Scores, the Best Measure of Soldier Quality," pp. 38–45, General Starry takes the "values which the military profession must embrace" (p. 43) to be competence, commitment, candor, and courage. The current edition of FM 100-1 repeats these four C terms as individual values to be instilled in

each soldier and Army civilian and offers as the values of "The Professional Army Ethic" loyalty, duty, selfless service, and integrity. These eight terms, with obvious overlap among them, leave things rather mushy. This section of the chapter is an effort to sharpen these terms.

35. His title but not his name is mentioned—perhaps Jefferson just couldn't remember it!

36. Is the commander-in-chief a member of the Army, and does personal responsibility apply to that commander? As the civilian commander, the professional army ethic would apparently not apply, but this question probably calls for a qualified "guardhouse lawyer." President Harry Truman did make it clear that "the buck stops here."

37. These references to FM 22-100 are to the October 1983 version. This version is going through a revision and may be superseded shortly. Of course, the problems and suggestions in the 1983 version remain useful.

38. *Ibid.,* p. 97.

39. *Ibid.,* p. 99.

40. At a certain point in his *Confessions,* St. Augustine asks that the Lord remove his sexual desires to help make him pure, but adds quickly, "Not just yet, Oh Lord" (bk. VIII).

3. MILITARY HONOR AND THE LAWS OF WARFARE

1. Hobbes, *Leviathan,* chap. XV.

2. *New York Times,* 24, 25 July 1976, p. 26, p. 24.

3. Plato, *The Republic,* chap. (III, 413c), trans. F. M. Cornford, in John Perry and Michael Bratman, eds., *Introduction to Philosophy* (New York: Oxford University Press, 1986), p. 717.

4. *New York Times,* 6 June 1981.

5. *Ibid.*

6. The idea that respect is based on fear can be found in Plato's *Euthyphro.* It is also developed in Sidney Axinn, "Human Dignity and War," *The Philosophy Forum* 10, no. 1(1971): 31–52.

7. Richard A. Gabriel and Paul L. Savage, *Crisis in Command, Mismanagement in the Army* (New York: Hill and Wang, 1978), p. 93.

8. *Ibid.,* p. 92.

9. Material in this section is taken from Sidney Axinn, "Honor, Patriotism, and Ultimate Loyalty," in *Nuclear Weapons and the Future of Humanity, The Fundamental Questions,* ed. Avner Cohen and Steven Lee (Totowa, N.J.: Rowman and Allanheld, 1986).

10. Alfred Vagts, *A History of Militarism, Civilian and Military,* rev. ed. (New York: Free Press, 1967), p. 449.

11. FM 27-10, p. 4.

12. FM 27-10, p. 3, for the United States. For Great Britain, see *The Law of War on Land, being Part II of the Manual of Military Law* (London: Her Majesty's Stationery Office, 1958), hereafter cited as British Manual. The British Manual was issued by the Army Council, commanded by someone with an appropriate name for the subject, E. W. Playfair.

13. Hague Convention No. IV, 18 October 1907, art. 23, para. (e); reprinted in FM 27-10, p. 18.

14. FM 27-10, p. 18.

15. According to the *Random House College Dictionary,* rev. ed. (New York, 1975), the bullets were named after Dum-Dum, a town in India where they were made.

16. Francis Jennings, *The Invasion of America* (Columbia: University of South Carolina Press, 1975), p. 162.

17. Applying the universal fairness criterion can be much more complicated than the text leads one to believe. What can and cannot be universalized may be far from obvious, and the text gives almost no suggestion of these serious problems. For example: Would torture be acceptable if we agree that all persons may be tortured? No, because while *A* tortures *B* and remains untortured him- or herself, *B* cannot torture *A* and also remain untortured him or herself. Mutual torture would be a different case. This example is merely a slight indication of the questions involved. A careful analysis would have to consider the large number of important studies of just this matter of the meaning of *universalization* or *generalization* in ethics.

18. Henri Coursier, *Course of Five Lessons on the Geneva Conventions* (Geneva: International Committee of the Red Cross, 1963), p. 6. This publication was originally available in German, English, and Spanish.

19. Russell Weigley, *The American Way of War, A History of United States Military Strategy and Policy* (Bloomington, Ind.: Indiana University Press, 1977).

20. *Ibid.,* p. xxii.

21. FM 27-10, p. 183. This refers to the *Uniform Code of Military Justice,* art. 92.

22. My source is a story by William Safire, *New York Times,* 6 January 1983, p. A27.

23. *Ibid.*

24. This has been amended to clarify its application to women as well as men.

25. Quincy Wright, *A Study of War,* 2nd ed. (Chicago: University of Chicago Press, 1965), p. 160.

26. *Ibid.*

27. In his famous *Fable of the Bees,* Bernard de Mandeville gave an interesting psychological explanation of the ease with which people accept political goals that seem diametrically opposed to their own selfish interests. The wily politicians have flattered us into believing that there are two kinds of people, "the lofty high-spirited" ones and "the vile groveling wretches." The "lofty" ones are those who oppose their own selfish ambitions and prefer to act for the public interest; the "vile" ones act only for their own private pleasures. Flattery works. No one wants to be a "vile groveling wretch," and so we do what the politicians desire. It is easier to smile at than to refute de Mandeville's explanation.

28. Charles C. Moskos, Jr., *The American Enlisted Man* (New York: Russell Sage Foundation, 1970), pp. 148, 150.

29. To borrow a phrase from a book title used by the great French photographer, Henri Cartier-Bresson.

30. FM 27-10, p. 72.

31. This was a widely reported newspaper story at the time. The details may be found in *The Last Japanese Soldier* (London: Tom Stacey, 1972).

32. *Ibid.,* p. 8.

33. MQS 1. Training Support Package, "Ethics and Professionalism," pp. 6–35. This is a syllabus for ROTC Ethics Instruction, developed by the Ethics Unit when it was located at Fort Benjamin Harrison, Indianapolis.

34. Aristotle, *Nichomachean Ethics,* trans. W. D. Ross (Oxford: Oxford University Press, 1925), 1094b3.

35. In the section on loyalty in Chapter 12, we shall consider the definition of fanaticism.

36. I have seen the remark that, in 1871, 8,800 men were AWOL, but I have not been able to verify this. If true, that would be about one-third of the Army!

37. Gabriel and Savage, *Crisis in Command,* p. 43. My only criticism of their excellent study would be of their comment that the data present a paradox in that desertion rates for U.S. ground forces seemed to increase as the level of combat decreased" (p. 42). This is no paradox, considering Professor Weigley's data. It is apparently not battle dangers but factors such as boredom and contempt for their officers that lead to desertion. I think the authors would easily agree; their own work focuses on the contempt of enlisted personnel for the unprofessional officers in Vietnam.

38. *Ibid., p.43.*

39. *Ibid.,* p. 47.

40. *Ibid.,* p. 69.

41. *Ibid.,* p. 66. As far as the low loss of upper-grade officers is concerned, it has been noted that this was a small-unit war—platoon level rather than division, brigade, or battalion level.

42. *Ibid.,* p. 81.

43. Of course, Nathan Hale was the American soldier hanged as a spy by the British during the American Revolution. He is reported to have said, "I only regret that I have but one life to lose for my country."

44. The argument that morality is a matter of intentions not consequences is developed in the Stoic tradition and in the work of Immanuel Kant.

45. Maj. Thomas J, Kuster, Jr., "Dealing with the Insurgency Spectre," *Military Review* (February 1987): 29.

46. As reported in *New York Times,* 7 August 1986, p. A26.

47. Major Edgar C. Doleman, Jr. (U.S.A., retired), "Human Values in War," *Army* (November 1986): 31.

48. The idea that judgment cannot be taught is far from original here. It can be found, among other places, in Immanuel Kant's *Critique of Pure Reason,* trans. Norman Kemp Smith (New York: St. Martin's Press, 1963): "If understanding in general is to be viewed as the faculty of rules, judgment will be the faculty of subsuming under rules; that is, of distinguishing whether something does or does not stand under a given rule." "And thus it appears that, though understanding is capable of being instructed, and of being equipped with rules, judgment is a peculiar talent which can be practised only, and cannot be taught. It is the specific quality of so-called motherwit; and its lack no school can make good." "Deficiency in judgment is just what is ordinarily called stupidity, and for such a failing there is no remedy" (A 133, B 172, A 135, B 173).

49. This remark may soon be out of date. Chess computers now exist that may be programmed for different styles of play, called *normal, aggressive, desperate,* and *positional.* Also, the computer's style of play can be changed at any point during the game. (Chess players will recognize this as the computer developed by Newcrest Technology, Ltd., Super Enterprise model 210.C.) There still remains this last question of when to choose which style; however, even this last matter could be formalized, at least in a trivial way. By trivial, I mean a program in which one style would

be used on Monday and Thursday, a second on alternate Saturdays, and so forth, If we want a significant program, the text comment may still hold for a while.

50. There should be no surprise at finding Socrates used to illustrate military honor. He served in the armed forces of his city and had occasion to refer to his service with pride. And, of course, we can hardly imagine ethical theory in the West without Socrates.

4. HOSTILITIES

1. Language of the Geneva Conventions, FM 27-10, p. 12.

2. The Library of the International Committee of the Red Cross in Geneva maintains a stock of "soldiers' manuals" that give a brief summary of the laws of war. The copy on my desk is about 4 by 6 inches, 13 pages long, with a cardstock cover. It can fit easily into a soldier's pocket. These pamphlets are available in quantity at a very low price to any nation wishing to use them in training programs, and they are translated into many languages. On a visit in the spring of 1976, the librarian asked me which language edition I thought was their best seller at the moment. I guessed incorrectly: The answer was the Arabic edition. The Arab-speaking nations were about to go to war against Israel and, naturally, needed to teach the rules to their personnel—the same rules that the Israelis were teaching their personnel. The only difference is that some Middle Eastern countries use the red crescent in place of the red cross. In Iran, the red lion and sun are used. Of course, teaching efforts are not always perfectly successful.

3. Henri Coursier, *Course* of *Five Lessons on the Geneva Conventions* (Geneva: International Committee of the Red Cross, 1963), p. 6.

4. This is not the whole of the declaration, but it is the operational part of it. The text here is as it appears in the British Manual of Military Law, cited above in Chapter 3, note 12.

5. *Ibid.,* p. 7.

6. Roger Fisher, Letter to the Editor, *New York Times,* 13 March 1974, p. 41.

7. British Manual, p. 8.

8. FM 22-100, *Military Leadership,* October 1983, p. 130.

9. FM 27-10, p. 16.

10. Michael Walzer, *Just and Unjust Wars, A Moral Argument with Historical Illustrations* (New York: Basic Books, 1977), pp. 323–325.

11. Elizabeth Anscombe, "War and Murder," in *War and Morality,* ed. Richard A. Wasserstrom (Belmont, Calif.: Wadsworth Publishing, 1970), p. 46.

12. Reported in *New York Times,* 7 August 1986, p. A26.

13. Therefore, FM 27-10 has had a list of changes inserted in it; see Change No. 1, 15 July 1976.

14. The United States manufactured no chemical weapons from 1969 up to the recent approval of the new type of "nerve gas." In place of weapons that keep the chemical agent in one compartment, a 155-millimeter shell will have two nonlethal chemical components in separate compartments. While the shell is on its way to a target, the two components combined to form a deadly nerve gas. See *New York Times,* 20 February 1983, p. 25. See also references there to a bomb called "Bigeye."

15. FM 27-10, Change No. 1, p. 3.

16. British Manual, notes, p. 41.

17. FM 27-10, Change No. 1, p. 3.

18. FM 27-10, p. 17.
19. British Manual, p. 43.
20. These cases are reported in the British Manual, notes, p. 43.
21. FM 27-10, p. 34.
22. British Manual, notes, p. 41.
23. *Ibid.,* p. 40.
24. FM 27-10, p. 34.
25. British Manual, p. 42.
26. FM 27-10, p. 23.
27. British Manual, note 3, p. 103.

28. Viewed from the back of a truck, Cassino was my own first sight of the complete destruction of a town. I mention it only because the memory remains vivid even after more than sixty years.

29. *The Effects of the Atom Bomb on Nagasaki,* U.S. Strategic Bombing Survey, 1947. Unclassified, 1 May 1950, vol. 1, accompanying map.

30. *Hiroshima and Nagasaki: The Physical, Medical, and Social Effects of the Atomic Bombings* (New York: Basic Books, 1981), p. 382. In another section of this book, "Radiation Effects on Animals and Plants," we find, "It was said that rats remained the same before and after the explosion" (p. 81).

31. Mentioned by J. Robert Oppenheimer in his contribution to *Readings in the Philosophy of Science,* ed. Philip P. Wiener (New York: Charles Scribner's Sons, 1953), p. 430.

32. British Manual, note, p. 102.

5. PRISONERS OF WAR

1. Part III, British Manual, p. 45.
2. Theodore Ropp, "War and Militarism," in *Dictionary of the History of Ideas,* ed. Philip P. Wiener (New York: Charles Scribner's Sons, 1973), vol. 4, p. 501.
3. GPW, art. 12.
4. At an early stage of the war in Vietnam, the United States was criticized for transferring POWs to the South Vietnam government without such assurances. The International Red Cross should have been permitted to visit the POW camps of South Vietnam but was not. See comments on this incident below in this chapter.
5. GPW, art. 13.
6. FM 27-10, p. 35.
7. *Ibid*, p.35.
8. British Manual, note 1, p. 53. They attribute the quotation to Rose, *Life of Napoleon,* 9th ed., 1924, vol. 1, p. 204.
9. GPW, art. 13.
10. This incident is based on newspaper comment alone, but the photograph and story were impossible to ignore. The reader may recall that there were unusual restrictions on press coverage of the Grenada action. This was followed by the press and the Department of Defense (DOD) each criticizing the other for irresponsible behavior. DOD argued that restricting press coverage was necessary to maintain military secrecy, and the press argued that it had never violated confidential briefings and that the public had a right to know what the DOD was doing. For a debate on the matter of restricting press coverage of military action, see *Military Review* 47, no. 2 (February 1987): 70–84. See also the discussion in Chapter 12.

11. British Manual, p. 53, note 2.

12. GPW, art. 12; FM 27-10, p. 36.

13. GPW, art. 13. It seems so easily understood that there is no need for further explanation in FM 27-10, p. 36.

14. FM 27-10, p. 36.

15. British Manual, note 4, p. 51.

16. *Ibid.* The source given is 11 War Crimes Report (W.C.R.), p. 53. The full title of the WCR is *Law Reports of Trials of War Criminals.* Selected and prepared by the United Nations War Crimes Commission; 15 vols. 1946-1949.

17. British Manual, note 4, p. 51. References cited are Schmidt Trial, 12 W.C.R., p. 119, and also the JMT Judgment, p. 46.

18. *New York Times* May 24, 2005, p.A23.

6. SPIES

1. The Hague Rules, art. 29. One turns to the Hague Rules as the place to find a formal, internationally agreed upon written version of the military code. Of course, this version is now more than one hundred years old and does not deal with the most recent weapons and problems; however, it still gives us the principles and the meaning of the laws and customs of war on land.

2. The terms *restricted, confidential,* and *secret* were once classifications for information. They are no longer the current terms for security clearance levels.

3. Thomas Hobbes's *Leviathan,* published in 1651, is an analysis of the nature of individuals and governments. To be *sovereign* means to depend on yourself for your own protection. He takes humans to be essentially selfish and materialist. While we individuals "in the state of nature" have the right to be sovereign, to defend ourselves and give loyalty to no one else, it is too dangerous and stupid to do so. Our lives would be "solitary, poor, nasty, brutish, and short" (*Leviathan,* chap. XIII). The only way to stay alive and prosperous is to agree to give up our weapons on the condition that everyone else in the area does: We give our weapons to someone hence forward called the King. If we are rational and understand the danger of remaining individually sovereign, we "confer all [our] power and strength upon one man, or upon one assembly of men." Then, the King or assembly keeps peace between the members of this community because the citizens are in greater fear of the King's power to punish than they are enticed by benefits to be gained by war against their fellows. War is "the time men live without a common power to keep them all in awe [fear]. . . . All other time is PEACE" *(ibid.).* According to this notion of war, if we depend on ourselves for our own protection, we are at war with everyone else, With or without active hostilities, we are at war because war consists "not in battle only . . . but in a tract of time wherein the will to contend by battle is sufficiently known" *(ibid.).* Hobbes gives perhaps the first analysis of a "cold war" as what he called "a posture of war" *(ibid.).* I mention Hobbes here to base and explain the idea that all "sovereign" nations are either at hot or cold war with all other nations; therefore, the definition of a spy ought to cover cases of passing information to foreign nations, whether they are active belligerents or not.

4. FM 27-10, p. 32; UCMJ, art. 106.

5. FM 27-10, p. 33; UCMJ, art. 104.

6. Is betrayal always immoral? That depends on the nature of the situation and the intentions of the individuals involved. The German officers who planned

and almost carried out the revolt against Hitler during World War II would have been greeted as heroes by one side and as traitors by some on the other. Which side would have been right? Universal fairness required that Hitler be stopped, and the effort to do so should have made heroes of those officers. As we found in the conclusion to Chapter 3, we cannot escape the responsibility for choosing a moral style and deciding whether the situation calls for applying universal fairness or for obedience to the demands of a particular social group. This is a stuffy way of introducing the conclusion that respect for fairness to humanity should have made the German officers and enlisted personnel—revolt and "betray" Hitler.

7. Reported in *the Japan Times*, 6 March 1987, p. 4.

8. Even a brief and superficial history will list quite a few foreign as well as domestic cases in each of the last few years. The British have had a number of "Official Secrets" cases, India had a major scandal in which "secret military information was found in homes of government officials and others," and the Kohl administration of the West German government was shaken by high-level "leaks." Spying is hardly confined to larger countries: Syria caught and hanged an Israeli spy (Eli Cohen), who was said to have "gained access to the top echelons of the Syrian government" (*Japan Times*, 18 February 1987).

9. On 23 September 1949, President Truman announced that the Soviet Union had set off an atomic explosion. Julius and Ethel Rosenberg were sentenced to death in March 1951. Despite some international appeals for clemency, the sentence was carried out. The death sentence for passing secrets to a foreign power in peacetime is by no means routine. For example, Klaus Fuchs apparently was the (or a) British member of the network to which the Rosenbergs delivered their stolen papers. Fuchs was caught, tried by the British, found guilty, and sentenced to a term of fourteen years in prison; he was paroled after serving nine years.

10. British Manual, note 1, p. 109. The case reference comes from the Natzweiller Trial, 5 W.C.R., p. 54.

11. British Manual, note 1, p. 105.

12. FM 27-10, p. 33.

13. Reprinted in *ibid.*, p. 23.

14. *Ibid.*, p. 23.

15. Herodotus reports the use of a spy by the Persians against the Greeks at Thermopylae, and there is no reason to believe this is the earliest use of spying.

16. Obviously, a public call for volunteers might carry a severe risk of informing an enemy, so there can be no such requirement.

17. That the odd general now and again is elected president (Washington, Grant, Eisenhower) is apparently based on the public perception of skill and confidence rather than as a reward for sacrifice.

18. Being absent without leave is obviously nor the same as having a discharge.

19. British Manual, p. 105, note 2.

7. NONHOSTILE RELATIONS WITH THE ENEMY

1. Hague Rules, art. 34.
2. Hague Rules, art. 35.
3. FM 27-10, para. 472.
4. FM 27-10, para. 472.
5. FM 27-10, para. 472.

6. British Manual, para. 475, p. 135. The last part of this passage is quoted from the British Official Account of the Franco-German War, Part II, vol. 3, app. 172.b.

7. FM 27-10, para. 457, p. 166.

8. *Ibid.*

9. *Ibid.*, para. 453, p. 165.

8. WAR CRIMES, REMEDIES, AND RETALIATION (DIRTY WARFARE)

1. The story about the Army's experiment in releasing the agent *aspergillus fumigatus* in the New York City subway system was reported in the *New York Times,* 23 December 1976, p. 12.

2. Exodus 7: 19–12, 36.

3. FM 27-10, para. 2, p. 3.

4. British Manual, para. 650, P. 185.

5. Ibid., para. 651.

6. The classical place to find the distinction between persons and things is in Kant's *Fundamental Principles of the Metaphysics of Morals* [428].

7. British Manual, para. 652, p. 186.

8. British Manual, para. 650, note 1, p. 186.

9. FM 27-10, para. 495, p. 176.

10. FM 27-10, p. 177.

11. British Manual, para. 646, note 2, p. 185.

12. Ibid., para. 645, p. 184; FM 27-10, p. 177.

13. Quincy Wright, "Legal Aspects of the Vietnam Situation," in *Crimes of War*, ed. Richard A. Falk, Gabriel Kolko, and Robert Jay Lifton (New York: Random House, 1971), pp. 183–189. Quoted passages, p. 187.

14. Geneva Covolian Convention, art. 33.

15. British Manual, p. 181.

16. Ibid.

17. Quoted in Falk et al., Crimes of War, p. 101.

18. British Manual, para. 637, p. 180.

19. Ibid.

20. FM 27-10, para. 505, p. 180.

21. For example, consider the atmosphere at the trial of German Field-Marshal Alfred Kesselring in Italy. Large numbers of shouting relatives of victims were reported to have attended the trial of the general who ordered the Ardentine caves massacre. I have no sympathy for the general, and I agree with the relatives that the punishment was too mild. My point here is to stress that trials of war criminals are not always affairs of quiet, calm, and impersonal legal thought.

22. Various figures are mentioned in the literature. This number is given by Richard Falk in "The Circle of Responsibility," in Falk et al., *Crimes of War*, pp. 222–232. The number of civilians slaughtered is given on p. 222.

23. From the opinion of Chief Justice Harlan Fiske Stone in *The Matter of Yamashita* (327 U.S. 1, 15).

24. It must be mentioned that General Douglas MacArthur, commander of the forces that defeated General Yamashita's 14th Army Group, was said to be very anxious to have Yamashita's court-martial take place quickly. See William Manchester, *American Caesar* (Boston: Little Brown, 1978), p. 485.

25. "In the Matter of Yamashita, 1945," excerpt from Chief Justice Stone, who delivered the opinion of the Court (quoted in Falk et al., *Crimes of War*, pp. 142–143).

26. Chief Justice Stone's opinion, for the majority, reprinted in ibid., p. 146.

27. FM 27-10, para. 501, pp. 178–179.

28. Lieutenant Calley claimed that he "was not aware of his responsibility to refuse an illegal order." Statement made by Secretary of the Army Howard H. Callaway when he called this a "mitigating circumstance" and reduced the lieutenant's sentence of twenty years to ten years. *New York Times*, 17 April 1974, p. 11. Lieutenant Calley was originally sentenced to life and then received several reductions in sentence before President Nixon's pardon.

29. Falk et al., Crimes of War, pp. 160–161.

30. Ibid., p. 154.

31. Ibid.,p. 159.

32. Ibid.,p. 158.

33. FM 27-10, para. 505.

34. British Manual, p. 357.

35. FM 27-10, para. 508, p. 182.

36. British Manual, para. 638, p. 182. The phrase "one or more of the following punishments" suggests that if is combined with some of the others their order be carefully chosen.

37. FM 27-10, para. 509, p. 182.

38. *Japan Times,* 10 February 1988, p. 2.

39. Ordinarily, the need to accept civilians is a burden to an area commander. It would seem that finding dead civilians on Okinawa would be less of a problem than finding them alive and in need of adequate protection, shelter, supplies, and government. The advantage to the Imperial Army is far from clear, except in the case of spies. Of course, "suspicion" of spying without a trial is hardly a basis for execution.

40. British Manual, para. 631, note 1(a), p. 179.

41. FM 27-10, p. 4.

42. Definition given by Benzion Netanyahu, "Terrorists and Freedom Fighters," in *Terrorism, How the West Can Win*, ed. B. Netanyahu (New York: Farrar, Straus & Giroux, 1986), p. 21. Quoted in Col. Anthony E. Hartle, "A Military Ethic in an Age of Terror," *Parameters* 17, no. 2 (Summer 1987): 68–75.

43. Quoted by Michael Howard in his nicely prepared small volume introducing the thought of the author of the classic study of war, Clausewitz (Oxford: Oxford University Press, 1983), p. 50.

44. Alessandro Silj, Never *Again without a Rifle: The Origins of Italian Terrorism*, trans. Salvator Attanasio (New York: Karz Publishers, 1979). I mention this as the only study I have found that tries to give an extended sympathetic analysis of the subject.

45. See Jeremy Bentham, *Principles of the Civil Code*, 1830 (vol. 1 in his Work, ed. Bowring, 1843), in which he holds that "the law cannot grant a benefit to any, without, at the same time, imposing a burthen on some one else" (p. 301). For discussion of some consequences of this, see Sidney Axinn, "The Collective Sense of Equal Protection of the Laws," in *Social Justice: Bowling Green Studies in Applied Philosophy*, ed. Michael Bradie and David Braybrooke, vol. 4, 1982, pp. 44–54.

9. THE DIRTY-HANDS THEORY OF COMMAND

1. Karl F. Thompson, trans., in Karl F Thompson, *Classics of Western Thought: Middle Ages, Renaissance, and Reformation*, 3rd ed. (New York: Harcourt Brace Jovanovich, 1980), pp. 312–313.

2. Carl B. Klockars, "The Dirty Harry Problem," in *Moral issues in Police Work*, ed. Frederick A. Elliston and Michael Feldberg (Totowa, N.J.: Rowman and Allanheld, 1985), pp. 55–71.

3. Michael Walzer, *Just and Unjust Wars: A Moral Argument with Historical Illustrations* (New York: Basic Books, 1977).

4. *Ibid.*, p. 323. Walzer had given the problem an extended analysis in his "Political Action: The Problem of Dirty Hands," *Philosophy and Public Affairs* 2 (1973): 160–180.

5. Klockars, "The Dirty Harry Problem," p. 55.

6. Bernard Williams, "Politics and Moral Character," in his *Moral Luck* (Cambridge: Cambridge University Press, 1981), pp. 54–70. All the Williams references in this section are to this chapter.

7. Walzer, *Just and Unjust Wars*, pp. 323–326.

8. *Ibid.*, p. 326.

9. A historian of ideas, George Boas, has noted, "It is always the emotional coefficient of ideas that retains its potency after an idea has lost its descriptive meaning," in his article, "Vox Populi," in *Dictionary of the History of Ideas*, ed. Philip P. Wiener (New York: Charles Scribner's Sons, 1973), vol. 4, p. 500. Perhaps there are also ideas that have a significant emotional sense without ever having a descriptive meaning. The idea of guilt may have had just that history, or even less tangible than that, it may be a name for an emotion that does not exist. Without subscribing to complete "emotivism" in ethical theory, we can agree that at least certain terms are merely emotive but that, among those terms, at least some may be names for emotions that do not exist. This last is the category to which guilt is most safely assigned. (I am told that this view is idiosyncratic.)

10. Walzer, *Just and Unjust Wars*, p. 325.

11. Klockars, "The Dirty Harry Problem," p. 70.

12. Jean-Jacques Rousseau, *The Social Contract;* the quotations are from *Classics of Western Thought, The Modern World*, ed. Charles Hirschfeld and Edgar E. Knoebel, 3rd ed. (New York: Harcourt Brace Jovanovich, 1980), p. 194.

13. Immanuel Kant, "To Perpetual Peace, A Philosophical Sketch," trans. Ted Humphrey, in Immanuel Kant, *Perpetual Peace and Other Essays* (Indianapolis: Hackett Publishing, 1983), pp. 107–143. As in most scholarly work on Kant, this edition gives the Berlin edition page numbers in the margins, and I do so here in brackets, for the Kant references in this section.

14. Kant, "Perpetual Peace," [381].

15. *Ibid.*

16. *Ibid.*, [386].

17. See Sidney Axinn, "Kant, Authority, and the French Revolution," *Journal of the History of Ideas* 32, no. 3 (1971): 423–432. Kant's view referred to in the text may be found in translation by F. B. Nisbet, in his "The Contest of the Faculties," in *Kant's Political Writings*, ed. Hans Reiss (Cambridge: Cambridge University Press, 1970), p. 182.

18. *Kant's Political Writings*, p. 182.

19. Walzer, *Just and Unjust Wars*, p. 325.

10. TORTURE

1. Tony Lagouranis and Allen Mikaelian, *Fear Up Harsh: An Army Interrogator's Dark Journey through Iraq* (New York: New American Library, 2007), p. 247.

2. Michael Ignatieff, *The Lesser Evil, Political Ethics in an Age of Terror* (Princeton: Princeton University Press, 2004), p. viii.

3. Hebrews 13:3 in *The New English Bible* (Cambridge University Press: Cambridge, 1972). The King James version of the Bible gives a slightly different translation.

4. "Law, Ancient Roman Ideas of Law," in *Dictionary of the History of Ideas,* ed. Wiener, Vol II., pp.685-690.

5. *Ibid.*

6. Wells, Donald A., ed., *An Encyclopedia of War and Ethics,*Westport, CT: Greenwood Press, 1996, p. 59.

7. Department of the Army, *The Law of Land Warfare*, FM 27-18 (Washington, D.C.: U.S. Government Printing Office, 1956), p. 37.

8. Wells, *Encyclopedia*, p. 459.

9. *New Yorker,* 25 June 2007, p. 69.

10. Wesley K. Clark and Kal Raustiala, "Why Terrorists Aren't Soldiers." *New York Times,* 8 August 2007, op-ed, p. A19.

11. Lagouranis, p. 243.

12. Alan M. Dershowitz, *Why Terrorism Works* (New Haven, CT: Yale University Press, 2002), A short and clear presentation of the Dershowitz argument is in Sanford Levinson's collection, *Torture* (see Bibliography), as well as a criticism of it in that collection by Elaine Scarry. Dershowitz gives the strongest argument I can imagine for a very bad idea.

13. Yehezkel Lein, *Absolute Prohibition: The Torture and Ill-treatment of Palestinian Detainees* (Joint Report, Hamoked, Center for the Defense of the Individual, and B'Tselem, The Israeli Center for Human Rights in the Occupied Territories, Jerusalem, May 2007).

14. Michael Walzer, *Just and Unjust Wars, A Moral Argument with Hisorical Illustrations* (New York: Basic Books, 1977), p. 325.

15. The material on this matter is taken from David Luban, "Liberalism, Torture, and the Ticking Bomb," in *Intervention, Terrorism, and Torture: Contemporary Challenges to Just War Theory*, ed. Steven P. Lee (Dordrecht, The Netherlands: Springer, 2007), pp. 249–262.

16. *Ibid.,* p. 256.

17. *Ibid.*

18. Ignatieff, cited. p. 20.

19. *Ibid.,* pp. 23–24.

11. NUCLEAR DEVICES AND LOW-INTENSITY CONFLICTS

1. FM 27-10, para. 35, p. 18.

2. British Manual, para. 113, p. 42.

3. FM 27-10, Change No. 1, 15 July 1976, p. 5.

4. *Ibid.,* p. 2.

5. *Ibid.,* p. 3.

6. *The Random House Dictionary* (New York: Ballantine Books, 1980), p. 364.

7. This section is based on an argument given by Professor Richard Wasser-

strom at a meeting on nuclear warfare at the University of Dayton, Ohio, in 1983; it may have been published since. He is not responsible for this version.

8. The British Manual, para. 119, p. 43.

9. Karl von Clausewitz, *On War,* quoted in Michael Howard, *Clausewitz* (Oxford: Oxford University Press, 1983), p. 50.

10. Robert S. McNamara, "Blundering into Disaster: The First Century of the Nuclear Age," *The Brookings Review* 5, no. 2 (Spring 1987): 8.

11. According to Robert S. McNamara, "Even the use of battlefield nuclear weapons would bring greater destruction to the West than any conceivable contribution they might make to its defense" *(ibid).*

12. FM 100-1, 14 August 1981, p. 9.

13. Some of the material that follows in this section on low-intensity conflicts has appeared as the author's letter to *Military Review* 68 (October 1987): 86–87.

14. *Military Review* 68 (February 1987), p. 25.

15. Quoted in Alfred H. Paddock, Jr., *U.S. Army Special Warfare, Its Origins— Psychological and Unconventional Warfare, 1941–1952* (Washington, D.C.: National Defense University Press, Fort Lesley J. McNair, 1982), p. 2. Paddock cites a Department of the Army publication of 1962 on special warfare.

16. Paddock, *U.S. Army Special Warfare,* p. 2. Paddock's work is a well-done and most helpful history of the evolution of special forces. Its careful study is recommended. Paddock's subject, however, is the history of special forces, and he does not deal directly with the moral issues. His work is not responsible for the viewpoint taken in this chapter.

17. FM 100-1, August 1981, p. 26.

18. A similar question arises in police work, the matter of "undercover" operations. Professional opinion is not unanimous on this. See Fredrick A. Elliston and Michael Feldberg, *Moral Issues in Police Work* (Totowa, N.J.: Rowman and Allanheld, 1985), for a variety of discussions on general effectiveness, the effects on the police themselves, problems involving informers, political targeting and misuse of results, privacy issues, third-party victimization, and proposed guidelines.

19. Paddock, *U.S. Army Special Warfare,* p. 12.

20. *Ibid.,* p. 14.

21. See, for example, Immanuel Kant, "On a Supposed Right to Lie from Altruistic Motives," in his *Critique of Practical Reason and Other Writings in Moral Philosophy,* trans. and ed. Lewis White Beck (Chicago: University of Chicago Press, 1949), which contains the argument that it is wrong to lie, even to protect an innocent life.

22. Quoted by Hannah Arendt, "On Responsibility for Evil," in Richard A. Falk, Gabriel Kolko, and Robert Jay Lifton, eds., *Crimes of War* (New York: Random House, 1971), p. 494.

23. Paddock, *U.S. Army Special Warfare,* p. 49.

24. *Ibid.,* p. 49.

25. *Ibid.,* p. 9.

26. *Ibid.,* p. 158.

27. *Ibid.,* pp. 32–33.

12. CONCLUSIONS

1. "In the Zyklon B Case (In re Tesch and Others): I W.C.R. p. 93, the accused who were German civilians were found guilty of supplying poison gas for use in ex-

termination chambers, the victims being Polish, Belgian, Dutch, French and Czech nationals." British Manual, note 5, p. 182.

2. What follows in this text is so brief and oversimplified that interested readers are encouraged to consult the various references works available, as well as the classical contributions to the philosophy of law. One might start with the articles on natural law, analytic law, and jurisprudence in *The Encyclopedia of Philosophy*, ed. Paul Edwards (New York: Macmillan, 1967). Another helpful collection of well-done articles on legal theories as well as a great many other pivotal subjects is the *Dictionary of the History of Ideas*, ed. Philip P. Wiener (New York: Charles Scribner's Sons, 1973).

3. This point is well put in "Natural Law" by Richard Wollheim in the *Encyclopedia of Philosophy*. Essentially, his phraseology is used here.

4. Anatole France was the pen name of French writer Jacques Anatole Thibault, who received the 1921 Nobel Prize in Literature. His novel, *Le Lys Rouge (The Red Lily)*, appeared in 1894.

5. Russell F. Weigley, *The American Way of War, A History of United States Military Strategy and Policy* (Bloomington: Indiana University Press, 1977), p. 476.

6. *Ibid.*, p. 382.

7. *Ibid.*, p. xxi.

8. *Ibid.*, p. xxii.

9. *Ibid.*, p. xx.

10. *Ibid.*, p. 19.

11. *Ibid.*, p.281; p. 325.

12. Quoted in *ibid.*, p. 378.

13. Reported by Shunske Ikeda, "Japanese War Crimes in Asia," Tokyo, 1987, privately circulated.

14. *Japan Times Weekly*, Saturday, 12 March 1988, p. 6. This newspaper also mentions that China and some Western researchers allege that Japanese war criminals were shown clemency by U.S. forces after 1945 in exchange for information on germ warfare.

15. *Ibid.* "China's bitterness over the war revived when the then Japanese Prime Minister Nakasone visited Tokyo's shrine to its war dead." Whether the prime minister of Japan should visit the Yasukuni Shrine has been a politically divisive issue for some time in Japanese politics because of domestic as well as foreign reactions.

16. As noted in an earlier chapter, the Urakami Cathedral, the largest cathedral in the Far East, stood 600 meters east-northeast of the hypocenter of the Nagasaki atom bomb. It was the closest institution to the explosion. Because the attack was carried out at 11:02 A.M. (apparently a clear morning), 9 August 1945, three days after the first atomic bomb at Hiroshima, the suspicion that the cathedral was used as a target is hard to suppress.

17. Reported in Martin Hollis, "Reasons of Honour," *The Aristotelian Society Proceedings* 87 (New Series 1986–1987): 1.

18. Immanuel Kant, "Perpetual Peace," *Perpetual Peace and Other Essays*, ed. and trans. Ted Humphrey (Indianapolis: Hackett Publishing Co. 1983) [369]. Lord Acton is also known for repeating Kant's point. See Acton's *Essays on Freedom and Power* (Boston, Mass.: Beacon Press, 1938), p. 364.

19. *The Collected Dialogues of Plato, Including the Letters*, edited by Edith Hamilton and Huntington Cairns, Princeton: Princeton University Press,1961, *The Republic*, II.360 b.

20. *Ibid.* [414b].

21. *Beyond Good and Evil,* #146, trans. Helen Zimmern, in *The Philosophy of Nietzsche,* (New York: Modern Library, 1927), p. 466.

22. The quotations to follow are from two papers in this debate on military/media relations: "War, Television and Public Opinion," by Maj. Cass D. Howell, U.S. Marine Corps, and "A Familiar Refrain But Slightly Out of Tune," by Col. Wallace B. Eberhard, U.S. Army Reserve, Ret. *Military Review* 67 (February 1987): 71–79, 71, 80–84. Maj. Howell argues for the elimination of television from the battlefield, and Col. Eberhard holds that television should not be so restricted.

23. Major Howell's paper is somewhat reminiscent of Orosius's *Seven Books of History Against the Pagans.* The story behind Orosius's motives in writing his books may be apocryphal, but one version of it runs this way: St. Augustine was quite annoyed by the general feeling of the times that since conversion to Christianity, the world had gotten worse, that there were more calamities, more horrible events, than in the good old days before the Christian era. Perhaps it would be wise to return to the old Roman gods instead of continuing with this new one from Asia Minor. Therefore, Augustine commissioned a young scholar to write a history of all the terrible things that had occurred in the known history of the world before the birth of Christ and the problems since, thereby proving that things now were actually better than they had been. Orosius did his job impressively, collecting all the records of earthquakes, great fires, plagues, famines, wanton violence, and so forth. But a body in motion tends to continue in motion, and Orosius went on collecting calamities through to his own time. His conclusion was that while things were no worse after the birth of Christ, they also were not demonstrably better. This report was weaker than the boss desired but still something to throw at the doubters: At least, things were no worse. Reading Maj. Howell's article, one gets the impression that while he may have started out to show that the Vietnam War produced fewer war crimes than earlier wars that the American public had supported, he had to conclude, like Orosius, that at least this one was no worse.

24. *Ibid.,* p. 75.

25. Kant, "Perpetual Peace" [381].

26. *Ibid.,* the negative principle on [381] and the positive on [386].

27. Readers are encouraged to test themselves on the questionnaire in Appendix 3.

28. Immanuel Kant, *Critique of Judgment,* trans. J. H. Bernard (New York: Hafner Publishing, 1951), #28 [263], p. 102.

APPENDIX 1

1. There are widely reported cases, such as the *New York Times* report that "The CIA recent record [in 1978] includes the assassinations of Patrice Lumumba; Ngo Dinh Diem, the South Vietnamese President; Rafael Trujillo Monila, the Dominican Republic President; Gen. Rene Schneider, the commander of the Chilean Army," by John Stockwell, "A Call for Openness as an Antidote to the CIA's Secrecy," *New York Times,* 17 May 1978, op ed. A more recent example may be found in Bob Woodward, *Veil: The Secret Wars of the CIA 1981–1987* (New York: Pocket Books, 1987).

2. Alasdair MacIntyre, *After Virtue* (Notre Dame, Ind.: University of Notre Dame Press, 1981), p. 112.

3. A strong presentation of the virtue-centered view can be found in the thoughtful writing of Col. Malham M. Wakin. See his "The Ethics of Leadership II," in the very important anthology edited by him, *War, Morality, and the Military Profession* (Boulder, Colo.: Westview Press, 1986), pp. 200–216.

4. Kant's work on history may be found conveniently in *Perpetual Peace and Other Essays on Politics, History, and Morals*, ed. and trans. Ted Humphrey (Indianapolis: Hackett Publishing, 1983).

APPENDIX 2

1. The bibliography on the "just war" theory is very long, and the literature continues to grow. In the last decades, we have Michael Walzer's widely read and thoughtful *Just and Unjust Wars*. For a criticism of Walzer and an important work in itself, there is James Turner Johnson's *Just War Tradition and the Restraint of War* (Princeton, N.J.: Princeton University Press, 1981). Mentioning just these two is unfair to many other very helpful works. For examples, see the bibliography in Johnson's book.

2. Russell F Weigley's *The American Way of War: A History of United States Military Strategy and Policy* was published by Indiana University Press as a paperback in 1977. (The Macmillan edition appeared in 1973.) Although he limits his bibliography to "selected" works that bear on strategy, Weigley lists 188 items.

3. David Irwin, "New-Classicism in Art," in *Dictionary of the History of Ideas*, ed. Philip P. Wiener (New York: Charles Scribner's Sons, 1974), vol. 3, p. 364.

4. *Japan Times*, 12 April 1988, p. 8. The story comes from UPI-Kyodo News. One might note that we have no independent source to corroborate this *Pravda* story.

Brief Bibliography

Aristotle. *Nichomachean Ethics*. Translated by W. D. Ross. In *The Basic Works of Aristotle*. Edited by Richard McKeon. New York: Random House, 1941.

"Law, Ancient Roman Ideas of Law," in *Dictionary of the History of Ideas*. Edited by Philip P. Wiener. New York: Charles Scribner's Sons, 1973.

Ascherson, Neal. "The Death Doctors." In *New York Review of Books*, 28 May 1987.

Axinn, Sidney. "Honor, Patriotism, and Ultimate Loyalty." In *Nuclear Weapons and the Future of Humanity, The Fundamental Questions*. Edited by Avner Cohen and Steven Lee. Totowa, N.J.: Rowman and Allanheld, 1986.

———. "Human Dignity and War." *The Philosophical Forum* 10, no. 1(1971): 31–52.

———. "Kant, Authority, and the French Revolution." *Journal of the History of Ideas* 32, no. 3(1971): 423–432.

———. "Loyalty and the Limits of Patriotism." In *Political Realism and International Morality, Ethics in the Nuclear Age*. Edited by Kenneth Kipnis and Diana T. Meyers. Boulder, Colo.: Westview Press, an AMINTAPHIL Volume, 1987, pp. 239—250.

Clark, Wesley K., and Kal Raustiala. "Why Terrorists Aren't Soldiers." *New York Times*, 8 August 2007, op-ed, p. A19.

Coursier, Henri. *Course of Five Lessons on the Geneva Conventions*. Geneva: International Committee of the Red Cross, 1963.

Department of the Army. *The Army Field Manual* 100-1. Washington, D.C.: U.S. Government Printing Office, 1981.

Department of the Army. *The Law of Land Warfare*. Army Field Manual 27-10. Washington, D.C.: U.S. Government Printing Office, July 1956.

Department of the Army. *The Law of Land Warfare*. Army Field Manual 27-10. Washington, D.C.: U.S. Government Printing Office, 1956.

Department of the Army. *Military Leadership: Field Manual 22-100*. Washington, D.C.: U.S. Government Printing Office, 1985.

Dershowitz, Alan M. *Why Terrorism Works*. New Haven, CT: Yale University Press, 2002.

The Effects of the Atom Bomb on Nagasaki. U.S. Strategic Bombing Survey, 1947. Unclassified, 1 May 1950.

Elliston, Frederick A., and Michael Feldberg, eds. *Moral Issues in Police Work*. Totowa, N.J.: Rowman and Allanheld, 1985.

Falk, Richard A., Gabriel Kolko, and Robert Jay Lifton, eds. *Crimes of War*. New York: Random House, 1971.

Flower, Elizabeth. "Ethics of Peace." In *Dictionary of the History of Ideas*, edited by Philip P. Wiener. New York: Charles Scribner's Sons, 1973.

Gabriel, Richard A., and Paul L. Savage. *Crisis in Command, Mismanagement in the Army*. New York: Hill and Wang, 1978.

Hiroshima and Nagasaki: The Physical, Medical, and Social Effects of the Atomic Bombings. New York: Basic Books, 1981.

Hobbes, Thomas. *Leviathan*, 1651. Available in many convenient editions; for example, *Hobbes Selections*, ed. F. 3. II. Woodbridge. New York: Charles Scribner's Sons, 1958.

Howard, Michael. *Clausewitz*. Oxford: Oxford University Press, 1983.

Ignatieff, Michael. *The Lesser Evil, Political Ethics in an Age of Terror*. Princeton: Princeton University Press, 2004.

James, William. *Psychology: Briefer Course*. New York: Collier Books, 1962.

Jennings, Francis. *The Invasion of America*. Columbia, S.C.: University of South Carolina Press, 1975.

Kant, Immanuel. *Critique of Judgment*. Translated by J. H. Bernard. New York: Hafner Publishing, 1951.

———. *Critique of Practical Reason*. Translated by Lewis White Beck. New York: Liberal Arts Press, 1956.

———. *Grounding for the Metaphysics of Morals*. Translated by James W. Ellington. Indianapolis: Hackett Publishing, 1981.

———. *Kant's Political Writings*. Edited by Hans Reiss. Cambridge: Cambridge University Press, 1970.

———. *The Metaphysical Elements of Justice*. Translated by John Ladd. Indianapolis: Bobbs-Merrill, 1965.

———. *Perpetual Peace and Other Essays*. Edited by Ted Humphrey. Indianapolis: Hackett Publishing, 1983.

Lagouranis, Tony, and Allen Mikaelian. *Fear Up Harsh: An Army Interrogator's Dark Journey through Iraq*. New York City: New American Library, 2007.

Law of War on Land, The, Being Part II of the Manual of Military Law. London: Her Majesty's Stationery Office, 1958.

Levinson, Sanford, ed. *Torture, A Collection*. Oxford: Oxford University Press, 2004.

Luban, David. "Liberalism, Torture, and the Ticking Bomb." In *Intervention, Terrorism, and Torture, Contemporary Challenges to Just War Theory*, edited by Steven P. Lee. Dordrecht, The Netherlands: Springer, 2007.

MacIntyre, Alasdair. *After Virtue*. Notre Dame, Ind.: University of Notre Dame Press, 1981.

Manchester, William. *American Caesar: Douglass MacArthur* 1880–1964. Boston: Little, Brown, 1978.

McNamara, Robert S. "Blundering into Disaster: The First Century of the Nuclear Age." *The Brookings Review* 5, no. 2 (Spring 1987).

Mill, J. S. *Principles of Political Economy,* 1848. Excerpts reprinted in Wagner, Donald 0., q. v.

Moskos, Charles C., Jr. *The American Enlisted Man.* New York: Russell Sage Foundation, 1970.

Paddock, Alfred H., Jr. *U.S. Army Special Warfare, Its Origins—Psychological and Unconventional Warfare, 1941–1952.* Washington, D.C.: National Defense University Press, Fort Lesley J. McNair, U.S. Government Printing Office, 1982.

Ropp, Theodore. "War and Militarism." In *Dictionary of the History of Ideas,* edited by Philip P. Wiener. New York: Charles Scribner's Sons, 1973.

Silj, Alessandro. *Never Again without a Rifle: The Origins of Italian Terrorism.* Translated by Salvator Attanasio. New York: Karz Publishers, 1979.

Singer, Edgar A., Jr. *On the Contented Life.* New York: Henry Holt, 1936.

Smith, Major Daniel M. (U.S. Army). "The Army: A Search for Values." *Military Review* 60, no. 3 (March 1980).

Stromberg. Peter L., Malham M. Wakin, and Daniel Callahan. *The Teaching of Ethics in the Military.* Hastings-on-Hudson, N.Y.: The Hastings Center, 1982.

Vagts, Alfred. *A History of Militarism, Civilian and Military.* Rev. ed. New York: Free Press, 1967.

Wagner, Donald O., ed. *Social Reformers.* New York: Macmillan, 1959.

Wakin, Malham M., ed. *War, Morality, and the Military Profession.* Rev. ed. Boulder, Colo.: Westview Press, 1986.

Walzer, Michael. *Just and Unjust Wars: A Moral Argument with Historical Illustrations.* New York: Basic Books, 1977.

———. "Political Action: The Problem of Dirty Hands." *Philosophy and Public Affairs* 2(1973): 160–180.

Weigley, Russell K. *The American Way of War, A History of United States Military Strategy and Policy.* Bloomington, Ind.: Indiana University Press, 1977.

Wells, Donald A., editor, *An Encyclopedia of War and Ethics.* Westport, CT: Greenwood Press, 1996.

Williams, Bernard. *Moral Luck,* Cambridge: Cambridge University Press, 1981.

Wilson, Edmund. *Patriotic Gore: Studies in the Literature of the American Civil War.* New York: Oxford University Press, 1962.

Wright, Quincy. *A Study of War,* 2nd ed. Chicago: University of Chicago Press, 1965.

Yehezkel Lein. *Absolute Prohibition: The Torture and Ill-treatment of Palestinian Detainees.* Joint Report, Hamoked, Center for the Defense of the Individual, and B'Tselem, The Israeli Center for Human Rights in the Occupied Territories, Jerusalem: May 2007.

Index

Sidney Axinn is Professor Emeritus, Philosophy Dpartment, Temple University, and Courtesy Professor, Philosophy, University of South Florida. He is Past President of the American Society for Value Inquiry, and the author of *The Logic of Hope: Extensions of Kant's View of Religion.*